Ft. Mackinac

Ft. Snelling

Ft. Winnebago

Ft. Detroit

Ft. Crawford

Ft. Omaha

Ft. Dearborn

Ft. Wayne

Ft. Grenville

Ft. Pitt

Atkinson

Ft. Madison

Ft. Edwards

rth

Ft. Bellefontaine

Jefferson Barracks

ott

son

Ft. Smith

wson

Ft. Wilkenson

Richardson

Ft. McHenry

Ft. St. Stephens

p

Ft. Adams

Ft. Bowyer

PEDDLERS
and
POST TRADERS

PEDDLERS
and
POST TRADERS

*The Army Sutler
on the Frontier*

David Michael Delo

UNIVERSITY OF UTAH PRESS
Salt Lake City

University of Utah Press Publications in the American West, volume 28
Copyright © 1992 University of Utah Press
All rights reserved

∞ This symbol indicates books printed on paper that meets the minimum
requirement of American National Standard for Information Services—
Permanence of Paper for Printed Library Materials, ANSI A39.38-1984

LIBRARY OF CONGRESS CATALOGING-IN-PUBLICATION DATA

Delo, David Michael, 1938–
    Peddlers and post traders : the army sutler on the frontier /
David Michael Delo.
        p. cm. —(University of Utah publications in the American
West; v. 28)
    Includes bibliographical references and index.
    ISBN 0-87480-402-7 (alk. paper)
    1. Sutlers—West (U.S.)—History—19th century. 2. Frontier and
pioneer life—west (U.S.) 3. United States. Army—Military life—
History—19th century. 4. West (U.S.)—History. I. Title.
II. Title : Post traders. III. Series.
F591. D354   1992
355.1'2—dc20   92-53606
                                    CIP

To my wife, Iloilo
for unwavering faith

CONTENTS

A noble thou shalt have and present pay;
and liquors likewise I shall give to thee,
. . . Is that not just? for I shall sutler be
unto the camps and profits will acrue.

Shakespeare, *Henry V*

INTRODUCTION

Mother Ross . . . was given the exclusive right to sell beer in the Deer Park, Dublin, on a review day, and was also allowed to keep a sutler's tent in Hyde Park. She reaped more profit from these than from the Queen's promise that if her unborn child turned out to be a boy he would get a commission as soon as he was born.— Scouller, The Armies of Queen Anne

---

The sutler (and his post-Civil War counterpart, the military post trader) was a civilian peddler who offered comestibles and small wares to men under arms . . . for a price.

It's highly likely that he was in business soon after the first days of formal warfare, for he emerged from the multitudes of noncombatants known as camp followers. For at least twenty-five hundred years, camp followers filled the wake of conquering hordes, moving behind their fighting men like a shadow. And a great shadow it was, often exceeding its mercenary host by a factor of two to four. In 1577 European observers reported that the ranks of Spanish soldiers leaving the Netherlands swelled from 7,000 to 20,000 when camp followers were counted. As late as 1839 someone observed that of the 17,000 souls committed to the Afghan War, only 4,500 were soldiers: the remaining 12,500 were camp followers.

While the civilian horde that accompanied Alexander the Great was referred to as a noncombatant baggage train, Xenophon of Greece denigratingly characterized camp followers of the Peloponnesian War as a "host of useless mouths to feed."[1] Although its ranks contained dependents, scavengers, and prostitutes, the baggage train also held a number of highly useful male and female servants, such as contractors, grooms, grass cutters, mule and camel drivers, water carriers, snake charmers, dancers, conjurors, and sutlers. The men of the fighting force and their civilian supporters possessed such a symbiotic relationship that Charlemagne, during the Carthaginian war of the ninth century, ordered each combatant to provide his own baggage train.[2]

As the armies of European nation-states evolved, military leaders sought to minimize the dependence of their soldiers on ephemeral civilian support by absorbing camp followers' services into the military administrative structure. The sutler, who had been identified by that name as a dealer in consumables as early as the beginning of the sixteenth century, survived that assimilation.[3] As the centuries passed, he traded a portion of his independence for greater job security in the form of a quasiofficial status.[4]

The Prussian Army sutler, for example, was a recognized tradesman who possessed considerable latitude in camp. When the army rested during the blockade of Pirna in 1756, a soldier wrote that there were "swarms of sutlers and butchers, and all day long you could see long streets of stalls where food was being boiled or roasted."[5] He could move at will to sell his wares, and line officers provided him with escorts while he plundered enemy villages to improve his inventory.[6] The local commanding officer required only that the sutler observe an eight o'clock evening curfew and wear a light blue cockade in his hat at all times.[7]

The suttling profession was first officially recognized as an integral part of a military regime in England, in February 1717. British Army regulations not only controlled the hours of his trade; they set his prices and, for the first time, officially warned soldiers and officers not to partake in suttling activities.[8]

In America, the suttling profession of the sixteenth century mirrored its European cousin. From the French-Indian War of 1757 until 1820, the sutler offered goods as a member of the ranks of camp followers. In 1821, the Secretary of War and army leaders decided that because the sutler made a definite contribution to the welfare of the soldier, especially those on the frontier, he should be officially integrated into the military establishment. The position of the Regular Army post sutler and accompanying regulations went into effect in 1822.

Suttling quickly evolved into a profession. As quickly, the profit potential of the suttling profession politicized the appointment process. Slots were limited, and each sutler possessed a monopoly over his military post. Because of the importance of the military-post role, especially along the expanding frontier, the sutler's clientele included the local settlers.

Sutler numbers reached a peak during the Civil War. The ranks were swelled by those who served volunteer units, and most of those men were motivated more by greed than by politics. As a result, sutlers damaged the morale of the soldiers with whiskey, high prices, and shoddy quality. In 1866, as a direct result, the army abolished the sutler's slot.

Less than two years later, pressure from emigrants and isolated posts forced the army to reinstate a variation of the sutler's post in the guise of a military post trader. Once again, while the trader filled a void and made good money, he also caused trouble. Eventually, at the beginning of the 1880s, he found himself crosswise to the tide of history. He was defeated by the temperance movement in his struggle to retain his license to sell alcoholic beverages, and soon lost other key privileges. By 1890 the army staff said that the post trader stood out as a privileged rival of local citizens and advised Congress that he was no longer needed nor wanted.

By the mid-1890s the sutler had been replaced by the U.S. Army canteen, an establishment that became the post exchange system—the "PX." Like the bullwhacker and the stagecoach driver, the sutler, his institutions, and his way of life disappeared from the American scene. In the long run, his nemesis was not his poor reputation, the Temperance League, or the spread of the U.S. Army canteen, but the inexorable urbanization of what was once the American frontier.

The primary objective of this study is to shed light on the suttling profession in America and to describe how it changed. As implied by changes to his title, the sutler's profession passed through definable stages. Each stage is characterized by recognizable criteria, including the trader's background, the source authority for and the manner of his appointment, the character of contemporary military regulations, and the disposition of and tasks undertaken by the army.

Some elements remained constant throughout his American career. The boundaries of the sutler's freedom were set and controlled by United States government policy decisions and by U.S. Army regulations. The degree to which the average sutler was financially successful was determined by historical circumstance, and in particular, by the economic character of the times. In general, as time passed, the sutler trade became better established and more profitable. The most successful class of sutlers were post–Civil War entrepreneurs, a number of "gentlemen traders" who served the army between 1867 and 1890. Because suttling was a trade that attracted a variety of fascinating characters, many of the following chapters include profiles of the more interesting and notorious sutlers of the time.

The second objective of this study is to evaluate the contribution made by the sutler and the military post trader to the settlement of the American West. The profession was certainly not without its administrative problems, its controversies, or its scoundrels. After the army provided the sutler with stability and protection sufficient to earn a decent living, his unique position became highly prized and vulnerable to influence peddling. And most traders were constantly accused of price gouging and of illegally selling whiskey, not only to soldiers but to the Indians. Thus, throughout their century-long career, sutlers and post traders were stereotyped as blatantly unethical villains.

To date, in spite of the excellent record of numerous individual sutlers, the reputation of the profession has mirrored the actions of its more unethical contingent. The suttling profession deserves more praiseworthy consideration than it has been given, and those men who served with dignity and integrity deserve greater recognition for their contributions to America's heritage.

PART I

THE CAMP
FOLLOWER

Pre–1821

ONE

Early American Camp Followers

There was . . . an honest little Irish lieutenant . . . who owed so much money to a camp suttler, that he began to make love to the man's daughter, intending to pay his debt that way; and at the battle of Malplaquet, flying away from the debt and the lady too, he rushed so desperately on the French lines, that he . . . came a captain out of the action, and had to marry the suttler's daughter after all, who brought him his canceled debt to her father as poor Roger's fortune. To run out of the reach of bill and marriage, he ran on the enemy's pikes; and as those did not kill him he was thrown back upon t'other horn of his dilemma. —Thackeray, The History of Henry Esmond

Until Congress authorized the establishment of a professional army after the American Revolution, residents of American colonies relied on British troops and local militia to cope with civil disputes, Indian wars, and invasions by foreign powers. Because there was no standing American army for a sutler to follow, nor a permanent organization to which he could be attached, he practiced his profession solely during periods of hostilities. In place of receiving a private's per diem or an officer's salary, he was engaged by regimental officers as a civilian merchant. In return for the opportunity, he was expected to protect his wares and provide his own transportation and housing. Each time peace was reestablished and the irregular soldier returned to his former civilian pursuits, the sutler was dismissed. Like the troops he served, he was in the fight for the short haul.

From the French-Indian War through the Revolutionary War, the American sutler, like his European counterpart, made his contribution by hustling food and alcoholic beverages for his troops. Regimental orderly books and army regulations reveal that the sutler was a man who, given half the chance, would take advantage. He was not unlike his

professional ancestors, who accompanied the Athenians when they attacked Sicily. Those sutlers were so anxious to help that they took part
in pillaging and then sold their booty to sustain their trade.[1]

Scattered references to the character and the activities of the American sutler form a composite image of a man whom writers contemporary with the Civil War called *"a necessary evil." Necessary* referred to
the soldiers' needs for variety in food and for small, personal items that
the army either could not or chose not to provide; *evil* was the recur-
ring propensity on the part of the sutler to overrun the camp, take the
soldiers' money, and leave the generals with men who were too drunk
to fight. Behind the battle lines, half of the regimental officers skir-
mished with the sutler to minimize the damage he could do without
killing the fellow's enthusiasm for performing his job. The remaining
half of the regimental staff adopted more of a "free market" approach,
which meant that the officer in charge looked the other way or shared
the sutler's profits.

A glimpse of suttling activities during the French-Indian War is provided by the diary of James Walker of New Hampshire. He was employed by Colonel Goffe, one of many American colonial officers who
raised a regiment of colonists. Like his fellow regimental commanders,
Goffe chose his own sutler. He probably had a good one in James
Walker. First of all, Walker was the son of Andrew Walker of London-
derry, Ireland, a man who had come to America in 1734, and settled in
New Bedford. The elder Walker erected one of the first frame houses in
town and developed an orchard. He may also have operated an inn or
tavern; the town history implied that he entertained travelers. The task
of provisioning others, therefore, may not have been new to his son,
James. As the son of a tavern keeper, he would have known about
basic foodstuffs, credit, prices, sources of supply, and the importance of
being responsible and providing service if his family was to gain repeat
business with former guests. In addition to good background creden-
tials, Walker was Goffe's son-in-law.[2] Nepotism is an ancient creed.

From James's diary, it appears that he was hired in 1760, the closing
year of the war. He set out for Albany, New York, in June, to provision his trade. He used Albany as a supply base, and sent teamloads of
goods to his regiment, stationed at Fort Ticonderoga at the northern
end of Lake George. The trip from Albany to the post and back took a
full month, in part because the last leg of the trip traversed the length
of Lake George. James supplied his own boat and furnished his own ox

carts rather than wagons, because the soldiers needed all of the larger wagons for supplies.[3] Once he had arrived in camp and had unloaded his goods, he was given a location, specified by the Provost Marshal, where he could pitch his tent. Then he was permitted to sell his merchandise directly to the soldiers.[4]

It is easy to visualize a small, noisy area inside a military camp where a handful of men vied for business. They sold their wares from tents or stalls, called tabernacles, as they had done since the 1500s and as they would continue to do through the Civil War one hundred years later. Most sutlers sold comestibles. Sutler Josiah Brewer specialized in green Batteen cloth by the yard and thread, silk, and buttons.[5] Walker's journal indicates that he stuck to basics: sugar, cheese, and tobacco; barrels of rum and other spirits; boxes of chocolate; and soap. He also sold spruce beer, a contemporary concoction brewed by mixing, per barrel, a quantity of spruce-tree bark and water with five quarts of molasses. This drink was considered beneficial to the health and the convenience of the troops, and sold at a price of three coppers per gallon.[6]

All regimental commanders were instructed to appoint a sutler or a person to supply their troops with necessary stores.[7] At Fort Edward, situated about fifteen miles south of Lake George on the Hudson River, all of the sutlers in camp were licensed, even though permission to suttle did not guarantee that a sutler would be attached to a regiment. And like bachelors, unattached sutlers were camped together. No sutler was to pitch his tent or break ground or build a hut "within or without the lines" without first applying to the Adjutant Deputy Quartermaster General, under penalty of having all liquor and stores demolished. The quartermaster restricted the sutlers' marketing activities to a piece of ground referred to as "the center of the line of the army," and set the hours of suttling. Order and discipline in the camp were enforced by the provost guard. No lights were allowed at night, and soldiers were not allowed in the sutlers' area after retreat.[8]

In addition to the rules that defined the sutlers' activities, the military required all vendors to sell their wares at fixed prices. Each item was sold in British monetary units and adjusted for local inflation. A unit of cheese, for example, cost one shilling. A sutler who chose to disregard orders was escorted out of camp. When the men at Camp Edward voiced complaints about high prices, for example about the "extravagant price" of milk, the commanding officer simply adjusted the tariff downward to six pence, "New York currency, per quart."[9]

At the close of the French-Indian War, James Walker exchanged his suttling business for a commission as captain of a horse troop. He was appointed by Governor Wentworth and saw action during the American Revolutionary War. If Walker was kin to the governor, he did not reveal the relationship in his diary.

By the dawn of the American Revolutionary War, military laws of the U.S. Army more thoroughly defined acceptable and unacceptable sutler behavior. His duties and responsibilities were carefully delineated in manuals such as *The 1779 Regulations for the Order and Discipline of the Troops of the U.S.*[10] These early codifications demonstrated that high-ranking army personnel possessed a clear understanding of the sutler's role and held firm opinions as to how he should interface with the military establishment.[11]

Military officials instituted price controls, issued licenses, and regulated vending places and times, practices that had been established for the sutler in Europe at the beginning of the eighteenth century. To prevent unauthorized nighttime entertainment, the army restricted his operations to daylight hours—from reveille until nine at night every day except Sunday. Sutlers were to close their establishments during "devine services," upon penalty of being dismissed from all future suttling. [12]

In addition, the Continental Congress and army staff held regimental commanders responsible for the behavior of all vendors. They were to see to it that the sutlers supplied their assigned soldiers with good and wholesome provisions at market price. At the same time, these same officers were warned not to "extract exorbitant prices for houses or stalls let out to sutlers" or, for their private advantage, to "lay any duty or imposition upon or be interested in the sale of such victuals, liquors, or other necessities brought into the garrisons, forts, or barracks for the use of soldiers."[13] If any commanding officer was caught suttling, he would be dismissed from the service and forfeit a month's wages as a fine.

The need to include the sutler in regulations also indicated that the army command was aware of how disruptive the sutler could be if left to his own devices. In spite of regulations and close supervision, there was at least one large scam during the Revolutionary War that involved sutlers. On July 28, 1783, the Supervisor of Finance sent a letter to the

Continental Congress enclosing a note from the Paymaster General of the U.S. Army. The paymaster said that a number of sutlers and paymasters had colluded to swindle the pay of a large group of men who had been furloughed in early June. The pay these soldiers had expected for the months of February, March, and April arrived on June 15, but involved regimental paymasters failed to notify the men or their furloughing officers. In the meantime, regimental sutlers managed to sell and to obtain receipts from almost every officer and private "for the whole amount of their three month advance" prior to their having been furloughed.

When Congress discovered it had no grounds for legal prosecution, it decided to hold the men up to public shame. To that end, the Paymaster General was asked to provide Congress with the names of responsible regimental paymasters and camp sutlers, and to "put these same in the eastern newspapers with the above letter."[14]

Although the sutler was viewed by the army command as a major source of supplementary food and wares, he was not given special status and no regulation favored him. Any soldier or officer could bring any quantity of food or drink onto the premises of the camp or post except when Congress entered into a contract to furnish select provisions. To strengthen its independence from the vagaries of civilian food vendors, the army created the post of Commissary General of Stores and Purchases, one of several much-needed organizational positions. The first officer to hold the post, Joseph Trumbull, was given concurrent responsibility for subsistence supplies.

In November 1775, the American soldier's daily subsistence included protein, bread, vegetables, milk, and one quart of spruce beer or cider. Unfortunately, as time passed, the supply service broke down. Soldiers were forced to live more and more on bread and meat. When vegetables were lacking, General George Washington authorized farmers to establish markets at camp to sell produce.[15] Washington also authorized each brigade to engage one sutler who was to have a "suttling booth" for selling liquor at a fixed price. Since spirits were thought to be healthy, a gill of whiskey (two ounces) was included as part of the daily ration.

The overriding problem with spirits was how to regulate the rate and quantity consumed by the soldier. This problem plagued the U.S. Army throughout the eighteenth and nineteenth centuries. In the eighteenth century, a modicum of spirits was deemed beneficial, so the army issued a ration of rum, brandy, or whiskey on a daily basis. However, drunkenness was also an accepted mode of relaxation for all classes, and over and above his daily allotment the soldier was free to purchase intoxicants from his regimental sutler.

Because the average Revolutionary War sutler was no paragon of ethical behavior, he sold alcoholic beverages to anyone who had money, so any soldier with a supply of cash could drink his pay. In 1778, to discourage drinking, commanding officers raised prices for hard liquor to four shillings per quart, and reduced beer prices from one shilling ten pence to a shilling per quart. No other liquors were allowed within seven miles of camp. General Washington, like other commanding officers, tried on several occasions to ban all liquor dealers. He also instituted licensing to regulate prices and to keep unauthorized vendors from the soldiers, but none of his efforts succeeded for very long.[16]

The orderly book of the Jersey brigade at Pompton for January 27, 1781, noted that in response to a severe alcoholic situation the commanding officer issued a hard-line, "no exceptions," ban on alcohol. His rule applied to sutlers of either sex. "Any woman who shall presume to sell liquor shall be severely punished. And the brigade sutler will not sell any liquor to any non-commissioned officer or soldier without a written permission from the officers commanding companies." He extended his rule on the thirtieth of that month to a point two miles beyond the perimeter of the camp to deal with those who had tried to set up shop just outside of camp.[17] And once again, his regulation was pointedly addressed to sutlers of both sexes.

Historical references to female sutlers in American military camps are rare, but the U.S. Army may have had no fewer than European armies, where women vendors had a long tradition.[18] In the early 1700s, in the army of Frederick the Great of Prussia, female sutlers were free to perform the same services as their male counterparts. They, too, wore cockades in their hats. Many were licensed; many more were unofficial. Most were widows or soldiers' wives. Because a number of the women were reputed to have loose morals, the female sutler shared the term *Marketenderinen* (whores) with camp prostitutes, but they were respected and left to their own devices.[19] During maneuvers near Potsdam, for example, it is told that Frederick the Great and his staff spotted a hill with a good view. Upon reaching the top of this apocryphal mound, they came upon two stalls of Marketenderinen. The ladies informed the officers that the hill was occupied;

it was ideal for their trade. The generals, on the other hand, they observed, could watch their troops from any place they liked. With respect for an ancient trade, the king and his staff "beat a retreat."[20] During the American Revolutionary War, General Burgoyne finally forbid camp women from going to town because they smuggled too much liquor to the men.

The debilitating effect of alcohol was hardly a problem restricted to the American soldier. British officers often amused themselves by drinking, gambling, and quarreling at the expense of military duties.[21] In July 1777, British General Burgoyne banned liquor to his troops. He ordered all sutlers and others to cease selling liquor, and required officers to make a search of sutlers' huts and tents. Sutlers who broke the rules were taken prisoner, their stock was destroyed, and their dwellings were destroyed or burned.[22]

The occupational profile of the sutler-at-war changed during the course of the American Revolutionary War. At first, he was retained solely as a vendor of food, drink, and small wares to supplement army provisions, but American officials soon entertained the idea that the sutler had the potential to serve the army as a more general merchant. In 1776, the Continental Congress urged its military commanders to encourage sutlers to provide the men with hosiery, shoes, coarse linen, soap, rum, sugar, and wine, all of which were much needed. General Montgomery also suggested that he be used to minimize the need to deal with troublesome currency exchange rates and discount problems.[23] From his headquarters near Quebec, Canada, Montgomery sent General Schuyler a letter, in December 1775, to voice his complaint that local Canadian inhabitants wouldn't take Continental money. When he had distributed funds to the troops in Montreal, few outsiders would receive it. He suggested that instead of giving soldiers what amounted to discounted paper, the army use sutlers to bring "such articles as soldiers choose to lay out their money upon." Then the troop might be paid in Continental currency which would not be depreciated. The Continental Congress agreed.[24]

For centuries the sutler had been used as a source of supplemental food and liquor for troops in the field; no more, no less. His continued presence in the army was proof of the value of his services, and when he minded his manners, he made a significant contribution to the welfare

of the men. But, for the most part, suttling was a trade that still reflected the origins of its name, *soeteler*, a petty tradesman or soldier's
servant. The majority of those who filled the position may have had no
special training or background, but as good capitalists most sutlers
charged what the traffic would bear and sought a competitive edge to
increase their profits.

And the sutler was in an excellent position to make good money.
His most profitable items for sale, unfortunately, were various alcoholic beverages, so he possessed the potential to damage discipline in
the camp and reduce the combat-readiness of the troops. Because of his
dual potential for good and harm, the sutler was characterized
throughout American history by the highly descriptive phrase "a necessary evil."

Records of individual seventeenth- and eighteenth-century American
sutlers and their activities are scarce, and the historical record gives the
suttling trade scant attention. In the main, sutler-related information
describes his general operations and military regulations instituted to
control him during periods of hostilities. After all, the sutler was simply
a civilian who provided a logistical service for the army. Although he
was relied upon, his role was limited; he had little official status or was
not involved in battles or policy.

After the United States created a standing American army, the sutler's services were more heavily relied upon. As a result, the nineteenth-
century historical record provides much more detailed information
about the parameters of his profession as well as some detail about the
character of the men who suttled.

TWO

With America's Fledgling
Frontier Army

> *The various complicated and scandalous practices reported in the*
> *suttling line make it the Brigadier General's duty to direct reform*
> *effective the first of March. In the interval, traders will have time to*
> *close their accounts. Also, the Deputy Quartermaster General will*
> *have made one dozen set of standard weights and measures to be*
> *made of iron.*—General Wayne's Orderly Book, February 1, 1796

To many readers of American history the term *frontier*
evokes images of cowboys and cattle drives, cavalry
and Indians, and Conestoga wagons—scenes of the vibrant post-Civil
War West. This epoch has occupied a disproportionate share of America's attention, in part because of our attraction to excitement, challenge, and change.

If we envision a broader definition of America's frontier as the
boundary that separated land settled by or at least under the control of
Americans from that western portion of the country that was not, our
time frame must be extended from the well-known twenty-five-year period to four hundred years.

But there was no permanent army, hence no sutlers, on the American frontier until after the American Revolution. Heightened concern
for occupation of the frontier caused Congress to attempt to quash the
Indians who were resisting American settlement of the Ohio Valley. Because initial attempts, by General Josiah Hamar in 1790 and by Major
General Arthur St. Clair in 1791, were disasters, Congress created a
standing army in 1792. Once across the Appalachians, the army re-

15

mained on the westering frontier until that frontier ceased to exist a century later. For the purpose of this study, therefore, the American frontier is defined as the period from 1790 to 1893.

During this period the enlisted man found himself serving as America's spearhead pioneer, and the army ended up playing corporate host to the sutler. Wherever the army went, so went the sutler; and whatever the army did, the sutler served as a witness, if not as a participant. It is the interaction between these entities—the army, the sutler, and the frontier—that forms the focal plane of our story.

In March 1792, when Congress created the Legion of the United States, General George Washington selected "Mad" Anthony Wayne to command it.[1] Two years later, in the summer of 1794, Wayne led two thousand men into the Ohio Valley where he was joined by fifteen hundred Kentucky volunteers. Then, on August 20, near what is now Toledo, Ohio, their combined forces encountered and defeated an allied force of native American Indians in a decisive encounter known as the Battle of Fallen Timbers.[2] The victory, the subsequent Treaty of Greenville in 1795, and the establishment of the army at Fort Greenville, some thirty-five miles northwest of the present town of Dayton, Ohio, temporarily cleared the way for American settlement in the Northwest Territory. To confirm its intention of remaining in control of the region, the American army garrisoned a series of forts in the Northwest Territory.[3]

The army's first frontier assignment was to keep the peace. Its soldiers built new roads and military posts, protected pockets of frontier settlers, enforced the laws, and attempted to reduce Indian aggression. Historian Francis Paul Prucha labeled these wilderness battlers as America's "agents of empire."[4]

Between 1792 and 1807, however, the army consisted of less than three thousand men. When partitioned to garrison a dozen frontier posts across the border, individual posts were left with an average of less than sixty men. In spite of the discrepancy between the available manpower and the magnitude of the assignment, Congress consistently sidestepped requests to increase the army's roster.[5]

To maximize the mobility and independence of individual units, U.S. Army commanding officers sought a reliable supply of basic foodstuffs and necessities. This was a difficult objective because the supply procurement process of the period was riddled by incompetence, bribery, nepotism, and fraud.[6] So, in their need, officers turned to an age-old source of supply: the sutler. Older soldiers, merchants, and the few who had served as sutlers during the Revolutionary War obtained informal appointments from regimental colonels and post commanders and headed west.

To suttle on America's frontier with America's fledgling army was equivalent to operating a marginally profitable business in an unstable environment—what entrepreneurs refer to as a high-risk business. In the past, as long as the army was engaged in hostilities, the sutler knew he was needed and he found ways to make his trade profitable. After a short time on the frontier, the sutler learned that the situation was quite different. Many discovered that for each dollar of profit they had envisioned, they stood an equal chance of spending more than a dollar's worth of effort, if not assuming more than a dollar's worth of debt.

Consider the sutler's situation. On the one hand, as one of a number of civilian camp followers who had made their way to the frontier to serve the army, he was virtually on his own. A good portion of his concerns derived from his informal association with the army. Camp followers received indirect protection from the army's proximity, but they were required to set up their shops outside the stockade. Like the laundresses, blacksmiths, cobblers, and tailors with whom the sutler was collectively classified, he was welcome to make a small profit as long as he obeyed regulations.[7] The army readily admitted that it had need of his food and wares, but it made no room for him in its organization and wanted no responsibility for his welfare.

Not that living inside the post would have been that much better. The frontier military post of the early 1800s was a crude and Spartan establishment, often fifty miles from the nearest town and hundreds from the nearest city. Officers and men inside the stockade were left to their own resources. Fort Wayne provides a good turn-of-the-century example.

A lonely outpost in the heart of Indian country where a soldier's life was hard and dull: that was the image advanced by Bert J. Griswold, author of the *Pictorial History of Fort Wayne*. The scene he creates could be replicated endlessly and do justice to any post on the frontier in 1800, especially when he wrote:

Quarreling, drunkenness, and insubordination were inevitable and incessant. Gambling persisted in spite of stringent regulations against card playing. There was difficulty in finding men capable of living up to the responsibilities of noncommissioned officers. Time and again men were promoted, only to be reduced to the ranks for drunkenness or fighting; their places had to be given to others just like them, who were usually disciplined in their turn. . . . Punishments were severe and brutal during the first years. . . . Flogging on the bare back before the troops at parade was almost the only recourse of court-martial and officers. Stoppage of the whiskey ration often accompanied such a sentence.[8]

On the other hand, to keep his job, the sutler had to satisfy the requirements set forth by the Adjutant General of the U.S. Army and obey regulations issued by local commanders. Because the frontier environment was more Darwinian than it was noble, the sutler's costs varied proportionally with the length of his supply line and the season. The market he serviced was unstable, and outside complications ranged from unlimited competition with Indians, half-breeds, traders, and squatters to sudden war. Indeed, to suttle on the frontier was to operate a business between the proverbial rock and a hard place. It was a profession in which only a few were going to be adept or successful.

Turnover during the early days of frontier suttling was understandably high. At Fort Wayne, for example, five sutlers tried their hand between 1802 and 1814. Even though three were related to the presiding or prior commanding officer, and three of the five had a background in merchandising, the position turned over on the average of once every three years.

Mr. Samuel Abbott, who was the sutler from 1802 to 1804, came from a family of prominent Detroit British traders. More importantly, his brother, James, was son-in-law to Major John Whistler, who commanded Fort Dearborn until 1810 and Fort Wayne in 1815 and 1816. Samuel Abbott's successor at Fort Wayne, James Peltier, another trader from Detroit, suttled there from 1804 to 1807.[9] The third in line, Dr. Abraham Edwards, was a son-in-law of Colonel Thomas Hunt, who once commanded Fort Detroit and then Fort Bellefontaine, situated close to St. Louis. Edwards held the sutler's position from 1807 until 1810. The fourth sutler, William Oliver, was a physician by training. Referred to as a "gentleman from Virginia," he held the suttling reins until George Hunt, another son of the aforementioned Colonel Hunt, arrived from Fort Madison in 1812.

Frontier post conditions forced the sutler of the early 1800s to be a survivor, a cunning man who could sideslip regulations if necessary; a man who could catch the scent of trouble before it arrived. Those who survived remained alert to sudden reassignment of their commanding officer and to revisions in local regulations, particularly those that governed the sale of whiskey. More than a few sutlers were kicked off a military reservation or had their huts destroyed because they overlooked or disregarded regulations related to liquor sales. But whiskey was so endemic to military post life that the intelligent sutler accepted rather than fought the frequent changes in local rules.

The main concern of all of the camp followers on any given day was the mood of the commanding officer. On the military frontier he was the source of law, order, and punishment, as well as the wellspring of favors. When a regiment was separated for duty, sent off to battle, or relocated, the officer in charge effectively became the commanding officer. These were the men the sutler had to know and please. In some instances, the task meant providing special favors, sometimes to the point of allowing the officer to become a silent partner.

A change in the commanding officer could be sudden and rapid. During the first decades on the frontier a commanding officer could be rotated to a new assignment every year or two. The army's organization and disposition were in constant flux, so a new post commander might suddenly appear, accompanied by family, relatives, and friends in need of jobs. To replace the current sutler was a simple act of authority. In short, the sutler had no job security.

Selling whiskey did nothing to improve the sutler's security at his frontier post, but no other commodity he sold rivaled its importance. In fact, throughout his professional career, alcoholic beverages were his best-sellers and his greatest source of profit. They were also his supreme source of trouble.

Every post commander in the early 1800s spent a considerable amount of time in playing police chief and judge, presiding over almost daily courts-martial. More than half of the discipline cases stemmed from a soldier's too frequent encounters with whiskey. Since the sutler supplied most of the whiskey, references to Regular Army sutlers and to sutlers attached to militia units in the late 1700s and early 1800s appeared most often in local regulations that dealt with controlling the availability and consumption of alcoholic beverages.

The manner in which spirits were controlled at frontier posts varied widely. A post commander might designate military personnel who could enter the sutler's premises by issuing permits to purchase. He might issue a list of personnel banned from the sutler's store, and place the store out of bounds to sick personnel. He might assign responsibility to the officers by requiring them to issue written permission on a per-case basis.[10] But because hard liquor was permitted some of the time, the line between acceptable and unlawful behavior was not always clear. In June 1813, a private at Fort Wayne purchased and consumed whiskey in the sutler's store even though he had only been given permission to purchase a pint of cordial. The captain saw him and seized the cup from his hand. When he smelled whiskey, he threw the liquid in the man's face and ordered him to the guardhouse. The soldier was court-martialed.[11]

When General Anthony Wayne's men were stationed at Fort Greenville, Ohio, the camp orderly book was replete with discipline problems stemming from the unauthorized consumption of alcohol. Wayne banned the sale of all liquor for select periods of time, and officers were forbidden to grant permission to any noncommissioned officer, private, or any follower of the army to purchase liquor on any pretense. Anyone detected selling liquor was charged with willful disobedience of orders and was punished accordingly.[12]

When General Wilkinson commanded the military post at Detroit, he installed this same stringent control to cope with what he termed a general condition of "desertion, licentiousness, drunkenness, and disorderly conduct." He also imposed martial law. Interestingly enough, when his sutlers complained, Wilkinson modified his order.[13]

Wilkinson's radical measures were no more effective than the temporary, half-hearted controls that most commanding officers employed to minimize drinking. The most effective method to enforce post and regimental rules was to punish the sutler. Sutlers Isaac Vanhist and Nathaniel Reader of Fort Wayne were charged with selling spiritous liquors to soldiers of the legion, contrary to orders issued January 24 and July 6, 1794. Both men were ordered from camp without the liberty of returning as sutlers. That same summer, sutler William Shannon and his soldier colleague, Matthew Gill, were charged with disobedience of the general order prohibiting the sale of whiskey. They also had attempted to defraud a private of his twenty dollars of discharge money by overcharging him. The civilian sutler, Shannon, received a light sentence: he was allowed to leave camp. Soldier Gill, however, was given one hundred lashes on his bare back and drummed out of the service.[14] The lesson was not lost on others.

As a point of interest, the majority of orders issued by U.S. Army general staff officers to control the sutler during this "settling-in" period, from 1784 to 1821, withstood the test of time. Garrison orders set forth under "Mad" Anthony Wayne can be found virtually unchanged in army regulations as late as the 1880s. Not that Anthony Wayne was necessarily an innovative commander; on the contrary, he relied on established practice and principles established by preceding commanders, including those created by the First Duke of Marlborough and Frederick the Great. Both of these commanders defined the boundaries of acceptable behavior for their camp followers. In essence, the rules that were shaped in Europe during the early 1700s were used in the U.S. Army throughout the 1800s.

One of the more obvious adaptations of early sutler regulations was the use of Marlborough's concept of grand sutler and petty sutler.[15] On February 27, 1796, General Wayne called all of his officers to a noon meeting at the Adjutant General's quarters to select a grand sutler for the troops. "The extortions, abuses and excesses daily committed by the swarm of petty traders and smugglers who creek [*sic*] into the village," he said, "render such an arrangement indispensable as well to the preservation of good order and the support of discipline, as to the comfort and accommodation of individuals."[16]

The person elected to the office of grand sutler was provided the power to issue licenses to all dealers and traders.[17] In turn, he was held responsible to ensure that the cantonment received a constant and competent supply of "sound and wholesome groceries and provision, with a suitable assortment of dry goods." His duties included procuring vegetables in season, stall- and grass-fed beef, and mutton. Prices, unless altered by a board of officers, were to remain fixed. He would also ensure that no whiskey was introduced to the cantonment under his authority and that no sale of spiritous liquor was made to enlisted men except with the written permission of a commissioned officer. If complaints were registered against him, he would be removed. Any sutler who failed to cooperate with these rules, added Wayne, "shall be turned out, his property confiscated and he will never be able to deal again with the troops."[18]

To extend control over his sutlers, Wayne used a device employed by Napoleon Bonaparte, Frederick the Great, and George Washington:

he licensed them. And in May 1795, when Wayne prepared to conduct the Greenville Treaty with the chiefs of the Indian tribes he had bested at the Battle of Fallen Timbers, Adjutant General John Mills told all traders, sutlers, and storekeepers to vacate every post and garrison west of the Miami of the Ohio. They were to remove all stores, goods, wares, and merchandise on or before the fifteenth of the month or forfeit everything. A few, mentioned by name, were to remain for trading.[19] The order was pointedly designed to "stop the increase of sutlers and to ensure sobriety, peace and harmony between the Indians and the soldiers during the pending Treaty." This was Wayne's way of admitting that the only way he could fully control the sutlers was to select a few of the trustworthy and ban the rest.

Licensed or unlicensed, every sutler who wished to sell his goods to soldiers on the frontier faced a variety of local garrison orders. These regulations described the boundaries of the sutler's daily routine, including how, when, and to whom he could issue whiskey, what items he was supposed to stock, and his hours of operation.[20] Occasionally an order dealt with a more fundamental issue, such as hygiene. An 1802 "Ordinance for the Government of Sutlers or Inhabitants residing in the Vicinity of Fort Wayne" upbraided civilians—and specifically sutlers—who occupied the public ground near the fort for having allowed "refuse and filth" to accumulate in the streets and around their dwellings. The order demanded that they clean up the "puterfaction" and keep the streets and dwellings clean. Those who remained negligent would be "denied the privileges they enjoy" and be treated as the good of the service of the United States requires. A few days later, the Officer of the Day was instructed to confine any sutler or inhabitant who ignored the ordinance and report their names.[21]

The sutler could also benefit from his post commander's autocratic whims. When the commandant of Fort Wayne noticed that his officers were "sliding into primitive habits," a condition he defined as dining without tablecloths and eating without benefit of utensils or plates, he ordered each man to set aside half a month's pay and purchase "two table cloths and two towels," from Mr. Abbott, the sutler. Those who needed knives, forks, or plates were also to purchase one of each.[22]

When the men complained about the quality and price of liquor, sugar, and tea sold by sutler Peltier, Fort Wayne's commanding officer, Captain John Whipple, took time to explain the situation to his men. When the trade of the company was given to Mr. Peltier, he said,

Peltier agreed to trade on the same principles used by the prior sutler, Mr. Abbott, but Peltier's costs were higher.

Although some articles are high, Mr. Peltier does not get the advance Mr. Abbott did, owing to the highness of transportation. Instead of getting a boat load brought to this place for forty dollars, which is the customary price in spring and summer, it has cost Mr. Peltier more than one hundred dollars. In the spring and summer when transportation is cheap, he must lower his prices accordingly. It will happen that a trader cannot always get the best flavored liquors and sugars, but the C.O. does not wish any soldier to trade with Mr. Peltier contrary to his own inclination.[23]

A century of new opportunities was offered to sutlers when the Army of the United States created a series of permanent frontier military posts. As with any social institution, change came slowly, but as of 1810 sutlers must have sensed the potential for a permanent position. Military post commanders were beginning to select one sutler to serve as their official trader, and communications such as Whipple's notice to his men indicated that the army was beginning to pay attention to the complicated nature of suttling. Whipple's hands-off attitude and his deference to "Mr. Peltier, the sutler," implied that the trader's status at the post was on the rise.

Yet the sutler was still defined as a camp follower. As such, he would remain a civilian outside the military system. He continued to be suspect, with good reason, of being opportunistic and unethical, and with the exception of the occasional in-law, the sutler's influence was limited. He still had little if any social relationship with his commanding officer. In fact, continuance of a sutler's services was contingent on a post commander maintaining what Anthony Wayne referred to as a balance between good order and discipline versus comfort and accommodation.

Army-wide reliance on sutlers for a steady supply of provisions was the catalyst for the formation of new bonds between the sutler and the military establishment. The sutler's advantage over suppliers based in Washington, D.C., was his motivation to do a good job at the post itself. In time, he eventually became accepted as a professional.

In the early 1800s, however, the sutler had a ways to go. He would need to overcome obstacles far more difficult than temperamental post commanders and periodic changes in regulations before he could begin to think in longer range financial terms and job security.

THREE

Risks, Losses, and Retreats

Mr. Kinzie [sutler] was taken at Chicago and brought to Detroit during the war. Every possible attempt was made by British agents to attach him to their interests and when they found this unsuccessful, they sent him in irons to Quebec where he continued a long time in captivity.—Governor Lewis Cass

F or the sutler who confined his business to the frontier post garrison, the risk of doing business was directly proportional to eccentricities of the reigning commanding officer and to the occasional policy surprises issued by the Adjutant General. For the sutler who pursued the more lucrative fur trade with local Indian tribes, the risk of doing business, especially during the period immediately preceding the War of 1812, was considerably greater. Aside from the possibility of losing his goods, if not his hair, the trader could count on serious competition, not from French or British traders (although they wielded heavy influence over the Indians until the War of 1812), but from the U.S. government.

Between 1796 and 1822, the American government carried on its own retail trade with the Indians. A series of government-owned and -operated "factories" (essentially warehouses) of Indian trade goods provided cheap trinkets and tools at prices slightly above the cost of manufacture. The government's trading objective was to placate and befriend the Indians. Government officials were also concerned that Indian furs should be placed in the hands of U.S. traders rather than those of the French and British.

The individual who represented the government was the factor. He spent his time transporting goods to his assigned frontier post, trading with the Indians, and shipping furs back east in the spring. Between 1796 and 1809, government factories were established at Forts Wayne, Detroit, Chickasaw Bluffs, Stephens, Chicago, Bellefontaine, Natchitoches, Arkansas Post, Sandusky, Madison, Michilimackinac, and Osage. After the War of 1812 the system expanded to nearly two dozen outlets.[1] The quality of the goods was reputedly poor and shipments were unreliable, so many factors lost money. Finally, in 1822, under severe pressure from influential members of the fur-trade industry like business tycoon John Jacob Astor, the government licked its wounds, absorbed its losses, and bowed out of the Indian trading business.

While the factory system was in operation, however, a factor was often the frontier sutler's closest neighbor and competitor. The results of such proximal relationships produced mixed results: at Fort Dearborn, there was immeasurable trouble; at Fort Madison, the factor and the sutler went into business together.

When Fort Dearborn was built in 1804 on land now occupied by downtown Chicago, an Indian trader named John Kinzie was appointed as post sutler. His original name was McKenzie; he was a Britisher, born in Quebec, Canada, in 1763. A silversmith by trade and an Indian trader by preference, Kinzie had been in the northwest area since the 1780s. He possessed a good reputation and was highly respected by the Indians. The Sioux called him Shaw-nee-aw-kee, silversmith. He knew their language, and at one time or another, he established branch trading posts at Rock River, Milwaukee, and St. Joseph. He had also been an Indian trader in the area since 1795.

Kinzie was a survivor. He had a post at the Miami Rapids during the peak of the conflict between the first waves of American settlers and the Seneca. After the Battle of Fallen Timbers, Kinzie served as an interpreter at the 1795 Treaty of Grenville. And when General Wayne took control of the entire region, Kinzie protected his interests by becoming an American citizen.[2]

Kinzie's first years at Fort Dearborn went well. As sutler, Kinzie flourished. He enlarged and improved his home, built a dairy, baking ovens, and stables, and erected quarters for his employees, "the Frenchmen." He also entertained men of power and privilege. Governor Lewis Cass was among the distinguished guests at his home.

As an Indian trader, he supervised a thriving trade in the heart of Illinois, and as the local justice of the peace, he performed the first wedding ceremony at the post by joining in matrimony trader Samuel Abbott and the daughter of Fort Dearborn's commanding officer, Major Whistler.

After several years of relative calm, the government factor at Fort Dearborn, Matthew Irwin, informed the Secretary of War that the commanding officer, Captain Cooper, had appointed his own son as the official post sutler. The surgeon's mate had been made a partner, and First Lieutenant Thomas Hamilton—the commanding officer's son-in-law—was also somehow involved. No one, said Irwin, controlled their prices or activities. John Kinzie continued to operate his store, but those soldiers who wanted to purchase anything from him were punished. With bristling righteous indignation, Irwin claimed that three-fourths of every soldier's pay was spent at the post sutler store; profits therefore must have been immense. To support his claim, he reported that a man from Ohio had offered the surgeon two thousand dollars for his share of the enterprise.

Irwin documented his allegations by enclosing a list of comparative prices between "Cooper and Whistler's" store and "J. Kinzey's [*sic*]."[3]

ITEM	COOPER	KINZIE
Whiskey	.50/qt.	.375/qt
Tobacco	.75/lb.	.50/lb.
Brown Sugar	.25/lb.	.1675/lb.
Black ball	.50/stick	.25/stick
Shoe brushes	.75/pr	.50/pr

(Prices are in fractions of a dollar.)

After the Secretary of War verified the facts, he brought formal charges against Cooper, Whistler, and Hamilton. Captain Cooper was relieved of command on July 5, 1810, and replaced by Captain Heald. Captain Whistler was ordered to Detroit, while his son, Lieutenant William Whistler, was sent to Fort Wayne. Cooper's son-in-law, Lieutenant Hamilton, was charged with conduct unbecoming an officer (at some point in the brouhaha, he allegedly challenged Kinzie to a duel) and was transferred to Fort Bellefontaine. He ended up at Fort Madison on the banks of the Mississippi, in what is now Iowa.[4]

On May 5, 1812, Irwin sent another of his inflammatory letters to the Secretary of War. This one accused Kinzie of keeping Fort Dearborn officers from a reconciliation with the Indians, and alleged that Kinzie had interfered with the duties of the Indian agent. In reference to the "dangerous character of the man," Irwin said that Kinzie was not to be trusted. As an example of Kinzie's penchant for foul play, Irwin said he had smuggled goods into the country from Canada. Earlier that spring, Irwin had accused Kinzie and Forsyth of having bribed a man in Washington four hundred dollars a year to ensure that they were given the sutlership at Dearborn.

The antagonism between Kinzie and Irwin may have tainted Kinzie's attitude toward a salaried interpreter at Fort Dearborn, a close associate of Irwin's named Lalime. One day around 1809 or 1810, just outside the post grounds, Kinzie and Lalime exchanged words, then fought. Lalime had a pistol; Kinzie had his knife. Lalime shot Kinzie, but Kinzie killed Lalime. There were no known eyewitnesses. A military investigation cleared Kinzie of criminal conduct, but the soldiers, who had liked the translator, extracted some revenge by having Lalime's body buried in full view of the Kinzie home.

The relationship between the factor and the sutler at Fort Dearborn was the antithesis of that at Fort Madison. The Fort Madison factor, a veteran named John W. Johnson, and the sutler, George Hunt, side-stepped the problems of competition at a small, isolated post, and formed a partnership.

George Hunt was the son of Colonel Thomas Hunt, a career officer with the First Regiment, United States Infantry.[5] The colonel had served during the American Revolution and then commanded Forts Defiance, Wayne, and Detroit. In 1803, Colonel Hunt commanded Fort Bellefontaine, and in 1807 he led the original contingent of troops to build Fort Madison.

Colonel Hunt's progeny and their spouses were heavily involved in suttling. Of his three sons, Thomas, George, and John Elliott, and two daughters, Ruth and Elizabeth, at least two sons and both his sons-in-law were frontier post sutlers. The first to represent the family in suttling was Ruth's husband, Dr. Abraham Edwards of Detroit. The couple was married in 1804, after having met either in Detroit or during Colonel Hunt's relocation to Fort Wayne the year before he was assigned to Fort Bellefontaine. Although Colonel Hunt did not appoint his son-in-law as sutler while he commanded Fort Wayne, it's reasonable to suspect that Edwards used his familial position to acquire the position, which he filled from 1807 until 1810.

After Colonel Hunt died in 1808, his sons, George, and Thomas Hunt, Jr., asked Captain Zebulon Pike to write to the Secretary of War on their behalf. Both Pike and the Secretary of War had known the Hunt boys' father well.[6] A short time thereafter, George arrived at Fort Madison as sutler. (Son Thomas was not mentioned again.) Four years later, when the post was abandoned in the fall of 1812, George Hunt went to Fort Wayne to serve as sutler until 1814. His brother, John Elliott, clerked for him.

George's second sister, Elizabeth, married James G. Soulard (1798–1878) of St. Louis in 1820. For the first two years of their marriage, the couple resided at Fort Snelling where James acted as the post sutler.

Of the family's suttling activities, most is known about George while at Fort Madison. This post was one of two constructed solely to protect local government Indian factories. The original factory depot for the region was located at Bellefontaine. To improve the effectiveness of the trade, two new posts, Madison and Osage, were established closer to the Indian tribes. Had the government not sought the Indian trade, neither post would have been constructed.[7]

Lieutenant Hamilton (Captain Cooper's son-in-law from Fort Dearborn), and his wife, Catherine, were also at Fort Madison. They probably considered the assignment cruel and unusual punishment; the post was a one-story, rough-log barracks and stockade, tucked away in the heart of hostile Sauk Indian territory and garrisoned by fifty men and officers of the First Infantry Regiment. The post was guarded by pickets five feet high and by sentinels who stood guard night and day.

The post store, which sutler George Hunt built and operated, was located to one side of the post gates. Hunt's bread-and-butter trading goods were basic foodstuffs: refined sugar, coffee and tea, chocolate, molasses, pepper, butter, bacon, rice, cheese, raisins, tobacco, and snuff, and a variety of alcoholic beverages.

The U.S. goverment factory store, built by the troops, was situated on the other side of the post gates, opposite Hunt's store.[8] It was operated by factor John Johnson, who issued credit to the local Sauk, Fox, and Iowa Indian tribes in the fall in exchange for pelts in the spring. He also traded tools (and probably weapons). As per his instructions from his superiors, he sold at prices that covered his expenses and gave him a minimum of profit. The Indians often ridiculed his goods, but they nonetheless continued to trade with him.

In 1811, Johnson proposed that Hunt journey up the Mississippi past Galena, Illinois, establish a trading post, and trade factory goods for lead. Hunt accepted the offer, hired five Frenchmen, and headed up-river. On the bank of the river, close to the source of lead, he built a storehouse and a lead house, and began to ship two thousand pounds of lead per day by canoe to Johnson. While Hunt was thus engaged that fall, the War of 1812 broke out. Winnebago Indians, retreating from the first armed battle of the conflict, the Battle of Tippecanoe, camped close by his store. The following morning, they arrayed themselves in a manner that meant they were friendly and wanted to trade. When the white traders were exposed and armless, the Indians shot, scalped, and mutilated every white man in the camp except for Hunt, who they thought was Saginash—English. They nonetheless broke open his trunk, took his shirts and all of his goods, and then celebrated with the contents of a barrel of whiskey they found cached beneath the floor of Hunt's room.

During the subsequent scene of drunkenness, Hunt escaped and made his way to Fort Madison. He arrived January 4, 1812, after a bone-chilling 250-mile trip. Lieutenant Hamilton (who had been forgiven his indiscretion at Fort Dearborn in 1810) had been promoted to captain and was in command of the post when Hunt straggled in. "George Hunt is here a poor distressed creature," wrote Hamilton, "without a cent or a good suit of clothes."[9]

In August, Fort Mackinac was taken by the British. The loss caused General Hull to call for the evacuation of Fort Dearborn. On the morning of August 15, ninety-six men, women, and children, including protesting post sutler John Kinzie and his family, exited the post. All too soon, a scout preceding the caravan discovered that hostile Indians were laying an ambush. Defenses were hastily prepared, but the troops were overwhelmed. Of the ninety-six evacuees, only forty-three survived. The fact that no one in Kinzie's family was killed and that none of his property at the post was ever burned was a tribute to his relationship with the Indians.[10]

In September 1815, at the conclusion of the war, Kinzie served as an interpreter at the Treaty of Spring Wells, which was conducted near

Detroit. A year later, Governor Cass sought assistance to get Kinzie appointed as manager of the Indian agency at Chicago. In July 1816, Kinzie returned to Chicago, but he was unable to reestablish his Indian trade and soon fell into bankruptcy. He continued to act as an interpreter, but as of 1821 he wrote to his son, John, that he was paid only one hundred dollars for subsistence while he had acted as interpreter to an 1821 treaty. He found employment as a subagent for the Indian Department, and later as an agent for the American Fur Company. He died in January 1828 at age sixty-one.

Fort Madison was also among the frontier posts that fell to the Indians during the first year of the War of 1812. The post was hardly designed to withstand siege or a major attack, so when two hundred Sauk and Fox Indians surrounded Fort Madison the month following the Fort Dearborn massacre, the small garrison set fire to the post and escaped down the Mississippi.[11] George Hunt's Fort Madison flight from the Indians was a curtain call of his escape upriver the year before. He eventually wrote an account of the last days at the post.[12]

In addition to uninsured business losses sustained by veteran sutlers like John Kinzie at Fort Dearborn and George Hunt at Fort Madison, sutler vulnerability to irreversible loss during hostilities is further illustrated by the hardships suffered by Alabama sutler Benjamin S. Smool.[13]

Smool suttled at least from 1809 to 1815. During the War of 1812, he served the Second Regiment, U.S. Infantry, at Fort Bowyer, Mobile Point, Alabama.[14] American soldiers and officers caught up in the War of 1812 supplemented their rations with such commodities as they could afford to buy from their sutler, including fresh vegetables, fruits, coffee, liquor, and tobacco.

Smool assumed the risk of selling merchandise to the men of the Second Regiment on credit. Extending credit was part of doing business, because at this time in history the American soldier was paid in an irregular fashion. If the single-market sutler declined to extend credit, he would not have been able to serve the men properly and his sales (and profits) would have been severely restricted. All sutlers traded heavily on credit, with the hope that their regimental officers would allow them fair treatment at the pay table. Smool also built a storehouse to protect his merchandise. Since he was physically positioned within the boundaries of the post, he constructed his building on post grounds.

Smool's faith in his officers was well placed. The commanding officer, Major Chamberlain, asserted that it had been his custom, and that of other officers in the Second Regiment, to permit his soldiers to trade with the sutler near the time when pay was due, for "one half to three-quarters of pay, and on pay day see the sutler paid."[15]

The first signs of trouble arrived in the spring of 1814, when it became apparent that the British would attack and had the wherewithal to overpower the fort. The commanding officer, Major Chamberlain, ordered Smool's building destroyed so that neither it nor the goods inside would fall into enemy hands. His decision was justified when soon thereafter the fort fell to the British.

The soldiers of the Second Regiment were disbanded in 1815, but because the paymaster had no coin, the men were discharged "on certificate." That situation left Smool with a handful of worthless accounting sheets that contained the records of credit sales to an entire regiment for nearly a year.

Smool quickly discovered that no one was going to help him recover his losses, and there was no court of appeals. Under army regulations of the time, a sutler had no means of compelling the payment of debts contracted. Sutlers also routinely sustained heavy losses by the death and desertion of indebted soldiers. In Smool's case, his losses utterly destroyed his business.

Nearly twenty years after the war, the tenacious Smool was allowed to file a claim against the government for the value of his building and destroyed goods. During litigation of this claim, Major Chamberlain testified that Smool's services had been quite important to his men. His troops had received many comforts and conveniences from the sutler's store "which they could not have procured from any other," he said. The sutler's assortment and stock were "always extensive and well calculated to contribute to the comfort and necessities of the regiment." This assessment was echoed by the regimental artillery officer, Lieutenant A. L. Sands, who confessed that soldiers "were dependent upon the sutlers for all their comforts, which could not have been elsewhere procured while they were kept without pay."[16]

Commander of the U.S. Army, Major General Alexander Macomb, took the occasion to define the extent to which the army would assume liability for sutler equipment and goods by rejecting Smool's claim. When forts are spacious enough, he said, a specific area could be set aside for the sutler's buildings, but Fort Bowyer was a small place and sutler Smool had elected to build his storehouse without the permission of the commanding officer.[17] The value of his services notwithstanding, when a sutler did something on government property on his own, he must suffer the risks of war.

The sutler of the early 1800s was well aware that he was in a high-risk business. Competition from his own government was probably a nasty blow to his profit margin, but since he volunteered to accompany soldiers on the frontier, he couldn't complain about the sudden appearance of hostilities, be they against Indians or the British. In the midst of turmoil, the independent sutler maintained his supply lines and his credit. But the risks, the kind of eventualities encountered by Kinzie, Hunt, and Smool, kept their prices high. The average soldier's lament about "systematic gouging" by his sutler—a recurrent theme through the nineteenth century—was not always due to some rascal's desire to get rich quickly.[18]

In 1818, similar experiences by other sutlers would form the basis of a series of recommendations to the army to stabilize the suttling business. The sutler's horizon was getting brighter, but on the eve of battle in 1812, relief was still a decade away.

FOUR

Suttling on the Mississippi

I intend giving up the suttling at the Council Bluffs, finding that, at the present prices, being 50 percent on Phil'a [delphia] prices, I cannot make it an object [worth the] risk sinking money.—John O'Fallon, Letter to General Thomas A. Smith, 1822

During the period immediately following the War of 1812, America's western borderland, which included the Mississippi River Valley, was the scene of rapid change. Large numbers of American settlers were assimilating large new parcels on both sides of the river. As they grabbed up the land, these new frontiersmen bought out, drove out, and lobbied to relocate the reluctant but fearful Indian tribes of the region.

Because the Mississippi valley had become the new frontier, it was also the focus of considerable military activity. The army was expected to continue to maintain the peace between warring Indian tribes, restrain whites from disturbing the Indians, and enforce the law by arresting murderers and whiskey peddlers. When not thus occupied, the army was to stabilize and then reestablish control over the Mississippi River Valley and the thousand-mile frontier. For these purposes the U.S. Army was allotted less than ten thousand men.[1]

To stabilize the Mississippi valley region, the army first needed to deal with the Indians who had sided with the British in the War of 1812. The tactic it chose was the old stick-and-carrot approach:

treaties laced with gifts and intimidation followed by trade goods and the reminder that the army was not far away. The first treaty, executed at Spring Wells, Michigan, on September 8, 1815, settled affairs with eight Indian tribes, including the Chippewa, Ottawa, and Potawatomi. Soon thereafter, Territorial Governor William Clark supervised the execution of twelve additional treaties.[2] Trade was then renewed. To enable traders to introduce goods up and down the Missouri and Mississippi rivers, Indian trading factories were reestablished at reoccupied forts, at the mouth of the Illinois River on the Fox River–Wisconsin trading route, and between Lake Superior and the Upper Mississippi River.[3]

The army reestablished control over the American frontier's lengthy western and southern borders by reoccupying a number of forts taken by the British during the War of 1812 and by constructing a series of new posts. Because of the shortage of men, most of these posts were garrisoned by less than 200 men; most, in fact, were manned by a single company of 50 to 60 soldiers.[4] An 1817 profile of military posts showed Fort Hawkins with 34 men, Fort Scott with 117, and Fort Gaines with 25. Fort Crawford and Fort Snelling both had fewer than 100 men each.[5]

When conflict arose with Indians in unrelated incidents hundreds of miles apart, post garrisons were either thinned or stripped to develop an adqeuate force to meet the situation. On occasion, a regiment was permanently relocated. One thousand of the twelve hundred men Andrew Jackson had used to invade Florida in 1816 were redistributed to Camps Bellefontaine, Osage, and Clark on the frontier. The following year, all but 170 of the 850 men at Fort Bellefontaine were reallocated to other frontier posts.[6] Frontier posts thus became garrisoned on an "as-needed" basis while the U.S. Army spent considerable time on the move.

At this point in the development of the army, the sutler was attached to one or two regiments. Wherever the men went, so went the sutler. To adequately provision a fluctuating number of men on the move, the trader had to maintain a balance between credit, supply lines, sales, and inventory. Those sutlers assigned to units stationed along the Mississippi found it advantageous to shift their base of operations from East Coast cities like Philadelphia and New York to St. Louis. Situated at the confluence of the Mississippi and Missouri rivers, St. Louis, during the first several decades of the century, quickly became the heart of the West and the jumping-off spot for Far West exploration.

Yet even the sutlers who enjoyed the advantages of the proximity of this large supply center were tossed about by military, economic, and natural forces beyond their control. In addition to fluctuations in the location and size of their immediate market, sutlers suffered from East Coast bank failures, whose collapse generated a tidal wave of panic that quickly inundated St. Louis. The Mississippi and Missouri rivers also proved to be new hazards with which sutlers would have to reckon. One notable Mississippi valley trader named John O'Fallon discovered that when one entered a high-risk business like frontier suttling, even common sense and well-honed business skills were not always enough to guarantee success.

John O'Fallon was a good example of a new, rising breed of army sutler—the gentleman trader. He came from a good family with impeccable political and social connections, and he had acquired a good education. Before he entered suttling, his excellent personal reputation was enhanced by a distinguished military record. In addition, Mr. O'Fallon acquired the motivation to become a financial success. Unlike the lives of the majority of the eighteenth-century sutlers who preceded him, who never accomplished more than a passing entry in colonial, county, or military records, O'Fallon's life was well recorded.[7]

John O'Fallon's father was Dr. James O'Fallon, an Irishman who brought a heritage extending back to the A.D. 1014 Battle of Clontarf when he emigrated to America and settled in North Carolina in 1774. During the American Revolutionary War he served as the principal surgeon of the General Hospital of the United States and, soon after, married Frances E. ("Fanny") Clark, the youngest daughter of John and Ann (Rogers) Clark. The marriage made Dr. O'Fallon a brother-in-law to George Rogers Clark, the Virginian renowned for his frontier military leadership and achievements, and to William Clark of the Lewis and Clark 1804 expedition.[8]

When Dr. O'Fallon died in 1793, he left two sons, John, age two, and the newborn Benjamin. The boys were raised by William Clark at his home in St. Louis. Because Clark served as the governor of Missouri Territory until 1820 and was Missouri's Superintendent of Indian Affairs until 1838, both lads were provided with numerous opportunities to succeed or fail.[9]

After John O'Fallon graduated from college in Lexington in 1810, he was pressed by his friends to enter the army. More than likely he received encouragement from Major Croghan (father of Colonel George

Croghan), a close family friend. O'Fallon entered the army during the early days of the War of 1812, and was assigned to General Harrison's army at Vincennes, Indiana. By March 1814 he had been promoted to captain of the Second U.S. Rifle Regiment, a unit he commanded as of May 1815. At the close of the war, he was in charge of Fort Malden, in Canada, opposite the mouth of the Detroit River.[10]

Congress trimmed the army when the war was over. O'Fallon discharged a lot of his men and feared that he would lose his command, so he wrote influential men, including a number of congressmen, for an appointment as U.S. Indian agent or a U.S. government factor at the new military post near Green Bay. He simply said that he was captain of a rifle regiment, but too poor to go back home.

As it turned out, O'Fallon was one of four captains selected to be retained in the army, but he nonetheless resigned his commission on July 31, 1818, and returned to St. Louis.[11] A month later he was on his way up the Missouri River, following a portion of the trace that his uncle, William Clark, had taken fourteen years earlier. Instead of pushing against the current as an explorer for the president, John O'Fallon was sutler to a segment of a large army expedition.

O'Fallon had teamed up with the sutler at Bellefontaine, an old friend and ex-army captain named Lewis Bissell, who had served from 1808 to 1816. Fort Bellefontaine was the largest St. Louis military installation and staging post for military troops, so business there would have been good. As sutler to a new series of posts, O'Fallon saw an opportunity to extend, perhaps double, their business.

O'Fallon's familiarity with suttling came from his years in the army, and he gained insight into its profit potential from his brother, Benjamin, who suttled for General Clark during the 1813 expedition to Prairie du Chien.[12] In St. Louis, O'Fallon asked General Smith to recommend him to the Secretary of War. Smith was glad to do so, adding that O'Fallon was "a man of business and deserving of confidence."[13]

The new position with the expedition included the responsibility of serving as special paymaster. With his social and military background, he was certainly trustworthy enough, and since he would be traveling back and forth between the new western posts and St. Louis for supplies, the added responsibility made sense. In subsequent decades, the practice of using the sutler to support (sometimes supplant) the paymaster was a common frontier practice. The sutler usually had a lot of cash on hand and had the ability to bail out the post commandant when the army paymaster was late—a not uncommon occurrence.

The posts that O'Fallon was to serve would be established by a force later known as the 1818 Yellowstone expedition.[14] This military foray up the Missouri was undertaken by three separate contingents including a scientific unit under the command of Major Stephen H. Long. The tactical objective of the expedition was to place a military post at the Mandan Indian village sixteen hundred miles up the Missouri River. Secretary of War John C. Calhoun believed that from this location, the army could control the Indians in the Northwest, repel British influence, and protect, if not expand, American fur trade.[15] The strategic military objective was to take possession of the Northwest wilderness.

O'Fallon headed upriver in the company of a rifle regiment of the first contingent. He used a keelboat, probably manned by Frenchmen from St. Charles or St. Louis and in keeping with local practices. Since sutlers were not permitted to use army equipment, O'Fallon brought his own boat, the *General Jackson*. He also had horses follow the boat on land, because as the expedition hauled itself upstream at a rate of about seven miles per day, he made periodic return trips to St. Louis, accompanied on occasion by a few officers.[16]

On the journey, O'Fallon had his hands full. He played backup for the army contractor when the former ran out of whiskey, had one or more employees serve as "express" (mail carriers) to St. Louis, and toward the New Year of 1819 he paid the troops as special paymaster. As the surgeon for the troops commented:

> Capt. O'Fallon commenced paying the troops to the 31st December 1818. The prompt and regular Manner in which they have been paid, conduces much to reconcile them to their Secluded Situation. All who have discharged, have reenlisted.[17]

On October 18, 1818, fifty days out of St. Louis, the rifle company camped on an island called Isle des Vaches (Cow Island), sixteen miles north of present-day Omaha, Nebraska. Following army tradition, the camp was named Cantonment Martin after the captain who was in command.

Scurvy struck hard at Cantonment Martin. During the winter of 1818–19, half of the twelve hundred men became ill and more than one hundred men died.[18] The army nonetheless kept the men on the island until the following summer. John O'Fallon's employees continued to supply the men through the winter. In January 1819 O'Fallon returned to St. Louis, then headed east to purchase additional trade goods.[19] On the way back, he visited the home of David Meriwether, nephew of Meriwether Lewis of the 1804–06 Lewis and Clark expedition.

O'Fallon told David Meriwether that he was organizing a keelboat to send up the Missouri River that coming summer (of 1819). He would be attending to a rifle regiment of eight companies and the six hundred men in a regiment of infantry. He invited Meriwether to come along in his employ as a combination Indian trader and sutler, and offered to pay him two hundred dollars for the first year and three hundred dollars the second year. Remuneration would include all of the lad's expenses except clothing.

John O'Fallon was a close friend of the family. The nineteen-year-old probably leaped at the opportunity to go on such an adventure. David began his journey as supercargo (overseer) on a keelboat carrying goods to St. Louis. The goods were probably supplies that O'Fallon had earmarked for the voyage up the Missouri. He had them brought down the Ohio and the Mississippi to St. Louis by keelboat.[20]

Once this first task was accomplished and Meriwether was safely in St. Louis, he called on O'Fallon's partner, Captain Bissell, at Bissell's house outside Fort Bellefontaine. Bissell sent Meriwether up the Missouri by himself, with a rifle regiment of the Sixth Infantry in another keelboat that was owned by their suttling company. In Meriwether's diary, he said that both O'Fallon and Bissell were courteous gentlemen, so he remained in their employ for three years.[21]

Even though General Atkinson was in charge of the expedition, O'Fallon appeared to report to General Thomas S. Smith of Fort Bellefontaine. In April 1819, he advised the general that one of his boats had arrived safely at Cantonment Martin and that he would be happy to continue to sell the government whiskey at four dollars per gallon. He explained that the government contractor had run out of whiskey, so he was supplying the troops. The expedition's plan, he informed Smith, was to depart St. Louis on May 1. O'Fallon said he doubted the troops would get under way until mid-June. He was correct and, on June 28, wrote again that he was still waiting to depart. "The Rifle Co for which [General Atkinson] appointed me started last week. . . . I think I will be able to leave here on the 15th of next month."[22]

General Atkinson arrived in St. Louis in the spring of 1819. By the time he found Major Long on the Missouri River, Long's men had buttoned up at Engineer Cantonment for the winter. As in the winter of 1818, the troops were hit hard by scurvy. In the following spring a flood destroyed the encampment.[23]

The expedition had been so slow to accomplish its mission that Congress cut further funding. As a result, the army relinquished the idea of reaching the Mandan village and built its furthermost post at Council Bluffs, the point at which they were then located.

Lewis and Clark had had a powwow with local Indians in 1804 at Council Bluffs. It was located a few miles above Fort Lisa, a private post that controlled trade between 1812 and 1823 with the Omaha, Otoe, Pawnee, and other local tribes. Council Bluffs (later called Fort Atkinson) was patterned after the old blockhouse and palisade pattern, except that the compound was considerably greater. Each side was two hundred yards long, and its perimeter was defined by a fence with three gates. Posts similar to Council Bluffs evolved into small villages, each with a sawmill, quarry, Indian agency, laundry, hospitals, barns, stables, and a sutler's store.[24] Soldiers enforced local law and removed one major obstacle to settlement by building a network of roads. The men also explored, surveyed, and mapped unknown regions.[25] Troops also assisted government factors (until 1822), cut their own wood, loaded and unloaded cargo, drilled, removed white settlers from Indian lands, guarded the lead mines of Illinois and Missouri, and went on punitive expeditions against Indians. To increase the stability and permanence of their fort, they tended gardens to reduce the threat of scurvy. They also herded stock and hunted and fished to offset delays of contracted supplies.[26]

Bissell took charge of the trading post at Council Bluffs and found business good. By 1816, frontier troops had come to expect to see a sutler at their post, and they had come to rely on him to supplement provisions provided by the Commissary and Quartermaster Department. Colonel Alexander McNair and his brother, who supervised construction of the first sutler store at Fort Crawford in 1816, supplied its soldiers with flour, beans, pork, salt, candles, clothing, whiskey, soap, tobacco, coffee, and miscellaneous articles.[27] As to why the sutler was provided the option of carrying staples like coffee, sugar, tobacco, and other "delicacies," David Meriwether learned that the army did not provide them to soldiers as part of rations: the men were required to buy them out of their pay.[28]

Whiskey was another portable commodity supplied by the sutler. In fact, by the late 1810s most aspects of a soldier's life at outposts along the Mississippi and Missouri rivers had not changed very much from the patterns in vogue at Fort Wayne twenty years earlier. Courts-martial, fines, restrictions, and imprisonment remained abundant, and amusements were limited to gambling, horse races, shooting contests, an occasional library or band, and constant drinking.[29]

By the summer of 1820, David Meriwether had been acting as Indian trader in the Council Bluffs area for about a year. He had traded with the Pawnee and had carried out reconnaissance on a wagon road to New Mexico. In June, he and his black slave, Alfred, set out for Santa Fe on an exploration to check on wagon routes for his employers. He was accompanied by a party of Pawnees that included Chief Big Elk. Somewhere near the head of the Canadian River, they encountered a troop of Mexican soldiers who killed everyone except Meriwether, Alfred, and three Pawnees. Meriwether and Alfred were arrested, taken to Santa Fe, and thrown into jail.

The year 1820 was an equally bad year for O'Fallon. A month after Meriwether was incarcerated, the thirty-year-old trader saw his dreams of becoming a wealthy sutler shattered. An entire boatload of cargo had been lost to the black waters of the Missouri a few miles above Fort Osage. O'Fallon wrote General Smith of his loss. Referring to the incident as "a prodigious, nay incalculable loss," he asked that if any packages were picked up along the shore, they be directed to his agent located at Fort Osage.

Like any young entrepreneur, O'Fallon refused to be daunted by a turn of bad luck. He commenced purchasing again as best he could in St. Louis and planned to start another keelboat upriver by the first of August. In the meantime, he voiced his hope to General Smith that in light of his troubles the officers would be more liberal with him in prices, at least until he was reinstated.

The loss turned out to be ruinous. Even though there were upwards of one thousand men at the post, O'Fallon showed beginning doubts about continuing as sutler. In his July 27, 1820, letter to General Smith, he wrote, "I am engaged in starting on another boat with such articles as will replace the cost as far as this place will enable me," he wrote. "I must [wind?] up my [concession?] up the Missouri as soon as I can with safety. I consider it vastly better to make small profits without care and anxiety than great ones with those inconveniences."[30]

The following January, after first informing the general that he'd received information that the army was about to be reduced to six thousand rank and file, he addressed his situation as sutler to Council
Bluffs. "I discover that we have only had the semblance of distress as
respects our money affairs and that its reality is fast approaching us in
all its horrors. . . . Since the loss of my boat, having been completely
deranged in my calculations, I have had to resort to every shift to maintain my credit, but I hope in the course of the summer to be clear of
debt unless some unlooked for reverse intervenes."[31]

O'Fallon's cargo could not have chosen a worse time to go floating
downriver. Two years earlier the Second United States Bank back East
had failed. Between 1819 and 1821, its death throes shook St. Louis
with such force that they generated a panic. Money became scarce and
depression set in. Across the river, in Kentucky, property that once sold
for eight thousand dollars was worth five hundred. Prices in St. Louis—
a town that had tried to establish itself as a wholesaling center—were
now 15 to 20 percent higher than those in Philadelphia or Baltimore.
From St. Louis, O'Fallon remarked to General Smith that "few merchants can leave here for the eastward and hardly anything can command reasonable prices."[32]

O'Fallon's plight was similar to that of the local landholders and
general merchants. Their usual pattern, which O'Fallon most likely followed, was to stock up with goods on eastern credit and then push purchases on credit to increase the rate of sale. Unlike local free-trade merchants, however, O'Fallon was unable to raise his prices. He didn't
have the freedom; his prices were set by a group of officers at the post
who formed the Council of Administration.[33]

The official appointment of John O'Fallon as sutler to Council
Bluffs by Secretary of War John Calhoun was signed September 28,
1821, but by the following summer, O'Fallon advised General Smith
that he had had enough.[34] The failing Bank of Missouri had taken all
his cash money. He had settled with the bank by accepting good mort-
gages, but without capital he expected that this would be the last year
he would supply Council Bluffs. Above all else, the Council of Administration had set his retail prices as 50 percent on Philadelphia prices—
too low to make suttling "an object, nay risk, [worth] sinking money."
He candidly informed the general that the prices, as they were now
fixed, "will not more than pay the invoices of this establishment." He
ended his letter on a philosophical note by saying, "Times are now bad

enough[,] but could be much worse."[35] On February 13, 1823, he re-stated his disappointment over the army's position to General Smith. "I had made a proposition to General Atkinson about 18 months since[,] both liberal and reasonable as regarded myself to which I had believed had been acceded; but it appears that the General afterwards sanc-tioned the last reduction [in prices]. I am sure now convinced that the General officers and Council of Administration conceived they were only performing their duty; and that, had I been an officer in this place, it is quite likely, I would have done."[36]

Money could still be made at the suttling business, he believed, espe-cially since one could trade with the Indians while supplying the post, but the margin was insufficient to compensate him for the risk of trans-portation "and all the extra inconveniences attending the maintaining of a store at so remote a point." In the spring of 1823, O'Fallon wrote Smith that he was busily occupied with farming and making whiskey in Louisville, Kentucky, with his half-brother. The product of this latter occupation, he added, was an article that he was able to sell "at a sav-ing price as fast as can be made."[37]

David Meriwether also left the frontier. After having spent a full year in jail, David and his slave were released by the Mexican governor under the condition they would never return. His arrival back at Coun-cil Bluffs was celebrated, and he was immediately reengaged as a sutler at five hundred dollars per year.[38] He opened trade with the Osage and Iowa Indians at Fort Osage forty miles below the Kansas River, near Sibley, Missouri. But 1822 was his last year.

David Meriwether returned to Kentucky, married, raised a family, and became active in local politics. In 1850, he replaced John Calhoun as senator from Kentucky and, in 1853, was appointed the first gover-nor to the Territory of New Mexico. When he traveled to Santa Fe this time, he made his journey in the company of General John Garland, commander of the Ninth Military Department. Meriwether; his son Raymond; his new chief justice, James J. Davenport; two new Indian agents; a doctor; and a number of civilian employees joined them at Council Grove, Missouri. The travelers arrived in Santa Fe on August 8, 1853, where Meriwether was inaugurated the same day. It must have pleased him to have been sworn in as governor in a town where he had spent a year in jail thirty years earlier.

Meriwether served as New Mexico's territorial governor from 1853 to 1857. During the first year of his term, he accepted the Gadsden

Purchase from Mexico. Upon his return to Kentucky, he remained in the legislature until he was eighty-five years old.

John O'Fallon became a substantial St. Louis businessman and patron. He was elected to the legislature in 1821. By 1828, through inheritance, investment, and speculation, O'Fallon was wealthy enough to throw a party for 120 people, which included Generals Atkinson, Clark, and Ashley, and members of two prominent St. Louis trading families, the Choteaus and the Kennerlys. By 1830, John O'Fallon had became a prominent citizen of St. Louis. He donated the land on which St. Louis University (established in 1818) now stands, five acres for water works, and land valued at $223,000 for O'Fallon Park. O'Fallon presented Washington University two blocks of land and $45,000 for its new technical school for the mechanical and manufacturing enterprises. He also underwrote Washington University's construction of the dispensary and medical college.[39]

Although O'Fallon had owned slaves, in 1846 he was appointed president of a committee of one hundred to agitate for the abolition of slavery. He was also on the board of half the businesses in St. Louis, president of a branch bank of the U.S. Bank, and president of the committee to form the Missouri Pacific Railroad in 1849. Among other honors, he was the first president of the Ohio and Mississippi Railroad, and was elected president in 1850 of the North Missouri Railroad. As to his reputation, the old biographies said Mr. O'Fallon was highly esteemed and respected, a citizen who had "gained the affection and love of all." He died at age seventy-four, on December 17, 1865.

John O'Fallon was the first of a new breed of gentleman sutlers, but in his day sutlers were still considered camp followers. To make up for the deficit of protection and consideration that the army would not provide in their contractual relationship, O'Fallon used personal influence and his family name. They were not enough to overcome bottom-line problems. The combined loss of a load of cargo plus local bank failures left him without capital and at the mercy of an unyielding Council of Administration.

To add insult to injury, the year that John O'Fallon lost his cargo, 1822, was the last year the sutler would be regarded as a camp follower. And 1823, the year he turned over his business to his close friend and associate, James Kennerly, was the first year a new set of army regulations went into effect to assist the sutler.

PART II

THE ARMY POST
SUTLER

1821–1860

FIVE

Creation of the Army Post Sutler

> *The comfort or well-being of the troops . . . and the honor of the service require that the business of suttling should receive a character of permanency, fairness, and respectability which heretofore it has but infrequently possessed.—Chief Surgeon Joseph Lovell, United States Army, American State Papers, Military Affairs*

When John O'Fallon notified General Thomas A. Smith in January 1821 that the army would soon be reduced to six thousand men, he was right. The statute to cut the U.S. Army from a peak of 10,024 men to 6,183 men was passed under a rationale which held that a frontier post needed only 100 men and that the country needed only twenty-five to thirty posts.[1] Congress was saying that the need to control postwar costs was more important than any extant or near-future threat from any known external power. Republicans were also saying that they felt more comfortable with a smaller standing army.

General Winfield Scott and Secretary of War John C. Calhoun had argued in vain against the cuts. They then submitted a plan that kept the officer corps intact, so that in time of danger the army need only be fleshed out with enlisted men. Their plan was rejected and nearly half the organizational units of the army, with their officers, were dropped from the rolls.

In the interim, John Calhoun created the position of Commissary General and added a Subsistence Department. He also created the post of Surgeon General and a new set of army-wide regulations that covered the status and the functions of the army sutler.

The Commissary General instituted a new army provisioning system in June 1819 that made the army responsible for obtaining its own supplies.[2] Up to 1818, each military unit had relied on contractors for supplies, but the system was corrupt and lacked reliability. When matériel was in desperate need, major contractors failed to show, in part because some diverted moneys to other ventures and in part because contracts for supplies were controlled through the Treasury Department, not the War Department. To further improve local health conditions, the new Subsistence Office directed garrisons at frontier posts to cultivate gardens to reduce scurvy and to raise livestock to reduce supply and foraging problems.

With General Scott, Calhoun devised a new set of general army regulations. Effective 1821, the new regulations covered everything from conduct and dress to the care of arms and the conduct of the affairs of the post sutler. General Scott said that every pertinent subject had been reduced to analysis and systematized into institutions. The body of regulations, later modified by the War Department only in reaction to reports from senior officers and the Inspector General, established precedents that remained relatively intact for decades.[3]

The new regulations marked the first occasion that the army staff, rather than Congress or individual post commanders, had addressed the status and role of the sutler. Until now he had been grouped with the laundresses, blacksmiths, and carpenters as a camp follower. Twenty-eight paragraphs of Article 41 of the "Systems of Martial Law, Field Service, Etc.," [4] justified the need for the services of the sutler, described the degree of freedom he would be allowed, and defined his new relationship with the U.S. Army. The regulations also assigned responsibility for supervising the sutler's affairs to a cadre of officers known as the Council of Administration. Each post had its own council, an arrangement that survived until the early 1890s, when the sutler era came to a close.

The unusual amount of attention directed to the suttling profession sprang from a recognition that this civilian trader played a significant role in the comfort and well-being of the troops, particularly those stationed at remote outposts. The seed of this recognition may have been planted by the army's first Surgeon General, Joseph Lovell. Upon his appointment in 1818 (to the position he held until 1836), he submitted a lengthy report to Secretary of War John C. Calhoun, recommending changes in the kind of food the army fed its troops, especially its men on the frontier.[5] His comments directly affected the role and status of the sutler.

The bulk of American servicemen, said Lovell, were stationed along the western border, far from cities and villages. Although the sustenance they received was in some ways more nourishing than that provided the men of the French and German armies, it was his opinion that the food was insufficient and useless when diarrhea and dysentery set in. Experience in the late war had shown him that these debilitating illnesses had rendered service on the frontier quite unpleasant and unpopular, and had caused, Lovell claimed, "more desertion than all other reasons together."

The men who garrisoned frontier posts—especially the officers—were all too often dependent on occasional supplies obtained from irregular followers of a camp; and, too often, money alone could not produce a decent meal. The men had access to some goods through hucksters residing outside the camp, but only at very high prices. The situation was one that, in Lovell's words, "frequently required the equivalent of a Captain's pay to discharge the mess-bill."

The Surgeon General appraised the sutler as having "nearly as much importance to the health, comfort and convenience of the army as the nature of the component parts of the rations." His comments were not atypical of a Regular Army officer at the time. The commanding officer at Fort Bowyer during the War of 1812, Major Chamberlain of the Second Regiment, and his artillery officer, A. L. Sands, told General Macomb that not only had their troops received "many comforts and conveniences from the sutler's stores" which were otherwise unobtainable, but the soldiers had been "dependent upon the sutlers for all their comforts . . . while they were kept without pay."[6]

Lovell informed the Secretary of War that commanding officers had repeatedly tried to obtain and secure regular sutlers, who, by being provided "the exclusive right to sell to their corps, might be able and willing to furnish them regularly at a low rate." Unfortunately, the army was paid in such an irregular fashion that the sutler could not count on enough steady income to enable him to conduct business and still meet his bills. Under those conditions, the offer of a monopoly to the sutler was worthless.

The Surgeon General then extended his argument to destroy the myth of the vendor's greed. The sutler's high prices, Lovell said in his report, were not a symptom of avarice, but a direct side effect of the army's payroll practices. He had known "an honest and faithful man [to] lose from eight hundred to one thousand dollars by the death, desertion, and discharge of soldiers who had not been paid for many months, and some of them for two years." As a consequence, the sutler was "soon obliged to quit his business, and in the meantime, to charge an enormous profit to make up for his losses."

The sutler's losses, continued Lovell, did not include the additional financial burden he was forced to assume by the necessity of borrowing money or purchasing at long credit and, of course, at a great advance (the markup or interest rate). He understood that it was probably impractical to try to pay troops more regularly, but he strongly recommended that the army adopt some measure to "secure the sutler his just and authorized demands."

Article 41, known under its separate title as "Orders and Regulations Having Influence to the Appointment of Sutlers," gave the sutler the security he needed and considerably more. The preamble of Article 41 said that the comfort or well-being of the troops and the honor of the service required that "the business of suttling should receive a character of permanency, fairness, and respectability which heretofore it has but infrequently possessed."

To institutionalize the civilian sutler in its ranks, the army was prepared to vest his appointment in the hands of the Secretary of War. Prior to 1821, the commanding officer of the regiment or detachment of the fort made all appointments. The army was ready to provide the sutler with a true monopoly over his trade at his assigned post, in direct opposition to an earlier recommendation made by the Inspector General's office to open the position to all comers and to vest licensing in the hands of the post commander. The regulations required the army to provide the sutler a "definite and respectable rank," and to regulate his business with fixed and uniform regulations to ensure fair and equitable treatment.[7] Above all, the army would guarantee the sutler a moderate but certain profit.

In return for this commitment and concessions, the army expected the sutler to secure and provide "competent supplies of necessaries for both officers and men" in an orderly flow. The regulations would also free provisioning from the heretofore "secret interest of those who supervised subsistence supplies to the interior."

Sutler appointments would henceforth be made by the Secretary of War upon whatever recommendations he found valid. Temporary appointments that arose due to vacancies could be made by the commanding officer of the post, but even those were subject to later validation by the secretary. The sutler's appointment was good "during the pleasure of the Secretary of War," a phrase which implies that the sutler's tenure might be subject to sudden termination, especially after a new Secretary of War was appointed. Sutler appointment books, maintained by the Secretary of War, show that a number of sutlers appointed from the 1820s through the 1850s were removed when new political appointments automatically canceled their licenses. The majority quit voluntarily; only a handful of sutlers were removed because of poor performance.[8] The sutler was vulnerable, nonetheless, to a general court-martial and could be suspended or dismissed by a court approved by the commanding officer for violation of any provision in Article 41. If he was found guilty of conduct highly prejudicial to good order and discipline, he could be fined up to twenty-five cents for every soldier at the post and imprisoned until the fine was paid.[9]

In addition to being bound by army rules and regulations, the trader was tightly supervised by the Council of Administration. This council was composed of three officers (other than the commanding officer), plus a fourth officer who served as secretary. The council possessed the power "to prescribe the quantity and kind of clothing, small equipment, or soldier's necessities, groceries, etc., etc., which the sutler may be bound to keep on hand, to supply the probable wants of the officers and men at the post." To carry out its responsibilities, the council was authorized to "examine the sutler's books and papers, and, on actual inspection, to fix the tariff, or prices of the said goods, or commodities."

The council was given the added responsibility of inspecting the sutler's weights and measures, a task most likely attributable to problems that General Anthony Wayne experienced in 1796. Wayne ejected an unknown number of sutlers from his camp for having tampered with weights and measures. His order to rectify the situation read: "Various complicated and scandalous practices reported in the suttling line make it the Brigadier General's duty to direct reform effective the first of March. In the interval, traders will have time to close their accounts." The Deputy Quartermaster General was to have one dozen sets of standard weights and measures made of iron.[10]

The Council of Administration was required to log the minutes of each meeting in a book that was to be forwarded to the commanding officer for his review and approval. Decisions he approved were immediately posted in local regulations; decisions he disapproved were

Council of Administration Tariffs for Sutlers Goods,
Fort Gibson, 1845.[11]

ITEM	INVOICE	RETAIL PRICE	MARKUP [12]
	Cost/Dozen	*Cost/Item*	*Percentage*
Fancy Soap	$ 1.50	$ .25 ea.	50%
Hat	$ 3.25	$ .375	28%
Suspenders	$ 5.00	$ .75	45%
English Pocket Comb	$ 2.00	$ .25	50%
Cotton Flag Hanky	$ .75	$ .125	50%
Damask Table Cloth	$27.00	$3.00	25%
Woolen Gloves	$ 2.50	$ .50	58%
2 Blade Pocket Knife	$ 2.00	$ .25	50%
Coffee Mugs	$ 1.00	$ .1667	50%
Tomato Ketchup	$ 2.75	$ .50	54%
Lemmon Syrup (bottle)	$ 3.00	$ .50	50%
Pepper Sauce (.5 pint)	$ 1.00	$ .1875	55%
Sardines (box)	$ 6.00	$ .75	33%
Pillow Case Lining	$ .525/yd.	$ .75/yd.	30%
Rock Candy	$ .125/lb.	$ .25/lb.	50%
Lamp Oil	$ 1.25/gal.	$2.00/gal.	38%

returned to the council for further deliberation. If the council reached the same decision after a second round of discussion, its word was final. When the sutler became aware that final authority for his prices rested with the officers of the post and not the commanding officer, that knowledge affected his demeanor toward all officers. Because he needed to be on good terms with officers of the council, and never knew which individuals might serve next, he tried not to restrict officers' credit lines and allowed them leeway he might not have otherwise.

The sutler was required to post a notice of fixed rates in a conspicuous place in his shop for the information of his customers. Once again, this rule reflected the decision made at General Anthony Wayne's camp that a price should not vary for officers and enlisted men, nor should it differ solely because it was sold for cash or on credit.[13] The army also placed a ceiling on the amount of credit he could extend, thereby limiting a sutler's gross income. In former times, a commanding officer like Major Chamberlain might permit his sutler, Smool, to sell an enlisted man goods that were worth up to three-fourths of his monthly pay. The new regulations stated that a sutler could not sell to any enlisted man, within one pay period, goods that were worth more than one-half his monthly pay without the written consent of the commanding officer. On the other hand, the army was bound by rules of fairness to assist the sutler in collecting all moneys due him. When the paymaster arrived, he had to notify the sutler and invite him to sit at the pay table with his records and accounts.

As each man was paid, the paymaster settled outstanding liens by using a prearranged system of priorities. To cover lost equipment and pay irregularities, the government was given first consideration. Laundresses were second. The sutler, who was third in line, edged out the tailor, the blacksmith, and lesser tradesmen. When it was the sutler's turn, he presented his bill to the soldier. If the trooper admitted to the amount that the sutler said he owed, it was deducted from his pay "as a matter of course." If the soldier did not agree with an item or sum total, the sutler was required to provide a written bill or a signed and witnessed agreement. If he had maintained good records, his proof was a pay voucher the soldier signed each time he made a credit purchase. [14]

In return for the privilege of having a monopoly over post trade, the sutler paid a tax into the post fund. Tax rates, established by the Council of Administration, were normally ten to fifteen cents per month for every officer and enlisted man at the post. The Council of Administration was to meet once every two months to determine the average number of troops at the post and send the sutler a bill. If the average number of men at a post remained unchanged during the year, and that number was one hundred, the sutler paid twenty dollars every other month for the privilege of suttling.

The post fund, which was also fed by fines and miscellaneous amounts collected from the men, supported a variety of good causes, including the immediate relief of widows and orphans of officers or soldiers. It also went to "deranged or decayed" and disabled soldiers and officers discharged under circumstances that did not entitle them to pensions from the government. Any money left over after those disbursements were made went to the education of soldiers' children at the post school, the purchase of books for the post library, and the maintenance of a post band. [15]

To seal the army–sutler bond of mutual commitment, paragraph seventeen of Article 41 said that since the sutler's role was "a highly valued one," the commanding officer was strongly encouraged to "lend his authority, as often as may be necessary to protect, within his local command, the exclusive privilege, so purchased by the sutler" without further burdening the man with taxes or fees. The post commander was further authorized to make a suitably unused building available to the sutler free of charge, and if there was no house for him the sutler was to be allowed to erect one on the military premises. In comparison to the days prior to and during the War of 1812, the sutler had come a long way.

The army specified that its new rules applied to sutlers assigned to posts that were garrisoned by regiments and detached companies. Paragraph twenty-seven extended coverage of the regulations to those sutlers who served with troops of a regiment while they were on a march into the interior, during a campaign, or while on board transports.

The impact that Article 41 had on the professionalization of the suttling trade is difficult to overstate. This former camp follower, who was treated like a bastard child for hundreds of years, was now a recognized and integral part of the U.S. Army. He had a rank and a home—a specific army post over which he was lord of trade. His position was not the sinecure that some historians have held it to be, nor did the army provide him with a license by which he could amass a fortune. Yet after 1821, with his new sense of permanence, the sutler felt free to marry, to build a house, and to raise a family on the post. And because he was enveloped by the might and stability of the U.S. Army, he began to plan for the future, for he was protected not only by the walls of a fort, but by the power of an agency of the U.S. government. A fine example of one who thrived under the new changes was James Kennerly, a relative by marriage to John O'Fallon, who followed O'Fallon as sutler to Council Bluffs (Fort Atkinson).

James Kennerly (1792–1840) first arrived in St. Louis in 1813 at age twenty-three, with his brother, George Hancock Kennerly. The brothers came from a good Virginia family and had powerful St. Louis connections in their brother-in-law, William Clark, the territorial governor.

William Clark's notoriety has always been anchored in the role he played in the Lewis and Clark expedition, but he also held positions of

great power and influence in St. Louis from the time he was appointed
territorial governor in 1806 until his death in 1838. Clark ran against
Alexander McNair for the post of first governor of the state of Missouri in 1820, and lost, but he remained in St. Louis to devote the rest
of his life to his second profession as Superintendent of Indian Affairs.[16]
The year he lost the race for governor, his first wife died. He married
Mrs. Harriet (Kennerly) Radford, a widow and cousin of his first
wife.[17]

Those first in line for his patronage were his nephews, Benjamin and
John O'Fallon, and his brothers-in-law, Captain George Hancock Kennerly and James Kennerly. For a number of years, the Kennerly brothers resided at the home of William Clark, so the O'Fallon brothers and
Kennerly brothers knew one another intimately.

Benjamin O'Fallon and George H. Kennerly became Clark's most
trusted appointees in the Department of Indian Affairs. As Indian
agents, they worked closely with Indian chiefs and tribes, arranged
treaties, and kept Clark informed about the status of frontier racial relations.

The other two, James Kennerly and John O'Fallon, were inclined to
remain in private business. Between 1813 and 1815 they formed a partnership and operated a merchandising store in St. Louis. Kennerly then
had a brief partnership with Alexander McNair, the sutler at Fort
Crawford. When the partnership was dissolved, Kennerly reopened the
old St. Louis store in his own name and in a house owned by William
Clark. No later than January 1815, his obliging brother-in-law also appointed him as the U.S. forwarding agent for the government's factory
trading system in the Missouri area. His responsibility was to expedite
shipments of manufactured goods from the Department of Indian Affairs in St. Louis to Forts Osage, Edwards, Crawford, and Spandra
Bluffs, and to return with furs. He held this position at an annual
salary of four hundred dollars until the system was shut down in
1822.[18]

The following year—the year John O'Fallon sounded out James Kennerly on the position of sutler at Fort Atkinson—Kennerly was a trustee
of St. Louis and director of a bank. He was also a husband and father,
having wed Elsie Marie Saugrain on June 10, 1817. He may have
needed a job or fully agreed with O'Fallon's assessment that money
could still be made in the suttling profession, because O'Fallon recommended Kennerly to General Atkinson and Kennerly accepted the job.

James Kennerly also had access to enough capital to establish himself by teaming up with his brother, George. George provided capital and James performed the work. The arrangement worked well and lasted until 1837.

During at least his first three years at Fort Atkinson, James Kennerly maintained a diary of his daily activities. His record provides a detailed view of a sutler's life in the 1820s and illustrates the degree to which army regulations and the demands of frontier life dominated a sutler's existence.

Kennerly's wife and baby daughter escorted him up the Missouri River to Fort Atkinson in October 1823.[19] Colonel Leavenworth (who assumed command in 1821) and his wife greeted them upon their arrival. The Kennerlys were given comfortable quarters, and officers gave them vegetables. General Atkinson, on a tour of duty at the time, gave orders to have a sutler's house constructed. It was an auspicious beginning.

Kennerly took inventory of what remained of John O'Fallon's stock, then identified what he needed to purchase and placed an order with Bernard Pratte & Co. in St. Louis.[20] He also obtained merchandise from Mr. Cabanne, who operated an American Fur Company post a mile beyond Fort Lisa, which placed Cabanne's post seven to eight miles downstream from Fort Atkinson. Kennerly still made trips to Philadelphia and New York for major purchases, but when he was short of a necessary item, he borrowed what he needed from a number of close sources, including the Fort Atkinson commissary (fifty pounds of pork), the Council of Administration (a two-thousand-dollar loan), the army quartermaster (sixty pairs of glass for his house), and Cabanne's post (a keg of powder and eggs).

During his second month at Council Bluffs, Kennerly bargained with O'Fallon's agent, Mr. Reed, to purchase goods on hand and O'Fallon's sutler store. Kennerly paid Reed $275 for the building and took everything except twenty barrels of whiskey. Business must have been brisk, for Kennerly was nearly out of merchandise and whiskey before Christmas, so he purchased the balance of the whiskey from Reed. Over the Christmas holiday he sold a considerable quantity, and ran out of wine entirely.

As the year came to a close, he attended to his accounts. His financial transactions were effected by vouchers, because he was so far removed from a banking center. One sketchy paragraph in his diary indicated the complexity of his financial affairs. It read, "Gave Major O'Fallon a receipt for balance due Indian Department in full. Charged him with all payments made for Quartermaster Dept and Commissary. Settled with General Atkinson. Took his draft on Tray & Wahendorf for balance. Major O'Fallon will pay to General Clark—Major Langhan also—Capt Armstrong pays to B. Pratte & Co." If the number and content of journal entries indicates how Kennerly spent his time or reflects the priorities of his concerns, he spent an inordinate amount of energy in bickering with the Council of Administration over the retail prices of his goods. Haggling over prices was an appropriate concern, especially since prices determined whether Kennerly would make a profit, and the council's word was final.

Fort Atkinson's Council of Administration allowed a percentage markup on each invoice, then left it to the sutler to distribute such percentage as he deemed proper. According to Colonel George Croghan from the Inspector General's department, the Council of Administration at other posts placed a fixed price on each article. He had no opinion as to whether one approach was more correct, but stated that if either method was defective, "it must remain so until the Board changes it, for the Council of Administration knows no controlling power."[21]

Kennerly presented his first invoices to the Council of Administration on November 11, 1823, then waited until he could examine the fixed rates before he sent for his goods. The following May, when he handed over a set of invoices, the officer in charge told him that the council couldn't act on them because they weren't from Philadelphia, where the goods had been manufactured. It made no difference to the council that Kennerly had purchased the goods in St. Louis.

The council's refusal to accommodate normal purchasing practices created a conflict that quickly escalated. Kennerly wrote in his diary that the foreman of the council, Major Foster, was "very extravagant" in his ideas about mercantile transactions. Foster thought 6 percent was as much as merchants expected to make on their capital and that merchants in Franklin (a nearby trading town on the Missouri River) would supply goods on better terms.

Kennerly's notes said he flatly and "preemtorily" [*sic*] denied this, so he wrote the council "a short treatise on the subject of merchandising." He was nonetheless forced to open and to sell his late spring goods before the council fixed his prices, because his customers were clamoring for the goods.

The adjutant of the council advised Kennerly that the board had fixed risk at 4 percent of the price and the price at 50 percent of Philadelphia prices, and the colonel had approved those figures. Kennerly pronounced the ruling unfair and unjust and balked at opening crates of merchandise. As a result, Major Kitchen of the council paid Kennerly a visit to explain the council's deliberations. Kitchen's effort must have paid off, for Kennerly's diary testified that he "made out prices of goods."

The difference of opinion between Kennerly and the council as to what constituted a fair markup over invoice prices continued through the fall of 1824. On one occasion, Kennerly sent the council a letter asking for higher prices; on another, he wrote in his diary that the colonel and the Council of Administration could not agree on the price of either bread or flour, "nor the rate of lending funds to the paymaster." Once, the dispute became so heated that Colonel Woolly sent the adjutant to Kennerly's store to ask Kennerly whether he intended to be entirely independent or go by regulations. In the end, Kennerly agreed to abide by the regulations, but his profit margin must have been very tight. When a local trader offered Kennerly a deal on a Dearborn wagonload of goods, he tabled his decision until he could determine whether the council's prices would make it worth his time. After checking with the council, he turned the offer down. Only after the trader agreed to sell what he had for transportation costs, and to take back what didn't sell, did Kennerly decide that a little profit was better than none.

From a broader perspective, his tussles with the council and commanding officer about what he could and could not do peppered his diary as though they were a normal ingredient of family life. Many had to do with whiskey. On September 1, 1825, he requested permission to send liquor and groceries to meet the officers and troops returning from the Yellowstone expedition. The colonel refused to let him send liquor. He was allowed to use whiskey to pay the men he hired, but he was reprimanded by the commanding officer for selling whiskey to enlisted men even after being advised by junior officers that it was all right.[22] He also received letters from officers telling him not to credit their men more than the regulations allowed.

When the army wasn't reminding him of his boundaries, Kennerly was experiencing the usual collection problems. After sending out his accounts (billings) to the officers, he invariably received visits from those who wanted to complain. His diary shows that he pursued delinquent accounts in person. "Called on Gantt re his account," read one entry; "Promised order on Louisville for $251 and pay his accounts regularly and leave half his pay," read another. When he refused credit to an officer named Folger because the man had not paid his account, Folger "got hot, then cooled down." After a brief discussion, Kennerly jotted down the agreed-upon terms for Folger to catch up: "Offered to pay accounts for six months. Received half amount. Other to go to his credit."

James Kennerly's role as the post merchant included keeping the officers' wives happy. They occupied a portion of their time making social calls and taking rides to Cabanne's post on riverboats or in carriages. Frequently they visited Kennerly's store to examine crockery, clothes, and small luxuries. When a sutler's keelboat arrived, wrote Kennerly, there was a "flurry of excitement as the women sought to be the first to inspect the new wares." At these times he complained he was unable to unpack, because the crowd was so persistent.[23]

Aside from his extensive role as post merchant, Kennerly performed a variety of other duties. Some were valued for their social contribution; most were also profitable ventures. When the paymaster was short, Kennerly helped to pay the troops. He lent money to officers, held money and valuables for men on leave and on temporary duty, and bought notes. In short, he was the post banker.

It also became apparent from scattered diary entries that Kennerly had a number of men in his employ, at all times, to cut wood, unload his supplies from keelboats and barges, work in the store and on his house, and make repairs to equipment. As part of one arrangement he had with the commanding officer to raise one hundred bushels of corn (for fifty cents a bushel), Kennerly had a fellow raise the crop. He paid him ten dollars per month and two gallons of whiskey to have the crop planted.

The magnitude of Kennerly's problems with army regulations and collections of his accounts receivable over a three-year period, measured in terms of his business and position, was hardly worth the entries in his journal. Kennerly's trade was an integral part of the military establishment; he was looked upon by the officers of the post as a gentleman and a colleague; and aside from being the person who provided the troops needed services, Kennerly was a man of social position because he owned two slaves.

Kennerly and his wife dined at the colonel's home on numerous occasions. Once, he found it worth while to remark in his diary that only half of the officers had been invited to one of the colonel's social events attended by him and his brother, George. Social activities provided Kennerly with opportunities to develop ties to many of the prominent men of the fur trade and the army, as well as to politicians who visited and passed through the post.[24]

The Kennerlys held their own social affairs, including a dance after the construction of their house was completed. While James played sutler and host, his brother, George, provided color. According to his nephew's memory, George Hancock Kennerly was a dashing, bold, and romantic character who fought duels with pistol and sword on Bloody Island, Illinois. Known as a brave officer and unerring shot, he once faced Henry S. Geyer, who later became a Missouri senator. On May 11, 1818, George's uncle, William Clark, wrote the Secretary of War that Kennerly should be appointed as Indian agent on the Upper Missouri, because he possessed energy and vigor and had acquired fame for his gallantry as an officer in actions with the Mississippi tribes.

In his 1826 report, the now Inspector General, George Croghan, said that the sutler (Kennerly) "had a large supply valued at $20,000 and conducted himself satisfactorily." To Croghan, this meant that Kennerly had found a way to make his stay profitable. (Colonel George Croghan was also a nephew of William Clark.) As another author put it, Kennerly was "living the life of a country gentleman, as his forefathers had done in Virginia."[25]

When Fort Atkinson was abandoned in 1827 and its troops were transferred to Jefferson Barracks, James Kennerly and family accompanied them. He remained there as resident sutler, in partnership with his brother George, until 1837 when the post was abandoned. In the meantime, he built his wife and three children a fine residence on Persimmon Hill. In 1840, he died of an undisclosed illness.

SIX

The Evolution of Suttling, 1820–1840

I will not permit myself to speak of the system of suttling as it is now conducted lest I might commit myself. All I shall say for the present is let the Department of War know but one sutler to a Regiment of Infantry or let the door be opened to all who may choose to traffic with the soldier. —George Croghan, Report of Field Inspection, 1833

By 1840, twenty years after the army issued Article 41, the sutler had matured from a neophyte to a professional and had reshaped his business from a frontier venture into a profession. The manner in which the man and his trade evolved is discernable and measurable, because the attributes of the successful sutler were shaped by three factors: his need to stay in sync with changes that took place within the army, his need to stay one step ahead of a number of high-risk variables, and his need to deal with the increasing vulnerability of his position to political meddling.

Changes within the army were of paramount importance to the sutler. From his first days in America to his last, the sutler remained a military servant, and his world was bounded by the laws, regulations, and policies of the U.S. Army. Between 1821 and the end of his era, he was also leashed by the opinions and decisions of the Council of Administration. No matter how great his personal growth, he could never truly be his own master. And as in any large bureaucratic organization, those in the field were whiplashed by changes to policy and regulations from the home office. The post sutler, who was the subject of a number of these changes, must have wondered on more than one occasion exactly where, how, and to whom he was assigned.

Having primarily defined the sutler's position in terms of military posts in 1821, the army was forced to face the need to resolve jurisdiction problems between extant regimental and post sutlers. Who was the proper sutler when one or more companies were transferred from point A to point B, or when a new company stayed at one post and then another as it moved to a new frontier trouble spot?

John Culbertson of Pennsylvania became sutler to the First Regiment at Baton Rouge after he was discharged from the army in 1821. When his regiment was assigned to the Yellowstone expedition of 1818, he ascended the Missouri River with his troops, as had John O'Fallon. On October 13, 1823, Culbertson wrote an urgent letter from Fort Bellefontaine to Secretary of War John Calhoun to ask if he did not have the right to sell to the First Regiment wherever they went. At the moment, he said, his men were at Fort Atkinson, where the recently appointed sutler, James Kennerly, insisted upon "the exclusive privilege of supplying all troops that might be sent there."[1]

A fair amount of money was at stake. The First Regiment numbered 435 men. If $3.00 per month were expended on sutler supplies by each soldier—a reasonable expectation in those days since the private received $6.66 per month—the contended pot was $1,300.00 a month in sales. Apparently Mr. Kennerly was able to sway Secretary of War Calhoun to his claim that he "owned" the right to sales at his post, because he reaped the benefit from the extra business.[2]

Several years later, Inspector General George Croghan encountered a similar jurisdictional problem in New Orleans. Croghan, who examined conditions at fifteen to twenty frontier posts each year between 1825 and 1846, wrote that the post was supporting two sutler stores. The first was under the charge of the post sutler, who had been appointed by the Secretary of War; the other was under the charge of the agent of the regimental sutler, who, "having his appointment to the First Regiment, claims the exclusive privilege of suttling either in person or through an agent to all the companies of the regiment be they together or dispersed."[3]

The New Orleans commander had elected to deal exclusively with the agent of the regimental sutler, which was legal, but the other sutler was livid, and Croghan had no idea how to resolve the problem fairly. He asked the War Department for a ruling, because he was sure the issue would rise again.

He was right: the "overlap" problem did not go away. In 1828, Croghan reported another jurisdictional problem at Fort Howard. Major Gray originally had been appointed sutler to the Second Infantry in 1822, but when the headquarters of that regiment was relocated, he had his appointment changed to a post sutlership and remained at Fort Howard. He claimed exclusive suttling privileges for the post, while the infantry sutler of the First Regiment (also stationed at the post) insisted upon his right to suttle with the companies of infantry in that regiment.

Croghan became disgusted with the issue of suttling, and he was outspoken about who was to blame. "The respectability once attached to the post of sutler no longer obtains and is [declining] fast; this may be ascribed to the Department of War, which has in more instances than one, made appointments, conferring privileges that had long ago been granted by its own act to others then in the enjoyment of them." [4]

In all fairness, officers in the Department of War had tried to respond in accordance with endorsed field recommendations. The voices that the War Department heard, however, were inconsistent, and no one had sufficiently analyzed the problem to present a clear picture complete with adequate solutions. One change led to another, and then another. By the late 1830s the army's regulations that governed sutler appointments had undergone four significant changes:

1) August 4, 1828: "To put an end to collusions [sic] between post and regimental sutlers' rights and privileges, it is declared that Post sutlers are entitled to exclusive privilege of all troops stationed at posts to which they are assigned." The position of regimental sutler disappeared on the following December 31. Future sutler appointments were to be four years in duration; all existing appointments over two years were to expire on December 31, 1830; and all others would expire on December 31, 1832. [5]

2) April 12, 1831: The Secretary of War found it "inconvenient in practice to attach sutlers to posts instead of [to] certain portions of troops." All appointments were canceled. New warrants reassigned sutlers to companies.[6]

3) February 9, 1832: "There will be one sutler per post known as the 'Post Sutler.' If more than one is allowed, he will be the 'extra' sutler. If the garrison is reduced to four companies or less, only one sutler is needed." [7]

At this point, a frustrated George Croghan wrote from Jefferson Barracks, Missouri, to say that he was once again confronted with two sutlers at one post. One man he knew personally and liked: Mr. James Kennerly, "formerly an officer and subsequently for several years, sutler to the Sixth Regiment." The other he did not know: "Mr. Wallace, who has never rendered the state service." At that moment, Wallace suttled for only two companies of the Third Regiment, because the other two companies, which were just arriving from Fort Armstrong, had their own sutler, who was going to join them in a day or two.

"I will not permit myself to speak of the system of suttling as it is now conducted lest I might commit myself," Croghan wrote to vent his disgust. "All I shall say for the present is let the Dept of War know but one sutler to a Regiment of Infantry or let the door be opened to all who may choose to traffic with the soldier." [8]

In the fall of 1834, Croghan made eight recommendations to General-in-Chief Major General Macomb. He first proposed that sutlers be appointed at the regimental level, and that each man be required to furnish necessities to all companies of the regiment wherever they were or wherever they went. He then recommended that all sutlers be men of at least two years of prior service and that each be appointed by the colonel of the regiment with the consent of the General-in-Chief.

4) February 12, 1839: The Department of the Army issued a ruling strikingly similar to Croghan's 1834 recommendation. Troops in the field were allowed one sutler per regiment, per company, or per detachment unit. Extra post sutlers were no longer acceptable, and a sutler's term was set for three years, renewable. The Council of Administration was authorized to recommend appointments to the Secretary of War. [9]

Most changes within the army were communicated through new regulations. Regulations defined organization, operational procedures, and authority. When a regulation was issued because of the need to revise policy on a single issue, the regulation might contain a quantity of rephrasing or repetition from the preceding regulation. An 1835 regulation reconfirmed that the sutler was considered superior to enlisted men, but without line authority; that he was appointed by the Secretary of War for four years; that he could be suspended for improper conduct; and that he was not allowed to sell ardent spirits. This regulation was issued simply to say that "the post fund was to be assessed every two months, not to exceed fifteen cents per man per month."[10]

In addition to the sutler's need to adjust to procedural regulations, he was occasionally the subject of major policy decisions. One ruling, implemented in 1829, stated that each sutler was required to reside at or near the post to which he was assigned. The regulation was issued to stem a growing practice by sutlers to place a manager in their store and serve as an absentee landowner. The regulation said that if the licensed sutler farmed out his business and did not reside on post after three months from this regulation, the commanding officer was to inform the Secretary of War.[11] At least two sutlers lost their licenses because they ignored or chose to disobey this requirement, but Inspector Wool of the Inspector General's office wrote General Macomb in 1833 that the practice of allowing sutlers to farm out their business appeared to be permitted at most posts along the Great Lakes. He considered it a gross injustice to the soldiers, who, in essence, had to pay for the "extra rent" involved in having a middleman run the store. "If the public knew the army supported this principle," he said, "it would be an embarrassment to the administration."[12]

Of equal impact to the sutler's purse was the army's policy change in 1832 to substitute sugar and coffee for the liquor ration and to outlaw the sale of whiskey. The move was probably timed to assist the government's newly created Bureau of Indian Affairs, which announced its intention to suppress the whiskey trade with the Indians. [13]

The sutler was the target of the bill because he was the primary purveyor of spirits to the soldier. Since sutlers were under the thumb of the army and normally obedient to orders, control of the sutler should mean control of the flow of whiskey. The following year, however, Inspector General George Croghan advised his superiors that the order prohibiting the sale of whiskey by the sutler had "not been attended by the happy results expected from it." On the contrary, at Forts Howard and Crawford and at Jefferson Barracks, the rule, he said, added to, rather than lessened, "the vice of intemperance." The results had been antithetical: instead of being able to control liquor, local commanding officers now had to contend with "numerous victuallers of spirits" who, regardless of the consequence to the soldier, "vie with one another to sell their products at all hours of the night."

Croghan strongly recommended that the order forbidding the sutler to sell whiskey be rescinded and that the Council of Administration control the flow of camp liquor, but nothing changed.[14] Three years later, in his 1836 report from Fort Des Moines, Croghan repeated his observations and recommendations. The order to prohibit the sutler to sell liquor, he wrote, was "worse than useless." Everyone in the community sold liquor, so the sutler was the only one who suffered by the regulation. [15] That same year, as though to echo Croghan's logic, Colonel Taylor wrote from Fort Crawford that the post was completely surrounded by whiskey establishments, "whose object and business is to debauch the soldier."[16] Because of military indecisiveness for the next fifty years, the sutler's ability to sell alcoholic beverages flickered on and off as regularly as a neon sign.

As sutlers James Kennerly and John O'Fallon discovered during the first decades of the 1800s, selling or not selling whiskey wouldn't make or break a sutler, but prices per se could. And all of his prices were established by the post Council of Administration. To the sutler's chagrin, the council was devoid of businessmen; it was made up entirely of military officers, who were setting prices of goods they would eventually purchase as consumers. It would seem reasonable that they would want to keep the sutler's profits to a minimum. On a visit to Fort Snelling, Inspector Croghan once remarked that the extent to which prices were fixed by the Council of Administration was a matter outside his jurisdiction, but he included examples for review because he thought they showed "how far a Council of Administration can go in defiance of the law and of the senior officer in command."[17]

The Council of Administration was certainly not immune to bias. At Fort Crawford, it set prices below those of the local village of Prairie du Chien. Croghan remarked that when the sutler had been a retired military man, he had been allowed a decent "advance on prices" (markup). That was no longer the case, because members of the council no longer knew the sutler; he was often a stranger for whom they had "little community of feeling."[18]

As the decades passed, the sutler discovered that increased visibility was the price he paid for security and official status. Changes in army policy and within the military organization touched his trade, and he was forced to meet on a regular basis with the Council of Administration to secure acceptable prices on his goods. When he was a camp follower, he had been freer. He survived without much military protection; the only regulations he had to watch for were those directed at him by the local commanding officer; and he could regulate his visibility pretty much as he desired. As a result, he could stay in business—even illegally—as long as he kept an eye on the Indians and the Provost Marshal. Even during the first three decades of the 1800s, most army inspectors paid the sutler little mind except to mention on occasion that suttling appeared to be well managed by the Council of Administration.[19]

By 1830 a sutler's life had become complicated. His store and his home were located on the military reservation; he conducted extensive business with the officers' wives; and he was totally answerable to a group of officers who, collectively, had little experience in business or little sympathy for the sutler. Instead of hiding merchandise until the equivalent of the military police disappeared, he was required to present his invoices, fight for his prices, carry items that the board wanted, and extend credit to nearly everyone. By definition, the sutler of the mid-1800s had to be politically sharp and a sophisticated businessman.

Of course, not every element in the life of the frontier sutler underwent major metamorphosis in twenty years. Basic business concerns, which occupied most of the trader's time, remained fundamentally unchanged. They included the logistical and managerial skills needed to acquire, store, and sell merchandise at a price that, when collected, paid for all visible and hidden costs of doing business and left enough profit to make the whole affair worth while. The risk of conducting these routine activities on the frontier also remained high. The sutler remained far removed from a stable urban environment and its support services. He was exposed to a variety of debilitating and hostile elements, such as the vagaries of the elements—the kind that sank the cargo of John O'Fallon—and unpredictable hostility from the Indians, the kind who drove fur traders from the Rockies. Less physically onerous, but more damaging to his livelihood in the long run, were the problems attendant to serving a fluctuating and often unstable market, and in collecting what was due to him on some regular basis.

Situations that were life-threatening to sutlers were proportional to those experienced by the regiment to which they were assigned. This was especially true during the Civil War. Nothing in the records indicates that the sutler ever hesitated to accompany the army wherever it went, so either physical danger did not deter him or he routinely underrated the risk.[20] As a result, a few sutlers were killed in the line of duty, including a Mr. Dahlam of Florida.

The Treaty of Fort King was signed with the Seminoles in 1839. In that agreement, the army agreed to establish a trading post at Charlotte's Harbor, on the Caloosahatchie River. The task was given to a young lieutenant colonel named Colonel Stephen Watts Kearny. He selected a Mr. Dahlam, a sutler, to serve as the trader, and took twenty-six dragoons as an escort. In early July, Kearny left Dahlam on the riverbank to build his post.

Two weeks later, on July 23, 1839, Kearny returned in the company of a smaller number of men. They were armed, but they failed to establish a defense or night watch. At dawn, between 100 and 160 Indians attacked the sleeping band of soldiers. They killed 13 men in ten minutes; among them, Mr. Dahlam, his clerk, Mr. Morgan, and four men in his employ. Kearny and a few others survived by hiding in a canoe. Sutler Dahlam had packed in two thousand to three thousand dollars worth of goods and had carried about one thousand dollars in specie, so the Indians also got away with "good booty."

Later reports mentioned an Irish greyhound that belonged to Kearny, but which had developed a fondness for Mr. Dahlam. The dog must have returned to guard Dahlam's body after the Indians left. When the army burial crew arrived on the scene several weeks later, the corpses of most men were half-eaten by vultures and wolves. The dog was still there, and Dahlam's body was untouched.[21]

The sutler's market was not normally hazardous, but simply small and unstable. The majority of frontier posts like Brady, Winnebago, Howard, Snelling, Niagara, Armstrong, Gratiot, and Detroit were garrisoned by one to three companies, 50 to 150 men. Towson, Gibson, Leavenworth, and Snelling were larger, and Fort Atkinson was the exception with ten companies (500 men).[22] In 1832, the army's four regiments of artillery and seven regiments of infantry were composed of 106 companies, yet only two sutlers served more more than two to three companies at one time. Those sutlers were James C. Heron, who was assigned to six companies of the Third Regiment of Infantry, and James (and George) Kennerly, who served six companies of the Sixth Regiment of Infantry.[23]

In addition to the marginal size of his average market, the sutler never knew when a portion or all of the post garrison might be reassigned. Between 1812 and 1846, troops continued to move over long distances to cope with border problems, quell Indian scares, and explore and hold new territory. During the Winnebago scare in 1827, General Atkinson took six hundred men up the Missouri as a show of force.[24] He moved another one thousand upriver in 1832 to help the Illinois militia put down the Blackhawk Indians. In 1835, fourteen companies of men were assigned to Florida under General Clinch; two years later, his replacement, General Jessup, said he needed a total of six thousand men. To provide these troops, every western fort was stripped of its garrisons, including the six hundred men at Jefferson

Barracks. This leapfrog reaction made it constantly difficult for post sutlers to maintain decent stock levels, minimize spoilage of perishable goods, anticipate future needs, and maintain an even flow of income.[25]

The army also developed a pattern of abandoning old posts in favor of new ones constructed farther west. The pattern was referred to as the Principle of the Exterior Line.[26] Military detachments would enter the wilderness and construct forts at strategic spots, as on waterways and Indian trails. When the area was secure enough for pioneer farmers and townsmen, the soldiers moved farther west to new frontiers, and the older posts, no longer on the frontier, were abandoned. Each time a post was abandoned, the sutler lost his job. Although a few sutlers worked for more than one post in their careers, there was no automatic carryover once a post was closed.

Whenever the army moved into a disputed or troublesome region to establish control, it confirmed its authority over the land with garrisoned posts. Once west of the Mississippi, army troops moved along the early Overland and Santa Fe trade routes, made forays into the Southwest, and removed some of the myth of the "Great American Desert."[27] Major new posts were placed along main communication lines (Snelling), on the banks of rivers (Gibson), and at trailheads for western travel (Leavenworth). To the advantage of the sutler, these newer posts were larger, more permanent establishments. Fort Leavenworth and Jefferson Barracks became staging areas for major explorations; Fort Snelling was a stone fortress outlier in a timber and fur-rich country; and Forts Towson and Gibson were established on Indian reservations.

Another variable outside the sutler's control was the infrequency of military pay. The absence of funds among soldiers caused the sutler to deal extensively on credit and because it increased desertion, it directly increased his collection problems.

As Surgeon General Lovell had explained in 1818, because the men were paid on such an irregular basis—often only once a year because posts were isolated and paymasters had regular rounds—the sutler was forced to operate on credit. Regulations said that the sutler was allowed to conduct credit sales of up to one-half a soldier's monthly pay, but the situation contained a catch-22. If the sutler voluntarily restricted credit sales, he depressed his long-range income (accounts receivable); if he was liberal with his credit limit, he faced potentially horrendous collection problems. There were limits to which the smart sutler would go; like sutler Smool at Fort Bowyer, it was too easy to get burned. A few sutlers tried to have their cake and eat it, too. They pushed credit sales as far as (or beyond what) authorities and regulations allowed, and then demanded payment on a regular basis. Regulations said the army was duty-bound to assist the sutler, but many officers were not sympathetic.

Colonel George Croghan was one of the few men to consider the effect of credit sales on the officers and men rather than on the sutler. After his inspection of Council Bluffs in the mid-1820s, he suggested that it might be valuable to have the sutler exhibit a receipt in full to the paymaster every six months to show the amount spent by the men. At a minimum, he maintained that every officer must at least be required to pay his bill to the sutler before he was transferred to another post. "Many of the officers, especially the younger ones, are deeply in debt at many of the posts," said Croghan, "far beyond all immediate hopes of payment, at least from what they receive from the government—and why? The sutler, feeling that he is at the mercy of the officers (for any of them may become members of the Council of Administration) dare not refuse credit, and the officer, finding his credit good and no pressing calls for money, heedlessly runs in debt." Croghan asked his superior officers to review his previous reports, more than one of which he was certain recited instances "of the melancholy effects of this unlimited credit."[28]

The business of extensive credit sales increased collection problems for the sutler. The men did not normally contest the amounts they owed or refuse to pay the sutler, but many of the sutler's clients deserted, died, were transferred, or ended up missing. Henry H. Sibley gave up his sutlership at Fort Snelling (St. Paul, Minnesota) in the late 1830s mainly because many soldiers were transferred out before they had been paid, and they left without paying what they owed to him.[29] Even then, a soldier's debts were distributed in strict sequence—the laundress before the sutler. Regular Army officers posted signs during the summer of 1832 to announce payment to those who had served in the 1831 Blackhawk War militia. It seems to have been common practice for a volunteer officer and sutler to accompany the paymaster on the circuit. Sutler Tillton made the rounds and signed the disbursements of pay for the company of Captain Thomas McDow's Brigade of Mounted Volunteers when they mustered out on May 27, 1832.

According to Inspector Croghan, in his 1833 report, the infrequency of pay exacerbated the rate of desertion. The soldier was not an accountant and he did not keep track of his indebtedness. Once the enlisted men finally were paid, "they see the whole amount due to them by the government swept off by the sutler for they know not what, or rather for the payment of articles purchased some time before." Croghan characterized the results as "brooding and discontent" rather than as a lesson to the men that they needed to economize.[30]

Desertions posed a hopeless collection problem for the sutler. In 1823, 25 percent of all new recruits deserted within the year, and in 1825 the figure nearly doubled. Of 6,000 men in the service in 1826, 10 percent (636) disappeared, never to return; so this was not a minor, periodic irritation for the sutler. The rate of desertion climbed to 24 percent (1,450) in 1831.[31] On a more detailed level, the militia records of the Blackhawk War in Illinois reveal that a number of men from the company of Captain James Caldwell, First Regiment, First Brigade, Third Army, deserted in 1832. The assigned sutler, William P. Tillton, testified that six of the seven men who took off owed him between $4.00 and $11.50 per person, for a total of $46.25.[32]

As the years passed, sutlers faced one growing complication in their collection attempts: paperwork. Records of the Second Auditor's office show that the majority of sutlers who pursued claims of financial loss between the 1830s and the 1870s were turned down because the information the auditor's office needed to pay claims was not recorded on the muster rolls. Sutlers of the Fourth Rifle Regiment of the Louisiana Volunteers were denied $2,000 in Mexican War claims. A claim for $1,025 submitted by Fort Buchanan's sutler Elias Brevoort in 1856 was turned down (seven years later) because many of the names he included were not properly recorded.[33] The case load at the auditor's office hit a peak during the last years of the Civil War.

Beyond the sutler's need to adjust to changes in army regulations and policy, to watch for stray arrows, and to run after delinquent accounts, he had to be careful not to make too much money. Suttling was a small profession. In theory, as of 1840, only forty-two positions were available for review once every four years—twenty-six in the eastern division and sixteen in the western division.[34] As a result of the changes in regulations in 1821, the majority of post sutlers began to make a decent income. All too soon, word of their financial success became known beyond military circles, and competition for the few available positions increased. As the position increased in visibility, it became increasingly vulnerable to political influence. One of the first visible ramifications of political interference was the muddying of a previously straightforward process of sutler selection.

The revised army regulations of 1821 vested authority in the Secretary of War to appoint each sutler. Generals were a favorite source of sutler recommendations, because through the 1830s the majority of applicants were men with prior military service. A good number came from a class of officers who were dismissed when the military was cut back in 1815.[35] Colonel Croghan said the suttling system had been designed specifically to assist officers caught by those cutbacks. In his opinion, ex-military men were the only viable candidates for sutler. They were more reliable, they interfaced well with officers and the men because they were gentlemen cut from the same cloth, and they understood military procedures. In essence, they knew the score and stayed out of trouble.

Examples were numerous. John O'Fallon, who served in the War of 1812, became sutler at Council Bluffs with the assistance of General Thomas A. Smith. A letter from General Winfield Scott to Secretary of War Lewis Cass on November 19, 1832, requested, among other things, that Richard H. Bell, who had served with Scott as a captain in the Blackhawk War "nobly and gallantly," be given the appointment as sutler to Fort Monroe. William P. Tillton, the sutler with the First and Third armies of the Blackhawk War, received his appointment from General Atkinson, and E. C. March was appointed sutler to the Second U.S. Dragoons in the fall of 1833, after having been a colonel and quartermaster general to General Henry Atkinson.[36] Thus, when many sutlers were routinely referrred to as captain, major, and colonel, these titles were not sobriquets, but most often earned ranks.

In 1840 the majority of appointments still reflected recommendations made by commanding officers and officers of the post's Council of Administration, but civilians with a background in trading and merchandising were being appointed with increasing frequency. Recommendations for this new class of favorites emanated from congressmen, governors, and other high-ranking government officials.

By 1836, Inspector Croghan asserted that the suttling system no longer supported its original goals. Politicians had vied successfully with field commanders, generals, and the post's Council of Administration to appoint their relatives, friends, and the relatives of associates. In the early days, the sutler who was an ex-soldier had an advantage, but examination of more than a hundred sutlers who worked between 1800 and 1890 revealed a strong shift from a military background to a background in civilian trade.[37] "The original purpose," Croghan wrote to his superior, "was to provide cheap goods but also to provide a little profit for the support of many needy disbanded officers. The good has been lost from sight. Sutlers are now chosen from numbers the army knows not." He was ready to recommend that the whole system be done away with and to "return to the way things were before the war."[38]

One of Croghan's later reports contained a good example of his complaint. "The appointment or rather nomination of Mr. Schoolcraft as sutler [to Fort Brady]," he wrote, "although made by a regularly organized Council of Administration, has not been confirmed by the Secretary of War. I must confess that until this instance I did believe that the nomination of sutler by a Council of Administration was final and that the appointment via the Secretary of War was merely to prevent a future council from removing the man." [39] It was not clear why the secretary had failed to approve the candidate, nor was it mentioned whom he might have had in mind. The trend toward political appointments continued unabated until the mid-1870s, when the politically backed sale of post traderships for profit created a scandal that rocked President Grant's administration. (See chapter 12.)

When frontier-market expert Lewis E. Atherton compared pre–Civil War army sutlers and western merchants, he found that more than half of the latter class had started as clerks. They had been apprenticed to older men, and due to frugality and hard work "they knew their business." Sutlers, on the other hand, he said, were appointed through the Secretary of War and received their appointments through politics, so when the government changed, so often did the sutlers.[40] The implication was that the appointment process of sutlers discounted the backgrounds of candidates and was therefore not conducive to a stable military merchant regime.

In support of Mr. Atherton's contention that background was important, there exists the record of Hiero Tennant Wilson. Once referred to as a Chesterfieldian-styled sutler, Wilson suttled from 1834 to 1853, a full twenty years.[41] He was raised on a farm near Russelville, Kentucky, where he was born in September 1806. In his youth, he secured a position as clerk in a nearby store, where he learned mercantile life. At age twenty-eight, he traveled across the country to join his brother,

Thomas E. Wilson, the post trader and Indian trader at Fort Gibson in the Cherokee Nation, Indian Territory.

Hiero Wilson remained at Fort Gibson as second in charge until the late 1840s, then bought out Mr. Bugg, sutler at Fort Scott (Kansas), and obtained the post's sutler appointment. While Bugg traipsed off to the gold fields of California in search of richer diggings, Wilson set up shop. And he was well prepared. He had ten years of prior experience on the frontier, and had learned both Cherokee and Creek at Fort Gibson. At Fort Scott, he took the trouble to learn Osage so that he might deal with the Osage Mission (now St. Paul), about forty miles southwest.

The large-boned, round-faced Mr. Wilson was a refined gentleman in all aspects—kind, polite, neat, regular in his habits, and firm in his convictions—so he was admired, honored, and respected in the community. At six foot two and 206 pounds, he was called the Big White Chief by the Indians. He tended to his business by traveling to St. Louis, and sometimes to Philadelphia, every spring and fall to purchase goods. He eventually married Elizabeth C. Hogan, the daughter of General David Hogan.

Wilson retained his position as sutler until the post was closed in 1853. He then continued as a mercantile businessman, but also handled real estate (the Fort Scott Town Co.) and sold insurance. He eventually held a position in the first territorial legislature, was a commissioner of Bourbon County, and was a leading promoter to bring the Tebo and Neosho Railroad into the area. Wilson lived to see his eighty-sixth birthday.

But Atherton's contention that political appointments were detrimental to the army's suttling needs is not supported by the record. The intrusion of politics into the appointment process favored a shift away from sutlers with military backgrounds to candidates with merchandising or trading experience. And if the Inspector General's "frank, incisive and critical" reports are used as a barometer, the vast majority of sutlers performed brilliantly.[42] The most uncomplimentary entry about a sutler that can be located in any of his reports during a twenty-year span involved a Mr. Hunt (no known relation to the Hunts in chapter 3), whom the sutler at Fort Gratiot caught altering prices set by the Council of Administration. "Mr. Hunt is fine now," Inspector Croghan subsequently noted in 1833, although he was "severely reprimanded last fall."

The majority of Croghan's comments about sutlers were bland variations of the phrase "the sutler gives satisfaction." He didn't appreciate the fact that sutler Satterlee Clark at Fort Winnebago in 1834 was "but seldom there," even if his agent did give satisfaction. After all, sutler Clark retained the confidence of his troops, for he held his license through three four-year terms, from 1831 until 1842.[43] At Fort Winnebago, in 1842, Croghan found fault with the Council of Administration rather than with the sutler. Prior to the arrival of the commanding officer, the council had appointed Mr. Clark, a man who had neither money nor credit and could not fulfill his engagement. As a result, Croghan reported, there was "almost a total want of what are called soldier's necessaries."[44]

Croghan also reported good things he heard or discovered about a sutler. "Mr. Hulbert, sutler," he once wrote, "has an excellent assortment on hand which is sold in accordance to prices fixed by an active Council of Administration. Prices are fair and reasonable and officers and men give favorable reports on the sutler."[45] Croghan also called sutler David Jones of Fort Mackinac an "attentive, studious and respected" man, whose "profits are by no means commensurable with his services."[46]

Atherton's examination of pre–Civil War merchants also led him to suggest that because western tradesmen were far better trained than sutlers, they remained in business longer on the average than their military counterparts.[47] The longevity of a sutler, however, was determined by factors never encountered by autonomous western merchants. The sutler was appointed for a two- to four-year period. To be reappointed by the Council of Administration, he had to score high points in compliance, congeniality, and performance—not high profits. The camp-following peddler of 1810 held his post for an average of two to three years; the sutler of 1830 lasted five to ten years. The sutler's longevity on the job therefore quickly doubled after the inauguration of the position of army post sutler. After 1821, repeated appointments of the same sutler for up to fifteen to twenty years were not unknown. In addition to Hiero T. Wilson's decades at Fort Gibson and Fort Scott, Hiram Rich (at Fort Leavenworth), Franklin Steele (at Fort Snelling), and George B. Gooding (at Fort Towson) each retained their sutler licenses for twenty years.[48] (See chapter 7.)

The increase in the professional longevity of the army sutler between 1820 and 1840 was not due to an improvement in the sutler's training or skills as much as it was due to greater stability at military posts, better treatment of the sutler, and an improvement in the quality of the sutler's ethical character and social background.

Not often did the name of a sutler extend beyond the confines of his post or the day of his death, but sutler John Nicks lived on at Fort Gibson albeit in unusual circumstances. After serving with the army from 1808 till 1821 as a lieutenant colonel, Nicks was appointed brigadier general of the Arkansas militia. When the army built Fort Gibson in Oklahoma in 1826, he became its sutler and left his business partner, John Rogers, in charge of their joint enterprises at Fort Smith.[49]

In 1830, Sam Houston wrote to John Eaton, Commissary General of the Army, to ask that his name be considered as a candidate to replace Nicks if there was going to be a vacancy. He thought there might be, because he'd heard Nicks was having problems with the paymaster.[50] Nicks wasn't having problems at the time, but a year later the sutlership became vacant because Nicks died on New Year's Day of 1832. His widow, Sally Nicks, asked post commander Colonel Arbuckle for the opportunity to dispose of her deceased husband's ten thousand dollars worth of merchandise. Arbuckle agreed and appointed her as sutler. Mrs. Nicks was the first woman known to be appointed sutler to the Regular Army, as well as one of the first businesswomen in Oklahoma.[51]

Washington Irving, who passed through Fort Gibson about that time, remarked lightly on the essence of Mrs. Nicks's situation. Referring to her as the Widow Nix, a "plump, buxom dame," he said her husband had acquired a small fortune of twenty thousand dollars during his years as sutler. As a result, she had become "the object of desires of all the men." That evening, to Irving's amusement (or perhaps dismay), the widow was serenaded by the "ghastly QMaster," a Captain Clark, whose voice "broke the sleep of men, women and dogs throughout the fort."[52]

No amount of military protection or support can make up for an unprofitable enterprise, and a number of sutlers discovered that they couldn't sustain their post diplomacy requirements and stay ahead of their creditors. Without individual testimonials, it's impossible to ascertain all the reasons why pre–Civil War sutlers left their profession, but the difficulty of making and sustaining a satisfactory profit margin was among the most significant. That high profits automatically accompanied the job was a myth exemplified by a paragraph in Edward Coffman's *The Old Army*:

At some isolated posts, such as Fort Smith in the early 1820s, no other store was within fifty miles so if neighboring civilians wanted manufactured goods, the sutler's was it. There were small fortunes to be made by sutlers who catered to the needs of these frontier military communities. [53]

Statistics, a handful of manuscripts, and a dozen major secondary sources indicate that a sutler had an even chance of making a good living, but he had to have good luck and a lot of investment capital. Lewis Atherton estimated the value of goods at a western merchant store to be six to seven thousand dollars.[54] To serve six hundred troops at Fort Atkinson, James Kennerly had on hand an inventory valued at twenty thousand dollars. One Texas post sutler, who went broke in 1873 after a short period of time, allegedly owed his creditors between fifty and sixty thousand dollars. Credit from eastern wholesale houses was normally obtained without great difficulty, but terms were six months of credit, with the total sum payable in twelve months, and interest rates ranged between 6 and 10 percent after the first six months.[55]

Sutlers were encouraged to reside on post, but they needed cash to construct their own home, their store, and their warehouse(s). John Cleves Symmes, the sutler at Cantonment Davis on the Missouri in 1815, constructed his buildings after he reached the post. The vessel on which he made his trip upriver served as his store until the building was complete. The store, which could hold $9,000 worth of goods, cost him $270.[56] Army regulations of 1821 suggested that sutlers could have the use of a vacant building, but most references to sutler operations indicate that they built their own places, as did Symmes.

The sutler's vision of a "small fortune" often evaporated in the midst of credit instability, market instability, adversely low prices, logistical problems, competition, and Indian wars. These factors explain why, between 1820 and 1840, the majority of sutlers failed to apply to renew their licenses at the end of their terms.

When Symmes departed Cantonment Davis in 1816 for a post as sutler in Louisiana, he was unable to meet his wholesale bill in St. Louis. The regiment had eighteen months of pay due, but would not get paid until two more months had passed. The sutler who preceded Symmes at Cantonment Davis was still due money.[57] In 1832, General Atkinson acknowledged that James Kennerly's efforts in supplying his forces during the Blackhawk War might have been unprofitable, so he asked a Mr. Palmer to send over some of the sutler stores with the army's baggage: "He is already greatly [the] loser I apprehend by trying [to] furnish us."[58]

In the mid-1830s, Henry H. Sibley, a manager for the American Fur Company, sought a sutler's license because he thought the position would automatically enhance his position as Indian trader. He knew that a sutler was protected by his military post, paid no rent, and was exempt from a number of expenses other traders encountered in the trade. The sutler's guarantee of "security, comfort, and certain profit" was a "decided advantage over the regular Traders."[59] After a year as sutler at Fort Snelling, Sibley changed his mind. A number of Fort Snelling's troops were relocated in 1837, and Sibley lost money. Worse, the troops departed before they had been paid, so they left without paying outstanding sutler bills. Just before he quit, Sibley remarked that "the problems were as great as the profits," and he vowed never to undertake a sutlership again.[60]

A classic profitability problem was encountered by L. N. Bailey, a sutler who, as of 1828, had established a good record for seven years at Fort Dearborn (Chicago).[61] What he faced in 1828 may have been due in part to poor merchant skills or greed, but his letter to Inspector General George Croghan in 1828 was well constructed to make the reader sympathize with his plight.[62]

Bailey found suttling at Fort Dearborn to have been a reasonably profitable business until mid-1827. After that, he wrote, the position "didn't pay expenses by $100 per month." In May 1827, he had asked permission from the commanding officer to extend credit to the men based on extra pay due but not yet received. The commandant agreed. The company clerk provided Bailey with a list of the men, and when the men's pay was later received the orderly sergeant called for a list of charges from the sutler. Bailey heard nothing more. He received no notice about when the men were paid, nor did he ever receive any part of that money.

Bailey's second complaint also concerned the post's credit policies. In June 1828, a number of recruits from New York were added to the company. Some had been enlisted for a number of months, but had drawn no pay. Bailey advanced credit to the men, based on the back pay they were due. When those men were paid off in October, Bailey presented his accounts. He quickly discovered that the men had been told by the commanding officer that they only had to pay him four dollars per month unless they pleased to do differently. This was the standing order of the garrison. Many men who had outstanding balances from prior credit purchases "left the [pay] table with money in their pockets" (in Bailey's words), while they remained indebted to Bailey to the tune of $112. He was subsequently ordered not to issue those men further credit until they had paid him off.

A condition that exacerbated Bailey's problem was his reliance on whiskey to make a profit. From September 7, 1828, until he wrote his letter, Bailey had not sold one gill of whiskey, and only a small quantity of cider and beer. The whole amount of his trade at the post with the soldiers for eight months was $609, and the amount of profit allowed by the council was only 25 percent.

The men nonetheless were permitted to be in town from retreat to tattoo. As a result, as Bailey reported, "one grog shop received $800 for liquor alone." Sometime during the winter, Lieutenant Summer gave permission for each man in the company to purchase a pint of beer or a quart of cider a day, but the order lasted only four to five days, and then was revoked.

Bailey was desperate. He had tried to comply with the regulations of the post. His fuel bill alone, in that climate where wood was three dollars a cord, was considerable. He found the whole business, "as now managed," to be a life he was "unable to sustain," and unless "some beneficial alteration" could be made, he said he was going to be obliged to relinquish it altogether.

To minimize his exposure to financial loss, the astute sutler did what all large companies do today: he developed a diverse portfolio and different lines of business—some related, some unrelated. The first sideline that offered itself to the frontier sutler was the Indian trade. Anyone of good moral character was permitted to receive a license to deal with one or more Indian tribes, and, as Sibley knew, the sutler had an inside track because he was on a military post.

In the 1820s, the Jeffersonian ideal, whose objective was to assimilate American Indians into the white man's way of life, crumbled under pressure from population growth and frontiersman hostility. It was replaced by President Andrew Jackson's program of removal, based on the premise that only isolation from white Americans would ensure the preservation of the Indian.

The army was given the task of relocating Indian tribes from east of the Mississippi to west of the Mississippi. The process involved all sections of the frontier. In the South, the lands of the Cherokee Nation were stolen, and its people sustained inexcusable hardship during their journey to Oklahoma. Farther north, in the Mississippi valley, the Department of Indian Affairs was more successful in arranging peaceful

Indian Trading Licenses of Some Pre–Civil War Sutlers [63]

Thomas McNair (1815–19?)

John Dougherty (1820–45)

Dr. Abraham Edwards (1810–15)

John O'Fallon (1819–23)

George C. Kennerly (1818–30)

John Kinzie (1804–22?)

John C. Symmes (1815–18?)

Henry H. Sibley (1836–38)

treaties with the Sioux (in 1829), the Menominee (in 1831), the Winnebago (in 1832 and 1837), the Chippewa (in 1833, 1837, and 1854–55), and the Fox (in 1833 and 1837).[64] Nearly every relocation was accompanied by a large monetary award, because the U.S. government was purchasing tribal land. Knowing in advance when a move was due, unscrupulous Indian traders extended thousands of dollars of credit to the tribes in anticipation of those payments.[65]

The term *Indian trader*, per se, does not include sutlers, even though a sutler might possess a license to trade with the Indians; and many did so trade. In addition to sutlers like George Hunt, who worked with government factor John Johnson at Fort Madison in 1811, sutler John Symmes at Cantonment Davis held a license to trade with the Sacs and Foxes on the Osage River in 1815, and Thomas McNair, sutler to Fort Crawford in 1815–16, held a valid Indian trading license. Sutler James Kennerly, whose brother George was a subagent for Benjamin O'Fallon in 1826, was the Kickapoo Indian commissioner's secretary in the 1830s while he was sutler at Jefferson Barracks. Among other functions, he escorted bands of Indians to their reservations on the west side of the Missouri.[66] And when young Satterlee Clark was appointed to Fort Winnebago by General Jackson in 1830, he was under age, so he clerked for Oliver Newberry of Detroit as an Indian trader.[67]

It was difficult for a sutler on the frontier to ignore the profit potential of trade with the Indians, even though the risks (such as those mentioned in chapter 3) were sometimes greater.

Government contracts appealed to sutlers almost as much as an Indian trader's license. Perhaps the army viewed the sutler as a good organizer. He was a known entity. He may also may have been skilled in entering low bids. The army first purchased firewood from a sutler in 1832 at Fort Armstrong: three hundred cords at $2.98 per cord. Henry M. Rice, sutler at Fort Atkinson, obtained contracts for hay, corn, and oats in 1842, delivering nine thousand bushels of corn and seven thousand bushels of oats. Franklin Steele, who made his venture capital from timber, supplied Fort Snelling with wood, hay, oats, and beef for a decade. Several sutlers invested their capital in freighting lines. Two developed cattle ranches in the 1830s, an enterprise that became a major source of income for post traders after the Civil War. The replacement of the older military men by younger men with experience in merchandising as sutler may have accounted, in part, for the rather sudden appearance of entrepreneurial bent.

On a smaller remunerative scale, the sutler was often the local postmaster and banker. The first mention of a sutler assuming the role of postmaster occurred during the French-Indian War. John O'Fallon ran "expresses" between St. Louis and Council Bluffs, and sutler Franklin Steele assumed the postmaster's post at Snelling in the late 1830s as soon as mail lines were established.[68]

Every sutler willingly loaned money to the army. David Meriwether played banker at least once in the early 1820s before he left the frontier, when he covered a six-thousand-dollar cash loss after a paymaster's cash box had disappeared into the Missouri River. James Kennerly paid off the troops at Council Bluffs with his own funds. Indian agents occasionally wrote to Superintendent William Clark in St. Louis to ask for money to repay sutlers from whom they had borrowed money. Andrew Hughes told Clark he had borrowed three hundred dollars from Hiram Rich, the Leavenworth sutler (and late postmaster), to pay his interpreter, and in order to pay him back he had drafted a voucher using Clark's name. William Street, the Indian agent at Prairie du Chien, asked Clark where he could obtain funds at Fort Crawford. He considered the mail too unsafe, but believed there was "enough specie in the hands of the sutler and merchants to make the payment."[69]

By 1840, after four decades of suttling at military posts on the frontier, the sutler was a master at his trade. He knew the rules, the magnitude of his leeway, his limits, and what he had to do to stay in the black. As the army changed he kept pace, altering his practice as necessary to protect his profit margin yet maintain a stable level of service. Between 1822 and the onset of the Civil War, the character of the mythological "average" sutler changed. Greater numbers of men with merchandising experience entered the ranks. Once well ensconced in military life and the frontier-post military scene, these new sutlers began to plan for families and for the future. They became more conscious of long-range financial opportunities, and invested in a number of small entrepreneurial enterprises, carefully selecting those that made them more and more essential to the frontier community.

In the majority of cases, the sutler's community around his military post continued to grow. The army moved into areas of the continent previously uninhabited by whites, but America's land-hungry population followed on its heels. The pre–Civil War frontier post, like those established after that war, became the focal point for new settlement. And the pre–Civil War sutler-entrepreneurs established a pattern of diversity that eventually became the basis on which a few post–Civil War sutlers (post traders) would build substantial empires. Most sutler fortunes were developed at western posts between 1867 and 1880 (see chapter 12); a few notable exceptions (the topics of chapter 7) were created between the late 1840s and 1860.

SEVEN

Successful Pre–Civil War Sutlers

Marcus Whitman, guide and traveler who escorted many emigrant trains in the early days, estimated that the average overlander spent upwards to $4,000 at the four principal posts: Fort William, Fort Hall, Fort Bridger, and Fort Boise.—John D. Unruh, Jr., The Plains Across

The successful sutler of the middle 1800s—now a businessman who surveyed his growing menu of options with aggressive relish—was one of America's first frontier entrepreneurs. Not content to passively serve his garrison and hope that the post's Council of Administration would set prices that matched his sense of fairness, he took advantage of each opportunity that presented itself to make money. Although a number of sutlers who tried to develop profitable sidelines were unsuccessful, an equal number were partially successful. A handful, however, were able to put it all together and become wealthy men.

The success of this mid-nineteenth-century businessman depended then, as it does today, on three critical factors: location, location, and location. The landing of American troops at Vera Cruz in 1847, during the Mexican War, serves as a highly visual example. Just prior to the soldiers' unopposed landing, sutlers managed to get ashore where they set up shop. Imagine thirteen thousand troops landing on the beach, only to be met by a gang of merchandise peddlers. As recorded by General Scott, these sutlers, eager for fast profits, crowded their tents side by side along the beach and navy carpenters worked hastily to build floors, sides, and counters for these private enterprises, neglecting the pressing military business. Boxes of goods and fancy groceries filled the tents and a brisk trade began almost at once as soon as the troops came ashore.[1]

Occupation of the beach lasted two weeks.

Vera Cruz was a one-of-a-kind situation, and only a handful of frontier forts were blessed with locations that promised such excellent marketing opportunities for private enterprise. Within that handful, many became valuable to the sutler only after a market developed in the environs of the military reservation. The fur and timber industry caused rapid settlement around Fort Snelling (St. Paul), Minnesota, while the government's responsibility of managing the reservations of tribes in Indian Territory provided profitable contracts for sutlers at nearby posts like Fort Gibson and Fort Towson (both in Oklahoma). Self-contained military markets existed at Fort Leavenworth and at Jefferson Barracks, because those posts could accommodate more than a half-dozen companies at one time and occasionally accommodated more than a thousand men. These latter posts served as staging areas for troops. Of the two, Leavenworth grew larger, lasted much longer, and became far more rewarding for its sutlers.

From the sutler's perspective, the more lucrative forts were those whose locations attracted a large, diverse market. The majority of that type were situated on trading and emigration routes. In the mid-1840s, when Americans engaged in wholesale western migration, the U.S. Army began to buy up old fur trading posts on the Oregon and California trails. Then, in 1848, after the Mexican War, the army established more than thirty posts in Texas and another thirty farther west, in concert with the settlement of the Southwest. The sutlers at the few posts along the Oregon Trail probably did more business than all the posts in Texas, Arizona, and New Mexico combined.

Of the four east–west routes across the Continental Divide, the Platte River Trail out of Omaha and Nebraska City handled 90 percent of westbound emigrant traffic.[2] Thousands of emigrants, freighters, and military troopers paraded past these posts between 1845 and 1875. Marcus Whitman, a guide who escorted many emigrant trains, estimated that the average overlander spent nearly four thousand dollars between Fort Laramie (then Fort William, Wyoming Territory), Fort

Bridger (Wyoming Territory), Fort Hall (Idaho Territory), and Fort Boise (also Idaho Territory).[3]

In contrast, the numerous small posts in the Southwest (Military District no. 9) were a sutler's marketing nightmare: inaccessible, thinly settled, and surrounded by hostile Indians. The sutler who acquired a license to suttle at a post on the Oregon Trail had to be a drunk or a misanthrope not to become wealthy. By comparison, the sutler who accepted a post in the Southwest took his chances. He might not have much competition, but by the time he paid his freight bill and assessed the size and wealth of his market, he was lucky to break even.

In the mid-1800s, Southwest frontier posts were isolated in the extreme. Few roads connected them to supply depots. Before sutlers left the post, prudence and common sense required them to request an escort to protect them from roaming bands of Indians. Troops were paid irregularly, and on occasion, when a post was ordered to relocate, the settlement that had begun to develop around the post evanesced. The post garrison, not the area, became the market for the village and the reason for maintaining the settlement.

In 1853, Colonel Joseph K. F. Mansfield inspected the posts of Military District no. 9, which covered what is now Texas, Arizona, New Mexico, and California. His report for Texas was depressingly characteristic for all of the subsequent posts on which he reported. Troops stationed in the county of El Paso, Texas, he said, were 675 miles and in some cases 1,000 miles from the nearest trading town in the United States. Transportation costs for merchandise and sutlers' goods ranged from eight to fifteen cents per pound, "independent of the profits these traders must make on their goods in order to live," thus raising the prices of all articles brought from the States "from 100 percent to 400 percent."[4]

Prices remained high because there was limited competition, "in consequence of the limited sales and the danger attending transportation across the country infested with Indians." Mansfield believed that conditions were bound to remain as they were for some time to come. Officers could purchase food at contract prices, but "the other necessities and comforts of life to both officers and soldiers have to be purchased at the advanced prices above stated, or they are obliged to deny themselves what the troops at other posts enjoy."[5]

At Fort Massachusetts (Colorado)—as at Forts Defiance (Arizona), Los Lunes (Arizona), and Buchanan (Arizona)—the problem was primarily one of supply. All of the food for the settlements near Fort

Massachusetts came from Taos, New Mexico; all other supplies were brought in from Fort Union (New Mexico). Roads were impassable for loaded wagons. "This may be the cause of many deficiencies," noted Mansfield. The eighty-one men of the companies at Fort Massachusetts were obliged to purchase shirts, socks, and shoes from the sutler at high rates because the government failed to have these articles on hand for several months. "The sutler's prices, in consequence of the great transportation costs from the United States, are exorbitant and much beyond the ability to the soldiers to pay."[6]

The situation at Fort Union, headquarters of the Ninth Army in New Mexico, was not much different even if it was supposed to have served as a local supply house. Stores had to be freighted in from St. Louis or Fort Leavenworth. Kittie Bowen, the outspoken wife of Fort Union's Captain Bowen, let it be known that the "sutler prices exceed anything I have ever heard of!"[7]

Transportation costs from the depot at Fort Leavenworth to posts in the Southwest were steep, reflecting not only the miles but the risks. When possible, sutler wagons traveled with escorts and with larger quartermaster supply trains. Freight in 1854 to Fort Union was $7.96 per one hundred pounds; to Albuquerque, $10.80; to Fort Fillmore, $13.75, and to Fort Bliss, $14.00.[8]

At Forts Union, Massachusetts, Defiance, and Cantonment Burgwin (New Mexico), troops were paid irregularly, so cash was always short. Notes and drafts were practically worthless in New Mexico: the New Mexicans didn't like anything except silver. Even gold coins were suspect. The Treasury Department had expected to exchange treasury notes with traders, but they had little coin.[9]

Forts Union, Defiance, Massachusetts, Conrad (New Mexico), and Webster (New Mexico) were criticized as being poorly located. Forts Defiance, Massachusetts, and Webster were almost impossible to supply, and Forts Union, Conrad, and Fillmore (New Mexico) were located on private land. As soon as the hostile Indians were pacified, killed off, or placed on reservations, many posts were abandoned.[10] Not surprisingly, sutlers at Southwest frontier posts came and went almost as frequently as the enlisted men.

Yet a post didn't have to be off the main track to lose its value. Fort Kearny, on the Oregon Trail, had been the first in a series of posts across the United States that Congress agreed should be garrisoned for the purpose of protecting emigrants. In 1850, monthly mail service was established at the post, and during the 1860s the fort maintained facilities as a station for the Pony Express, Holladay's stagecoach line, and the telegraph. In 1871, the army decided that Fort Kearny was no longer needed. The Indians around the post were not a problem, for the Oregon Trail was being adequately covered by troops from Fort Leavenworth; the post was now "too near the frontier to be necessary to emigrants as a place of rest, repair," and it had been very expensive to maintain. It was two hundred miles from the nearest settlement, located on the wrong side of the Platte, and it was totally dependent on imported materials.[11] By 1875 Kearny was empty.

One young, gutsy sutler decided that it would be better to leave his unit and try his luck as a trader with a post of his own on a major route to California. His name was Major John Owens. He was attached to Colonel William W. Loring's Rifle Regiment of 600 men, which was bound for service in Oregon. The unit departed from Fort Leavenworth on May 10, 1849, with 160 wagons, a few families, 1,200 mules, and 700 horses. When the contingent made winter camp at Cantonment Loring, six miles north of where Fort Hall would be established, Owens quit, married a Shoshone, and started his trade.

Owens was thirty-three years old when he made the shift from sutler to pioneer storekeeper. He thought he had a good location in what would become Montana's Bitterroot Valley, and a good partner in his brother, but business was slow. He took in less than two thousand dollars during the first year. In his peak years his gross income exceeded ten thousand dollars.[12] He stuck it out, serving the area as the local banker, credit manager, and general merchant until 1871, when new mining activities took away his market.

Of all the pre–Civil War sutlers recorded by history, three stand out as highly successful frontier entrepreneurs: Franklin Steele, John Dougherty, and Hiram Rich. Each story is unique, yet the outcome of their circumstances is similar. Each served a long term as a sutler, each used the profits from his suttling business to fund one or more new ventures, and each became highly successful. Two of the three were known to have retired with considerable wealth.

Franklin Steele, a capitalist and businessman who was raised in Chester County, Pennsylvania, was sutler to Fort Snelling from 1838 to 1858. A combination of frontier opportunity and personal drive for acquisition and profits enabled him to become a highly successful entrepreneur. As he tells it, he arrived in Wisconsin Territory in 1837 at age twenty-four, a young man, healthy and ambitious, and ready to dare the perils of an almost unexplored region inhabited by savages.[13]

He selected Fort Snelling as his starting point and timber as his game. In September 1837, "immediately after the [Indian] treaty was made ceding the St. Croix Valley to the government," Steele started out from Fort Snelling in a bark canoe, accompanied by a scow loaded with tools, supplies, and laborers. He said he descended the Mississippi to the mouth of the St. Croix, and then ascended the St. Croix to the Dalles, where he had a log cabin built and put men to work felling trees. Or, as an early Wisconsin historian recalled, Steele started his lumber operations with an ox, a cart, and six half-breeds.[14]

In February 1838, immediately after another Indian treaty, he extended his cutting operations to the Snake River and, the following spring (of 1839), formed a corporation called the St. Croix Falls Lumbering Company with a group of men from Illinois and Missouri.

As his timber venture took shape, he also applied for and received the sutlership at Fort Snelling from President Van Buren. Fort Snelling had been erected in 1821, in the heart of Sioux and Ojibway hunting lands at the juncture of the Mississippi and the Minnesota rivers. The site, over 100,000 acres, was purchased from the Indians by Lieutenant Zebulon Pike for two hundred dollars worth of trade items and sixty gallons of whiskey. Fort Snelling was envisioned as one link in a chain of forts that the government planned to use to control the Indian trade and to protect American interests in the Northwest territories. The post became the hub of the Upper Mississippi fur-trade traffic for almost thirty years.

The first Fort Snelling sutler, Louis Devotion, arrived with the troops that established Cantonment New Hope, the temporary camp that preceded the post. His assistant, Philander Prescott, said that Devotion abandoned the business after a few years because the army would permit him a profit of only 25 percent, with no allowance for freight or waste.[15] James Soulard, a son-in-law of Colonel Thomas Hunt (see chapter 2), followed Devotion. He and his family lived in three rooms of the army's stone barracks. The sutler's store, which was constructed in 1823, was a simple rectangular one-room building, similar to the schoolhouse, roughly twenty feet by forty feet with a door in the middle and two windows, one on each side.[16]

At some early point in time, a Captain Leonard and a Mr. Ortley were referred to as post sutlers, and for four years beginning in 1828, the sutler was John Culbertson. He might have been the same sutler Culbertson who complained to the Secretary of War in 1823 about the conflict over a sutler's jurisdiction of troops. In December 1832, Culbertson gave up his suttling privileges. He did not want to reside at the post, and the army was beginning to enforce their 1829 ruling that sutlers must reside at the post at which they were trading.

In 1835, the *Register of Post Traders* shows that Samuel C. Stambaugh was serving as post sutler. Stambaugh, a journalist who hailed from Lancaster, Pennsylvania, had been the Indian agent at Green Bay, Wisconsin, in 1830, and he was a close ally of the Sauk and Fox tribes.[17] Stambaugh found that the sutlership was more work and less rewarding monetarily than he had anticipated, so he tried to sell his position to Henry H. Sibley of the American Fur Company outposts. But Stambaugh wanted too much for it. Instead, he and Sibley formed a partnership in 1836, in which Stambaugh would receive half the profits and Sibley would run the store. The agreement lasted until 1839, at which point Stambaugh's commission ran out and Sibley discovered he'd had a belly full of suttling.

Franklin Steele acquired the Fort Snelling sutler's license in 1839 and commenced his operations in February 1840, the year he also became postmaster. He stocked his merchandising venture with thirteen thousand dollars worth of goods from his lumbering profits, placed his name on a board across the top of the door, and announced the opening of "The Best Stocked Store in the West."[18] Aside from his basic dry-goods business, Steele carried berries, raisins, apples, cheese, sugar and spices, bread, butter, and jam. As usual for a frontier store, he stocked an assortment of clothing and sundries: suits, dresses, indigo, shoes, needles and thread, scrub brushes, brooms, candy, liquor, tobacco, pipes, and little luxuries.[19]

Fort Snelling was a small post, never garrisoned by more than two or three companies. The sutler who preceded Stambaugh had made fifteen hundred dollars to two thousand dollars per year,[20] but Steele was ambitious and had a nose for profitable investments. First, he formed a fur-trade partnership with his clerk, Norman W. Kittson, a fur trader who represented the American Fur Company at various posts in Iowa, Wisconsin, and Minnesota. Fort Snelling was the assembly area for the annual fur-trade catch before it was shipped to St. Louis. Between 1839 and 1843 he and Steele acted as fur-traders and general-supply merchants at the mouth of the Minnesota River.[21]

Steele, Sibley, and Henry M. Rice, another clerk who worked for Steele, became leading figures in the Fort Snelling–St. Paul area in the 1840s. Rice had come to Fort Snelling from Vermont in 1839. Sibley hired him to handle his Indian trade with the Winnebagos. Steele was already working closely with Sibley, sharing investment opportunities like partial ownership of the *Lynx*, a new 136-foot steamboat. Each owned one-eighth.[22] The year that Franklin Steele went to Baltimore, Maryland, to marry Miss Anna Barney, the granddaughter of Commodore Barney of the U.S. Navy, Sibley married Franklin Steele's sister.

In 1847, Steele and a number of new partners, including the Honorable Caleb Cushing of Massachusetts (a member of Congress from 1835 to 1843 and U.S. Attorney General in 1853), formed a company to manufacture lumber. Steele managed to cover the capital investment necessary to develop the enterprise by mortgaging his claim at the Falls of St. Anthony. He already had a ferryboat operation across the Mississippi River at St. Anthony and a waterpower claim for the falls. The sawmill and power at the Falls of St. Anthony attracted a considerable settlement. In 1848, the year he purchased Nicolet and Boom islands, he platted the town of St. Anthony. The village, based on the timber industry, thrived and was incorporated in 1855.

Steele leased his sawmill operations in the late 1840s, then became a partner in the Mississippi Boom Company and the Mississippi and Rum River Boom Company, two lumber boom companies in 1851. That year, he was elected president of the Board of Regents of the University of Minnesota, an institution to which he donated significant amounts of land and money in later years. He also promoted railroad development in St. Paul and built the first suspension bridge to span the Mississippi in 1854, connecting Minnesota and St. Anthony.

By the mid-1850s Steele had developed a reputation as a "skillful operator" in land, lumbering, and merchandising, and he was believed to have amassed a fortune. A local historian said that Steele, as a sutler, merchant, banker, land speculator, bridge builder, and politician, had perseverance and was an "entrepreneur of great energy and vision."[23] Seth Eastman, commander of Fort Snelling at the time, described Steele's home as a large and elegant dwelling with attached stables. His business complex included a storehouse and other buildings near the post. In February 1855, Steele County, Minnesota, was named for him.

The fur trade that Steele, Sibley, and Rice conducted was closely tied to the American Fur Company; thus, when the fur trade died down in the late 1840s, they turned their attention to land speculation. When Minnesota became a separate territory in 1849, everyone lined up for a share of the land. Steele set his sights on the Fort Snelling reservation and used his profits and equity in his lumbering operations to support this kind of venture. During the 1850s his brother-in-law, Henry H. Sibley, was a delegate to Congress, and it was generally expected that he would open the military reserve for settlement. But Congress balked and sold it off piece by piece until there were less than eleven thousand acres left.

On April 24, 1856, Steele offered seventy-five thousand dollars cash down for the majority of the land, including Fort Snelling. Authority for a private sale of military property existed in an 1819 precedent, when Congress empowered the Secretary of War to sell military sites that were no longer of value. Steele's associate, Henry Rice, obtained an extension of that power to cover Fort Snelling. Additional political maneuvering resulted in the Secretary of War giving a commission to a Mr. Heiskell to sell the land for top dollar. Heiskell and Major Eastman (the commanding officer of Snelling) offered it to Steele for ninety thousand dollars.

Everything was done silently. The sale was confirmed on July 2, and Steele, with backing from two partners, paid an installment of thirty thousand dollars on July 25. Six months later, Congressman Robert Smith asked for an investigation into the sale. The investigating House committee report, which exceeded 450 pages, resolved that the fort and adjacent land had been sold illegally: the Secretary of War was at fault; the agents were unqualified; the management of the sale was disadvantageous to the government; and John C. Mather (one of Steele's partners) had violated his duty. No one mentioned Franklin Steele.[24]

At first Congress left it up in the air, then brought suit to void the agreement. But the suit was set aside during the Civil War, and then dropped in 1865, and the post was reoccupied during the Slaveholder's Rebellion of the late 1860s. In 1868, Steele filed his own suit for $162,000 for back rent at $2,000 a month. Three years later, a board appointed by the Secretary of War recommended a settlement. Although Steele ended up with more land than he had purchased, he sold it all back to the government in 1872.

After Franklin Steele died in 1880 at age sixty-seven, his three daughters donated twenty thousand dollars for a plot of land in Minneapolis, to be known as Franklin Steele Square. In local historical documents, he is characterized as one of the state's most generous and public-spirited citizens.

In September 1848, while Franklin Steele was platting St. Anthony, a middle-aged Indian agent named John Dougherty was meeting with St. Louis capitalist and financier John Campbell to discuss opportunities in the suttling business at newly established posts along the Oregon Trail. The venture, it was thought, would be extremely profitable; and it was. Dougherty retired as a man of position and wealth—a posture that his years in the fur trade and with the government had not provided.[25]

John Dougherty was a Kentucky lad, born in Bardstown in 1791. At age seventeen, he left his home town and wandered down to bustling St. Louis. After a year or two of whatever a young lad found to do to pay his keep in a waterfront fur-trade town, he signed up as one of twenty-four oarsmen on the keelboat of an American adventurer named Thomas James. James's boat was one of thirteen in a 350-man expedition of the newly formed St. Louis Fur Company. The company belonged to Manual Lisa, one of the frontiersmen who had been with the 1804–6 Lewis and Clark expedition. Lisa's 1808 enterprise was not destined to go well. By the time the boats had reached the mouth of the Osage River, all but ten Americans, disgusted by the depletion of supplies, had turned back. A splinter group under the new leadership of Pierre Menard continued to the mouth of the Big Horn, then pressed on toward the Gallatin River (Montana). The expedition reached the three forks (Gallatin, Madison, and Jefferson) by February 1810. On April 3, 1810, the men began to build a fort. Beaver trapping was rich, but the Blackfoot Indians were on the warpath. A number of men had bad encounters, and then Dougherty's first canoe-load of pelts was lost when his craft hit a rock and sank. Menard finally ordered a retreat. The majority of the men returned directly to St. Louis. Colonel Andrew Henry, John Dougherty, and a few others went south across the mountains and wintered on the Columbia River, returning to St. Louis only the following spring.

Dougherty spent his next few years learning Indian lore and trapping, probably in the employ of the Missouri Fur Company. Alexander Doniphan said that Dougherty had the perfect face, form, and physique, plus that commanding, dignified ease and directness that Indians responded to so well.

In 1818, Dougherty became an interpreter for Major Benjamin O'Fallon, the brother of John O'Fallon, who outfitted at Council Bluffs. Dougherty and Benjamin O'Fallon joined the Stephen H. Long expedition at St. Charles. On July 19, at Franklin, a town on the Missouri, Dougherty, O'Fallon, and a Major Biddell left the military post and went to Fort Osage. Dougherty stayed at Osage for a while, then O'Fallon sent him to a Pawnee camp to retrieve a boy who had been stolen from his father. Dougherty also gathered tribes together for councils.

In 1819, Benjamin O'Fallon wrote to the Secretary of War to recommend that Dougherty become his assistant agent. He said Dougherty had "passed the prior eight years in the country between [St. Louis] and the Yellow Stone," and spoke several Indian languages as well. He believed that Dougherty should be paid for both his work as assistant Indian agent and as interpreter. Calhoun carried out O'Fallon's wishes by appointing Dougherty as subagent on December 23, 1819. He was paid $500 per year as assistant Indian agent, and $450 per year as interpreter.

Dougherty stayed at Council Bluffs (Fort Atkinson) until the summer of 1826, so he certainly knew James Kennerly well. He surely assimilated the basics of suttling by observing and listening to John O'Fallon and James Kennerly. On November 13, 1823, while at Atkinson, Dougherty married Mary Hertzog. He also bought a slave—perhaps to care for his bride. The year the post closed, 1826, he took Benjamin O'Fallon's place as Indian agent.

In 1827, Dougherty and his family accompanied Colonel Henry Leavenworth when he left Liberty, Missouri, accompanied by Brevet Major Daniel Ketchum's command in four keelboats, to found Cantonment (later Fort) Leavenworth. Dougherty had been assigned to the new post. In December of the following year, Dougherty's son, Lewis Bissell (most likely named after John O'Fallon's partner), was born, perhaps the second or third white child born in Kansas.

Dougherty continued to head up the Upper Missouri Agency, which included the Otoes, Pawnees, Omahas, Poncas, and other Indian tribes in the country west of the Missouri and north of the Northern Agency of the Western Territory. He held that position until 1839. His correspondence with officials back east underlines his concern for his job and for the Indians.

When William Clark died in 1838, Dougherty petitioned for his job as Missouri Superintendent of Indian Affairs, but the influence of the American Fur Company, which backed Andrew Drips, outweighed his, so Drips got the job. Dougherty remained as Indian agent for another year; then, as a substitute for the job he wanted but would never have, he entered the Missouri legislature as a Whig. Over the next few years, Dougherty invested in a general trading store and developed a cattle ranch from which he shipped beef cattle to posts along the Santa Fe and Oregon trails.

On September 16, 1848, Robert Campbell—that great source of St. Louis investment capital to so many entrepreneurs in the trading community of the West—suggested that Dougherty take the sutlership at Fort Childs (Fort Kearny). Dougherty not only agreed; he suggested they also try for the sutlership at Fort Laramie because the Indian trade there was extensive. Under the agreement, Dougherty would receive two-thirds of the profits and split it with the person in residence at the post; Campbell would retain one-third as a return on his investment.

Acquiring an interest in both post sutlerships was less difficult than it might have seemed. On October 28, 1847, Charles F. Ruff, who commanded Companies I and G of a regiment of Mounted Riflemen, established Fort Kearny on the Platte. Ruff had his wife and child with him. John Dougherty was his father-in-law.[26] Dougherty's nineteen-year-old son, Lewis, helped set up shop while Dougherty stayed at Fort Leavenworth, where he assembled his wagons for Kearny and Laramie. Dougherty transferred goods from the Missouri River to the posts, and brought back loads of buffalo robes. To make their freighting venture pay off, Campbell and Dougherty used their friendship with high-ranking officers at Leavenworth to secure civilian contracts for army supplies.

Dougherty also bid on the delivery of five hundred head of cattle to Fort Kearny, which was relocating to Grand Island. He had no trouble delivering them, because the Indians who frequented the area were all his friends. But there were other factors plaguing a freighter in those days, including high water, smallpox and other illnesses, drunken drivers, blizzards and heat waves, and breakdowns like busted wagon wheels that required repairs on the road. As the first big freighter on the Oregon Trail for the army before Lee, Waddell, and Majors, Dougherty probably faced them all.

Dougherty's son remained in charge of the Kearny store from 1848 to 1853, and then helped out in the Fort Laramie store where Dougherty and Campbell had established a partnership in 1849 with the post's first sutler, John Thomas Tutt. Tutt had received his sutlership from President Zachary Taylor in April 1849, built the first sutler store (which he improved in 1852), and stayed on until March 1857. His brother, H. L. Tutt, served at the store with him. During the first two years, Tutt said that he had averaged $170 per day from the Indian trade, and that in one year, nine thousand wagons and forty-two thousand people had passed in front of the post. He also said he'd had competition in the Indian trade from Kit Carson of Taos and Bill Bent of Colorado, who came up to sell mules in the summer of 1850.[27]

In 1851, Dougherty received the contract to take trade goods to the Laramie Peace Council, also known as the Horse Council. The council represented a major attempt by the American government to establish peace between whites and American Indians, and to reduce intertribal conflict by setting regional boundaries between a number of Plains Indian tribes. Dougherty also began to keep cattle near Fort Laramie for the Indian trade. Both he and Seth Ward are credited with the first herd in the area.

For a number of reasons, business declined rapidly in the late 1850s. Tutt spend a great deal of time away from Fort Laramie, and his business methods were allegedly sloppy. After Campbell got a look at the records, he wrote Dougherty that he felt he had been swindled. Campbell then withdrew from the partnership of Campbell, Dougherty, and Tutt in 1853. Both Robert Campbell and Dougherty's son, Lewis, asked Dougherty to sell out, but Dougherty kept his agreement with Tutt. He then turned over his affairs to his son. In March 1857, with eighteen months left on his three-year sutler's license, Tutt resigned. His action may have resulted from rumors that said the army was planning to abandon the post.[28]

Dougherty and Tutt's entire stock was purchased by one Seth Ward, Fort Laramie's most famous sutler, on March 19, 1857, for three thousand dollars. Out of the sutler game at last, the now retired sixty-four-year-old Dougherty bought an extensive tract of the Delaware Indian lands auctioned off at Fort Leavenworth in 1856. He added this tract to his holdings near St. Louis, his property in Liberty, the acreage he owned at Jatan, Missouri, and the land he owned in St. Joseph and Collinsville, Illinois. He also had constructed a twenty-thousand-dollar, two-story, brick mansion northwest of Liberty, which the Kansas City Star characterized as the "finest mansion West of the Mississippi River." For the few remaining years of his life, Dougherty managed his lands, his cattle business, and a banking business. He was a trustee of William Jewell College and became a community leader in Clay County, Missouri. At the time of his death, on December 28, 1860, it was reported that he had an extensive buffalo herd on his estate.

A quieter but equally successful sutler, Hiram Rich, started life on September 21, 1799, in Charlotte, Vermont. By 1829, at age twenty-nine, he had established himself as a trader in the growing trade town of Liberty, Missouri, situated on the Missouri River and not far north of St. Louis. He also married Julia Ann Wilson on the sixth of May that year.

A good portion of Rich's trade in the 1830s was with the Indians. In the early 1830s, Andrew S. Hughes, who worked for William Clark, Superintendent of Indian Affairs in St. Louis, paid Hiram Rich $300 for services probably related to Indian Bureau affairs. The draft that Hughes gave to Rich was written on Hughes's employer. More significantly, Rich was paid $7,977.30 in 1835 for provisions he forwarded to the Potawatomies, who were being moved to the Little Platte, Missouri, country.

By 1837, Rich's trading ventures extended to the South Platte River. He was granted a license on November 2, 1837, to employ eleven men to trade with the Arapahoes, Cheyennes, and Sioux at a point on the South Fork of the Platte about thirty miles from the mountains. The following year, on July 16, 1838, he received a one-year contract to supply rations to the immigrating Potawatomies in the Osage River subagency. He traded during the time that Pilcher was Superintendent of Indian Affairs. Pilcher wrote on August 14, 1839, that the contract with Rich had been one of necessity only. He felt that the government would soon be free of such contracts. "Those Liberty [Missouri] birds have feathered their nest," wrote Pilcher, "but I shall take measures to close their career."

If he closed Rich's Indian trading career, it wasn't until 1841, because on November 10, 1840, Rich received a one-year contact to hire up to twenty-three men to trade with bands of Sioux on the Upper Missouri. The following year he was appointed post trader at Fort Leavenworth, and in October was granted the appointment as postmaster. He succeeded Mr. Albert G. Wilson for both positions.

EARLY SUTLERS AT FORT LEAVENWORTH [29]

James Herron, 1829
B. G. Wallace and Major Alexander Morgan, 1830–1834
Major Alexander Morgan, 1837–1839
A. G. Wilson, 1839–1842
Hiram Rich, 1842–1862

Fort Leavenworth was established in 1827 to fill the void left by the abandonment of Fort Atkinson in 1826. The post developed rapidly and provided considerable employment opportunities. Once on the Fort Leavenworth military reservation, Hiram Rich built a home on Scott Avenue, a dignified colonial log house one and a half stories high, which became a post landmark. Here, the first governor of Kansas took his meals when Fort Leavenworth was the capital of the territory. One sign of the degree of Rich's financial security was his role on several occasions in the 1840s as "surety" for a local man who leased the Fort Leavenworth farm and had to take out a surety bond against his performance to provide a specified tonnage of vegetables to the troops.

On June 30, 1846, at age forty-seven, Hiram Rich had an adventure (probably one of many) in conjunction with his suttling responsibilities. He departed Fort Leavenworth for Santa Fe with General Stephen Watts Kearny, who commanded the Army of the West. The excursionary force consisted of the First Dragoons and fifteen hundred volunteers. As the odd chance of history would have it, among the troops was W. Clark Kennerly, the son of sutler James Kennerly (of Fort Atkinson, 1823–1826, and Jefferson Barracks until 1840). The command reached Santa Fe on the Fourth of July. Kearny permitted the men to buy liquor from the sutler that day to "celebrate as best they might." The profits probably helped to cover the loss of Rich's ox, which had died of heat stroke the day before.

The troops and Hiram Rich were gone for a year. The following September, newly commissioned Brigadier General Sterling Price, who was later commissioned as a general for the Confederacy during the Civil War, arrived in Fort Leavenworth after his journey from Santa Fe. Hiram Rich and a small escort were with him. Price had received notice of his promotion while en route, so the small contingent, under Price's direction, beelined it for Leavenworth. They carried only provisions and blankets, and covered better than forty miles miles a day for a week.

In 1851, while John Dougherty was packing his wagons at Fort Leavenworth with gifts for the Indians who would gather near Fort Laramie for the Great Treaty Council, Hiram Rich and his wife were entertaining David Mitchell, head of the St. Louis Indian Superintendency, and Thomas Fitzpatrick, the ex-fur trapper, guide, and interpreter who had conceived, planned, and obtained financing from Congress for the council. The following year, Rich was elected commissioner from Fort Leavenworth to join the delegation to Congress to urge the establishment of a regular territorial government. He was also elected secretary of the commission to receive and report the state of the polls at each of the precincts.

Rich maintained his position as the Fort Leavenworth post sutler for twenty years. Large numbers of troops gathered at the post before they shipped out to the West or the Southwest; extra men gathered there and departed on Stephen Watts Kearny's explorations; and a good number of emigrant settler trains originated at, or passed through, Leavenworth on their way west.

Even without emigrant traffic and transient troops, Fort Leavenworth maintained an average of four companies of troops, so Rich was able to count on an adequate and constant business. One soldier stationed at Fort Leavenworth wrote home in 1856 about living conditions at Fort Leavenworth. He said the men were paid every second month, that is, when the paymaster was in the vicinity. When that was not the case, they went without any pay for four to six months. When payday arrived, no one touched their rations. They all lived on "dainties" until their money was spent. "As regards myself," said the soldier, "I must confess I have not saved a cent, though I have never been short of money to buy civilian clothes, cigars, tobacco, etc."[30]

Although the trade with the Fort Leavenworth garrison and with its transient troops, emigrants, and local Indians may have kept Hiram Rich busy for twenty years, a few other sutlers discovered that the real money was in land speculation.

Sutlers Franklin Steele and John Dougherty weren't the first to apply profits from their suttling activities to land speculation and with bonanza results. Colonel John Nicks of Fort Smith (the same Nicks who, then a general, resided at Fort Gibson) and his partner, John Rogers, also found a winning combination when they blended land speculation and politics.

Fort Smith, Arkansas, was abandoned in 1824. John Nicks and John Rogers remained there, allegedly because Colonel Arbuckle had placed them in charge of the Belle Point works for the government flatboat that was used as a ferry. Then, Nicks went off to Fort Gibson as sutler. In his absence, John Rogers worked to get Congress to expand the garrison at Fort Smith to six companies. Rogers aligned himself with local politicians and obtained the names of five hundred petitioners. His persistent efforts bore fruit four years later. With the assistance of Arkansas politicians and Congress, the issue of maintaining or abandoning Fort Smith was linked to the 1836 question of frontier defense and the best way to create a network of forts linked by roads.

Rogers had 640 acres adjacent to the post on which he had hung a price tag of thirty thousand dollars. He advertised plans to convert 160 acres of his land into town lots, and said he would be willing to submit to an impartial appraiser if the government wanted to buy his land but thought his price was too high. Rogers appeared in Washington at the right time and received fifteen thousand dollars for 296 acres. Not entirely satisfied with this take, he sold two hundred tons of hay to the army at twelve dollars per ton, and when the town of Fort Smith began to assume shape next to the military post in 1838, Rogers platted it.[31]

Another alert opportunist was John Blair Todd, a one-time sutler and member of a loose 1857 coalition of traders that included capitalist Robert Campbell of St. Louis and Daniel M. Frost. Frost and Todd were both former army officers. They became partners in the fur trade, forming Frost and Todd, Inc., to compete with the American Fur Company. Todd, who was a cousin of Mary Todd Lincoln, used his connections in Washington, D.C., to succeed to the sutlership at Fort Randall. Frost already knew how to suttle; he had served as sutler at Fort Pierre under General Harney.[32] In addition to their Indian trade and the sutlership, they owned the largest wholesale warehouse in Sioux City. Todd believed their best opportunity for profits rested in land development. In December 1858, he accompanied several Yanktonnais Indian chiefs to Washington, D.C., where he helped them sell 115 million acres to the government. Todd immediately made claim to several excellent town sites in the name of a Todd and Frost venture called the Upper Missouri Land Company. This commpany established the town of Yankton, South Dakota.[33]

Highly successful pre–Civil War sutlers like Steele, Dougherty, Rich, and Nicks were not average men. They were ardent entrepreneurs who stood out from the forty to fifty other sutlers of their day. They played economic hardball. Not content to follow old patterns, they established their base of operations at frontier posts, then struck out on their own to find ways to improve their lot. And as they achieved their objectives, they directly and indirectly developed the country. As the country, like a blank parchment, was unrolled farther and farther west, this brand of successful sutler continued to make his mark and establish patterns that would be improved upon by other sutlers yet to appear.

Sixteenth-century sutlers dealt primarily in food and alcoholic beverages.
Engraving by Jan Visscher, from a painting by Philip Wouwerman (1619–68).

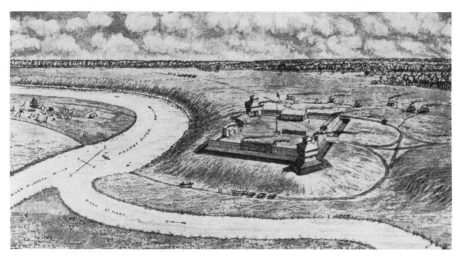

Fort Wayne, Northwest Territory, 1790s.

Upper left: David Meriwether, kin to
Meriwether Lewis of the Lewis and Clark expedition and sutler for John O'Fallon; first governor of New Mexico Territory, 1853–56.
Museum of New Mexico.

Upper right: Franklin Steele, sutler at Fort
Snelling, 1838–58. Minnesota Historical
Society.

Right: John O'Fallon. *History of St. Louis City
and County.*

A sutler's store at Harper's Ferry. Frank Leslie's *Illustrated Paper*, 1862.

"Bivouac Fire on the Potomac." *Harper's Weekly*, 1861.

CAMP PUNISHMENTS—TOO FOND OF WHISKY.—SCENE IN THE ARMY OF THE MISSISSIPPI.—[See Page 411.]

Above: "Too Fond of Whiskey."
Harper's Weekly, 1862.

Right: "Moseby's Guerrillas
Destroying a Sutler's Train."
Harper's Weekly, 1863.

Sutler's tent and customers, 1864. Library of Congress

Sutler's Row, Chattanooga, Tennessee, 1864. Library of Congress.

Payday in the Army of the Potomac, 1863: "A Descent on the Sutler." *Harper's Weekly.*

$ 2⁰⁰   Camp 2d Reg't U.S.S. Dec 24 1864.

To the Paymaster of the 2d Reg't U. S. Sharpshooters:

FOR VALUE RECEIVED, PLEASE PAY TO

ANDREW J. SWEETSER, Sutler, or Order,

The sum of *Two* _____ *Dollars* _____ *Cents,*

and deduct the same from my monthly pay at the next pay day.

Noyes Davis Co. K

Approved by _____

No. 533   R. Polkinhorn, printer, D st, bet. 6th and 7th str.

Camp 4th R. I. Vol April 26 1864

TO THE PAYMASTER U. S. VOLUNTEERS:

For Value received, please pay HENRY BUCKINGHAM, *Sutler of the 4th Reg. R. I. Vols., the sum of* _Two_ /2/ _____ *Dollars,*

and deduct the same from my next pay, and oblige

Witness, J. M. Moody   William Mathews Co. H

Civil War pay vouchers. Jade House Publications.

Upper left: John Collins produced prime saddles, served for twelve years as a sutler, and authored two books. Wyoming State Archives.

Upper right: Seth Ward, Indian trader turned sutler, was called pompous by one emigrant because he wore a diamond in his vest. Wyoming State Archives.

Left: John William Hugus watched the post–Civil War western migration from his post trader's store at Fort Kearny. Wyoming State Archives.

Fort Reno, Dakota Territory, 1867. A. C. Leighton's store is at far left, outside the fortifications. Drawing by Anton Schonborn. National Archives.

Fort Bridger, 1889. Wyoming State Archives.

Above: William Carter's home, Fort Bridger. Wyoming State Archives.

Left: William A. Carter, sutler at Fort Bridger, 1857–82, was called a capitalist and local genius. Wyoming State Archives.

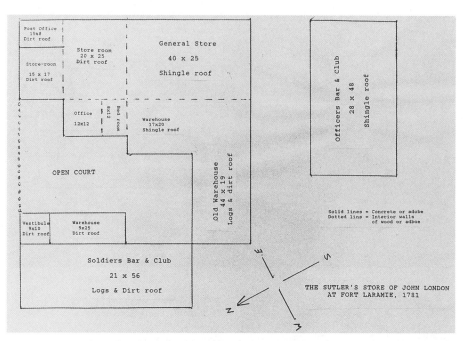

Post Office
15x8
Dirt roof

Store-room
15 x 17
Dirt roof

Store room
20 x 25
Dirt roof

General Store

40 x 25

Shingle roof

Office
12x12

Bed room
8x12

Warehouse
17x20
Shingle roof

OPEN COURT

Old Warehouse
44 x 19
Logs & dirt roof

Officers Bar & Club
28 x 48
Shingle roof

Vestibule
9x10
Dirt roof

Warehouse
9x25
Dirt roof

Soldiers Bar & Club

21 x 56

Logs & Dirt roof

Solid lines = Concrete or adobe
Dotted lines = Interior walls
of wood or adboe

THE SUTLER'S STORE OF JOHN LONDON
AT FORT LARAMIE, 1781

Floor plans for post trader John London's improvements, Fort Laramie store.
London Family Papers, University of North Carolina.

The home of John Collins and, later, John London, Fort Laramie. Mrs. Ray M.
Littler Collection, American Heritage Center, University of Wyoming.

Sutler W. H. Quinette, Fort Sill, Oklahoma, was a member of the officer's society on post. Fort Sill Museum, Fort Sill, Oklahoma.

James Kerr Moore, epitome of the successful gentleman post trader. Wyoming State Archives.

J. K. Moore leased the operation of his Fort Washakie hotel to a number of businessmen. Photograph ca. 1883. Wyoming State Archives.

Inside the sutler's store at Fort Laramie. Mrs. Ray M. Littler Collection, American Heritage Center, University of Wyoming.

Moses Waters's three-story building at Fort Riley, 1888. DeGolyer Library, Southern Methodist University.

PART III

THE CIVIL WAR SUTLER

1861–1866

EIGHT

The Civil War Sutler at Large

Mr. Sutler . . . will sell you . . . the latest novel for twice the sale price . . . or . . . a half-dozen rolls of cough candy, or quinine by the dose, or a pair of spurs, or a shirt, or perfumed notepaper. . . . In the way of cutlery, pocket knives and cork-screws he is sure to have, scissors usually, and surgical instruments occasionally. Great is the sutler. Like Shakespeare, he is "a many-sided man." Like Sam Slick's wife, one cannot live without him nor scarcely with him. —Charles Page, Letters of a War Correspondent

The story of the Civil War sutler is a tale of greed that was fed by opportunity and recorded by the deeds of those sutlers who served the U.S. Volunteers. These short-time sutlers bore little resemblance to the Regular Army sutler. They were camp followers who hoped to be in and out of a nasty fracas with an easy bundle of green before the odds changed against them. They quickly developed a ruinous reputation as scoundrels and callous profiteers who skirted battles and regulations with their wagons, and who pulled back their tent flaps with one eye on profits and the other on the Provost Marshal.

It's presumptuous to assume that *every* man who applied for—or who was invited to hold—the position of sutler with the volunteers harbored the hope of swindling his fellow man out of a dollar. There were harmless, honest, and hard-working peddlers who obeyed regulations and tried to provide good service, but the combination of significant profit potential and risks of wartime drew a rougher, more self-centered lot. In short, it was an ideal opportunity for a hustler. The annals of the Thirty-ninth Regiment of the Illinois Veteran Volunteer Infantry speaks to the two great passions of the regiment's nameless and foreign peddler. In anecdotal style, the author let it be known that their sutler was consumed first with a love for the taste of schnapps, which almost ruined him more than once because he went on sprees that generally lasted from seven to ten days. His second passion was to barter, in which his desire for gain often led him to be unscrupulous. ("It was only the monish, as he expressed it, that he wanted.") [1]

To help explain the financial expectations of the Civil War sutler, it is helpful to examine the role played by state-controlled forerunners of Civil War volunteers in earlier conflicts. After the War of 1812, state militia units were not called out en masse again until the Civil War, but a number of smaller, briefer frontier engagements involved state militia. Sutlers accompanied these militia, in particular during an unpleasant affair called the Blackhawk War.

The Blackhawk War was an unfortunate, but short-lived result of friction between a Sauk chief hostile to the United States and white frontier settlers who, in the main, displayed a disparaging if not antagonistic attitude toward Indians in general. Brevet Brigadier General Henry Atkinson, commander of the Regular Army's Right Wing of the Western Department, was called upon to direct a major part of the campaign. The force that assisted him that June of 1832 consisted of more than three thousand United States Volunteers—most of whom were Illinois militia.[2] When everyone is counted, three brigades of one thousand men each, two hundred dismounted militia, a mounted battalion of three hundred, and four hundred Regular Army troops rallied against one thousand Indian men, women, and children.[3]

The Blackhawk War lasted less than a few weeks, but the three thousand men mustered in during the latter half of June weren't mustered out until between mid-August and early September. The role that the sutler assumed during this limited affair is revealed in the amount of sutler debt that officers allowed their men. By examining the extent to which the sutler insinuated himself into the state volunteer organization, one can extrapolate forward to the next war dominated by volunteer organizations—the Civil War—and more easily understand the magnitude of what occurred there.

The muster rolls of the Illinois volunteer companies contained pay records, and the amount of sutler debt incurred by each officer and enlisted man was recorded in column ten, "Amount Due Sutler" (also spelled "settler" and "suttler"). An examination of the records of 1,318 men in twenty-four companies from the First and Third armies and two from the Second (an interim army) provided the following picture.

The pay records of twenty-four companies showed that 49 percent of the men who saw service were in debt to the sutler when they mustered out. Of 1,138 volunteers, 649 owed their company sutler a total of $7,493.06, an average of $11.54 per man.[4] The pay for a private was $6.66 for a thirty-day month, so the average indebtedness equals two months' pay for a private. The average service for companies called up in June 1832, however, lasted only six weeks.

Close analysis shows that two-thirds of all the men in debt owed an average of only $5.45—less than one month's pay for a private. (The privates of Captain Willcockson's Odd Company received an average of $1.00 a day for twelve days of service because of allotments.)[5] On the other end of the scale, several dozen privates owed more than $40.00 apiece, and the top 10 percent of all those in debt (sixty-five men) owed an average of $36.50.

The highest individual debt, $90.57, belonged to Captain James Craig, whose company mustered out September 14, 1832. (A captain made $45.00 per month.) Even his first lieutenant owed $46.25. The total indebtedness for twelve of the men in his company was $331.22, so the average per man was $27.60.[6] Fifty-four men in James Corder's company, the Second Regiment of the First Brigade, chalked up a total of $935.61, for an individual average indebtedness of $17.33.[7]

Based on the above figures, a sutler serving with a volunteer regiment in the future might expect that more than half of the men (perhaps three-fourths) of any company would make a purchase from him, and that most of those purchases (half the company) would buy on credit. His average customer, based on those credit records, would spend an average of $3.85 per month, nearly 60 percent of his pay. In the Blackhawk War, therefore, a sutler may have grossed a little more than one hundred dollars per month from an average company of 55 men (a company ranged in size from 28 to 118 officers and men), and if the above averages held true for all 3,500 troopers engaged for the ninety-day period of the war, the total sutler bill would have exceeded eighteen thousand dollars.

Spread over several dozen sutlers, the sum might not appear too excessive, but there were only five sutlers mentioned by name. The most prominent, William P. Tilton (also spelled Tillton), was appointed by General Atkinson and approved by the Secretary of State. He was the only sutler mentioned with the First and Third armies and may have come upriver from St. Louis with Atkinson's troops. Indirect reference was made to James Kennerly's support of the troops, but his name was not listed among the militia. (His suttling may have been limited to soldiers pulled from Fort Bellefontaine.) Another sutler mentioned prominently in payroll records was Daniel Wann. His name appeared in connection with three companies of the Independent battalions, and was once referred to as "Wann & Lytle." The fourth and fifth sutlers were O. Newberry (the sutler from Fort Winnebago) and P. Kingston, whose name appeared with two companies of the Second Army.

The rolls indicate that Mr. Tilton had the Third Army to himself; if so, he must have hired assistants. On the assumption that he served a majority of the seventy companies of the three brigades of the Third Army—as many as thirty-five hundred militia—for sixty days, his gross billing may have reached seventeen thousand dollars. During this time he lost less than two hundred dollars to men who deserted, a "shrinkage" of 1 percent. All in all, it was a very profitable war for Mr. Tilton.

Thirty years later, when cannons sounded the opening of the Civil War, sutlers were given another great opportunity to support volunteers—and to make good money. The strength of the United States Regular Army in 1861 was 26,000, so President Lincoln signed an enactment on June 22 to raise 500,000 volunteers to meet the Confederate threat. To promote rapid recruitment, the Union Army granted commissions to civilians who often possessed little military experience and who had no intention of remaining in the service after the war. Individuals who were selected for positions of leadership, including regimental colonels, were often locally prominent politicians capable of raising the necessary quota for a new brigade or regiment.

The militia regimental commander chose his own sutler, or had a group of his fellow officers select him. What could be more natural than for a patriotic leader or his supporters to pick a trusted neighbor, relative, or business associate? And if an officer formed a tacit partnership with his regimental sutler to share in the not-to-be-sneezed-at profits, at least the men were being provided for.

This simple bargain for mutual gain, formed in certain instances between the sutler and officer, paved the way for the biggest complaint against the Civil War sutler—unwarranted prices and unmerited profits. In the U.S. Sanitary Commission's December 1861 report to Secretary of War Edwin Stanton, high prices were mentioned as one of the sutler "evils" the commission believed had to be corrected to improve conditions in the camps. The prices of articles, it reported, were fixed by a Council of Administration in only about half of all the regiments. A dozen regimental staff officers heard of such a council for the first time only when a representative of the commission asked if there was such an institution in their regiments.[8]

The absence of a Council of Administration and other adequate controls created fertile conditions for corruption within those regiments and encouraged undesirable sutler practices. (Army regulations of 1821 did not apply to the sutler who was assigned to volunteer units.) In addition to the absence of adequate checks and controls on the sutler and his wares, whiskey was sold to whoever paid the highest price. Many men suffered and many men complained, but as long as military discipline was lax and the money rolled in, the sutler continued to conduct business as usual.

Had the number of volunteer army sutlers been manageable, their control would have been more easily accomplished, but 500,000 volunteers was equivalent to 573 regiments (using an average strength of 872 men), and the army authorized one sutler per regiment. Before the war was over, the Union armies enrolled nearly 2,000 separate regiments. A sutler might also be assigned to prisons and hospitals. Therefore, at any point in time during the war, the sutlers, with their clerks and assistants, numbered several thousand.[9]

Of 200 regiments inspected by the U.S. Sanitary Commission in 1861, 182 (91 percent) had a sutler. Of those, 103 (57 percent) were appointed by a colonel of the regiment. The Secretary of War appointed 63 others (32 percent). The majority of all sutlers were either political appointments or rubber-stamp approvals of recommendations made by regimental officers.[10]

From a sutler's point of view, the Civil War turned out to be simply a much larger version of the Blackhawk War. In terms of soldier mandays, the Civil War was sixteen thousand times larger than the Blackhawk War.[11] If gross revenues of the Blackhawk War were as high as eighteen thousand dollars, the estimated gross revenues taken in by Civil War sutlers—using a straight, unadjusted projection—would approach twenty-nine million dollars. According to estimates voiced by concerned politicians (see chapter 9), sutler gross earnings exceeded ten million dollars per year. Even allowing for poor data and political exaggeration, the correlation between the two conflicts was surprisingly good. The North finally won the war, at great cost, but it would appear that the sutlers made off with the prize money.

The Civil War sutler operated in the shadow of the volunteer army. When soldiers were on the march, he remained close behind, dealing from his wagons like the earlier New England peddlers who had disbursed their wares from mobile stores. When the men were bivouacked or encamped, he put up a store and advertised his private enterprise.[12]

His temporary site was a canvas tent, but when he knew he wouldn't have to move he constructed log sides for his canvas superstructure. Large hospital tents were often used because they were roomy enough for stools, tables, and a stove. At headquarters locations, supply depots, and winter camps, the sutler worked from a wooden hut or shanty that was sturdy enough to endure. After the war was over, government, commissary, and quartermaster buildings full of army supplies lined the streets of Chattanooga, and sutler's stores—little low wooden shanties—were everywhere.[13]

The most common sutler establishment seen in Civil War photographs was the canvas tent, open at the front with a wide board shelf that served both as a counter for serving customers and a showcase for goods. The sides of the tent came well down and were securely fastened. For added security, the sutler slept inside, in the midst of his stock.[14] As both a dry-goods dealer and grocer, he carried hundreds of items: fruit, flour, and sweets; checkers and playing cards; pencils, ink, paper, and stationery; hair restorer ("Grecian Compound" from Warner & Co., of Brooklyn); shoes, boots, lamps, and camping equipment; watches and locks; handkerchiefs and hundreds of drugs from Squibb, and from Charles Pfizer & Co.[15]

After having received his appointment, the sutler would visit a wholesaler or two to acquire the stock of merchandise he thought the men would need. His chief line of goods was perishable food—a collection of basic foodstuffs that ran the gamut from soda crackers, oranges, lemons, apples, raisins, candy, and cakes to loaf sugar, mackerel, salt fish, bacon, and ginger ale and other soft drinks.[16] One could buy sugar, molasses, or flour from the sutler as well as through the commissary.[17] The canning of meats, fruits, and vegetables was in its infancy at the time. Prices of these goods were so high that only officers could afford them, but the sutler found it profitable nonetheless to carry them.[18]

Veteran John Billings remembered sutlers carrying army regulation hats, cavalry boots, flannels, socks, and suspenders.[19] Another soldier recalled that when the boys wished to look good for review, they "blacked up their boots, scoured their brasses and to top the whole, put on a paper collar with white gloves procured by the sutler for the occasion."[20] Union officer Robert McAllister wrote his wife that he'd purchased an armor vest from his sutler. He doubted that he would use it. "It's too heavy," he wrote, "too warm and too inconvenient in the hot summer."[21]

The sutler business kept hundreds of manufacturers in business. Smoking supplies alone included cigars, snuff, pipes, tobacco cans and pouches, cigars, smoking and chewing tobacco, and matches. More than a dozen firms, including Campbell, Crane & Co. in Newark, New Jersey, Daniel Carruth from Boston, John Cotton, Ltd., in Edinburgh, Scotland, and Rigwood Smoking Tobacco in New York, supplied the sutlers' needs.[22] Advertisements for supplies were posted in daily newspapers such as the New York *Herald*, and in popular periodicals like Frank Leslie's *Illustrated Newspaper*.

The Union Army sutler was the envy of the Confederate soldier. One Confederate veteran remarked in his memoirs that the sutler's wagon, loaded with luxuries common in the Federal Army, was unknown in the Army of Northern Virginia. The nearest approach to the sutler's wagon, he said, was the "cider cart" of some old darky, or a basket of pies and cakes to split on the roadside for sale. That wasn't completely true, but in the South's collective memory, "plenty" characterized the North, "dearth" characterized the South. "Imagine the feelings of men half-famished," wrote one Confederate soldier,

> when they rush into a camp on one side while the enemy flees from the other and find the coffee on the fire, the sugar ready to be dropped in to the coffee, bread in the oven, crackers by the box, fine beef ready cooked, desiccated vegetables by the bushel, canned peaches, lobsters, tomatoes, milk, barrels of ground and toasted coffee, soda, salt and in short, everything a hungry soldier craves. Then add the liquors, wines, cigars, and tobacco found in the tents of the officers and the wagons of the sutlers, and remembering the condi-

tion of the victorious party, hungry, thirsty and worried, say if it did not require wonderful devotion to duty and great self-denial to push on.[23]

Another Confederate soldier, who stumbled upon an evacuated Union camp after his unit's victory at Seven Pines, wrote his folks about his luck: "Here were sutlers' tents filled with luxuries, oranges, lemons, oysters, pineapples, sardines, in fact almost everything that I could think of." He ate as much as he could, then filled his haversack with stationery, paper, envelopes, ink, and pens; puff-bosomed linen shirts, white gloves, and nuts, candies, and cheeses.[24]

The volume and diversity of the wares carried by the Union Army sutler indicated that he had little difficulty turning over his stock. One soldier recalled that the two sutler tents in his division always had their doors blocked by an "eager clamorous throng . . . checks in hand and held aloft eager to buy the inferior articles sold at prices so far above their value."[25] The Union soldier was not starving or threadbare: the ration furnished by the army was considered by most to be ample; so was the clothing. And the more thrifty soldiers sent money home via express companies. Some soldiers said that only a minority "squandered their last farthing" at the sutler's tent; others said that far more than a few "blew-in" all they had on the sutler after being paid.[26]

The sutler took nothing for granted. As part of his marketing, he kept a few luxury items of special taste on hand. In the fall of 1864 at City Point and Bermuda Hundred, a New York *Herald* correspondent noticed that the foods offered by the sutler included figs, jellies, and wines. He even had books, including *Harper's* and the *Atlantic Monthly*. The reporter also noted that sutlers timed their arrival in camp with the paymaster. This strategy, he concluded, tended to minimize the need to grant credit and "reduced the number of days when items would be physically available to men who saw nothing wrong with raids on sutlers."[27]

In general practice, every sutler was forced to sell up to half his merchandise on credit because funds were scarce. When a soldier requested credit, the sutler would have him sign a paymaster's order, then give him tokens that served as money. The paymaster's order was a check, made out to the sutler. It authorized the paymaster to pay the sutler the value of the voucher, usually just a few dollars. The usual order looked like this:

Camp _____day/month/186__

TO THE PAYMASTER OF THE U.S. VOLUNTEERS
    For value received, please pay to JOHN DOE, Sutler of the
____Regt. R. F. Vols., the sum of _____ dollars,
and deduct the same from my next pay, and oblige

Witness. *Soldier's friend*   *Private Soldier*   Co. K

In order for the sutler to collect outstanding debts, the credit information had to be recorded on the military payroll records. The payroll register was the basis of all claims adjudication. If the claim could not be verified, the sutler was denied payment. The sutler's concern to see that vouchers were properly recorded is understandable when it is known that in the early days of the war, the debt owed to the sutler was often the majority of what a soldier had been due.[28]

The use of sutler tokens simplified the process of extending credit. It was much easier for the sutler to issue tokens than to record each sale and each credit purchase. It also bypassed the acute shortage of metal coins. And since sutler coins were stamped with the name of the issuing sutler and the regiment he served, they were not interchangeable and thus prevented the holder from buying elsewhere.

The practice of using pay vouchers had a long history. During the War of 1812, the commanding officer at Fort Dearborn (Chicago), Captain Heald, told his troops that John Kinzie and (his brother-in-law) Forsyth were considered "the proper suttlers for the garrison," and would be as long as they furnished what was needed at reasonable prices. To seal the bargain, he said that no certificates of pay would be given to any other trader.

Metal tokens were first used in America by old Indian traders. Tokens and various forms of paper scrip were known on the eastern seaboard in colonial times. In 1820, a brass beaver token was issued to trappers in the employ of the Northwest Company, and the Hudson's Bay Company issued tokens to Indians in four denominations. Tokens in sutlers' stores appeared after 1851 with the establishment of Forts Union, Fillmore, Conrad, Defiance, Sumner, Garland, and Wingate.[29]

Civil War sutler tokens were made of brass, copper, or zinc; a few were made from hard rubber. They were normally available in denominations of five, fifteen, twenty-five, or fifty cents, and one dollar. The majority of these tokens were made in Chicago, Philadelphia, and Baltimore. In Maryland, F. X. Kochler sold tokens for about ten dollars per thousand.[30]

The soldiers resented the coins, in part because the sutler clerks used an old sales technique and said they were out of change. They wanted either to sell a dollar's worth of goods or give the customer sutler tokens or a sutler's ticket—cardboard scrip. Since tokens and scrip were good only at the issuing sutler's tent, the men used them as poker chips or in more frivolous ways. Near Fredericksburg, Virginia, in June 1862, John Faller wrote his folks that in the evening they had fun with the contrabands—blacks who had run away. "We get several to pat for the others while they dance. It's the most amusing thing since I came to Virginia. Since funds are scarce with us, we give them sutler tickets for dancing."[31]

A restriction on how much a soldier could purchsae on credit did not appear to thwart the soldier intent on filling his "limited but imperative" needs. One enlisted man, after having remarked that the sutlers were asking cash, added matter-of-factly that almost all of the men used tobacco, "and it takes a supply of money to stay with it."[32] Private Wilbur Fisk recalled that while the money lasted, the boys helped themselves to the sutler's butter at thirty cents per pound, "for getting trusted at the sutlers is pretty well played out."[33]

The sutler was reluctant to adjust his ways to abide by rules if they affected his trade. To find ways around restricting regulations, he pleaded ignorant and paid outright bribes. He looked for ways to extend the number of hours his tent could remain open and ways to use government transportation, and he curried favor by giving gifts to those in charge. Prior to and not long after an 1862 bill defined what he would be permitted to sell (see chapter 9), the sutler traded anything that brought a profit—Epsom salts, pretzels, Mexican spurs, gingerbread (reported to be composed chiefly of "sawdust, coal slack, tar, syrup, and chopped feed"), pistol cartridges, watch keys, pills, and joke books.[34] Of course, he always sold liquor.

Alcohol in every form remained a sutler best-seller. Profits from liquor alone might not sustain him, but he could not afford to ignore the ready market, especially since the soldier always consumed more than his share.[35] Supplies of beer, lager beer, wines, and liquors could easily be had from wholesale dealers located in New Jersey and Washington, D.C. Bininger & Co. alone, out of the nation's capital, carried "1849 Reserve" bourbon, "Zouave cognac," "Old Tom," "Regulation," "Night Cap," and "Peep-O-Day."[36] The troops had pet names for each of their favorite liquids. "Oh be joyful!" for example, lived up to its title until Major Hartshown saw fit to order its purveyors away from his regiment's camp.[37]

At 31 (15 percent) of the regiments visited by the representatives of the Sanitary Commission, the sutler was allowed to sell liquor; at 169 (85 percent), it was prohibited. However, in 177 (88 percent) regiments, it appeared that the men could acquire what they needed from sutlers "with a regular amount of freedom." Only in 23 regiments (11 percent) did the inspectors feel this was not true, which implies that of the 169 only 15 percent (23) enforced liquor regulations with any stringency.[38] On January 13, 1863, a sutler's clerk named Loomis was convicted of selling whiskey to the men of the 129th Illinois Infantry and expelled from camp. Several weeks later, after he formally apologized, Colonel Smith revoked the expulsion order and permitted him to return and remain in camp.[39]

Officers may have consumed more alcohol per person than enlisted men. Most sutlers had passes to carry liquor in their wagons for officers. By catering to the appetites of officers, the sutlers often acquired protection from the Provost Marshal. Protection was necessary because many smuggled whiskey into camp in barrels that they declared contained beer or cider, alcoholic beverages which were permitted.[40] Mr. Baker, in charge of the Provost Marshal's Detective Force, said that any endeavor to interfere with the itinerant saloon or bar of the sutler could "awaken the hostility of every drinking officer in the army." When Baker had attempted to suppress the traffic by seizing liquors not conveyed in accordance with orders, he was accused by general officers (including Brigadier Generals Moot and Revere) of seizing their private property. Brigadier General Patrick, Provost Marshal for the Army of the Potomac, had two of Baker's men arrested and attacked Baker's character.[41]

Nonetheless, Patrick issued a circular that forbade sutlers and traders to pass within the line of the army any liquor, wines, or intoxicating drinks—except as ordered by an officer for his personal use.[42] The order was a signal to the sutlers to be creative, so they dropped peaches into a bottle of whiskey and peddled the concoction as pickled peaches; and they shaped and painted tin cans to look like hymn books, filled them with whiskey, and sold them to pious soldiers under the label of "the bosom companion."[43]

Depending on what testimony is considered to be typical, the sutler who sold whiskey was a nefarious purveyor of debauchery or simply one of a number of enterprising merchants who strived to feed the desires of a ready-made market extant within an undisciplined and inherently weak system. "I have seen [a soldier] barter to the sutler a whole month's pay for a pint of whiskey," wrote a member of the Sanitary Commission. "I have seen him sell his last shirt to a comrade to obtain money with which to buy a single glass."[44] On the other hand, the commission reported that the volunteers were more temperate than the men in European armies, and that intoxication was acknowledged to be common only in six regiments.[45]

The sutler was certainly not the only supplier of alcoholic beverages; on the contrary, his competition was fierce. One lady peddler selling "sausages" did a land-office business when the troops discovered the skins were filled with bourbon. Trooper Augustus Meyers wasn't alone when he said he thought women sold more whiskey than the men; indeed, as previously noted, women have peddled whiskey and other commodities since the days of Frederick the Great's Prussian Army.[46] At the ferry where the Chesapeake and Ohio canal crossed the Potomac, a guard was posted to check passes and to prevent smuggling. He thought women did more whiskey smuggling than men. They had passes to visit sweethearts and relatives in the camp and always became indignant when he asked about liquor. One large woman with a fine broad smile made a tinkling sound with every movement she made. The soldier noticed she wore unusually large hoop skirts and asked her if she carried any liquor. Naturally, he was met with an emphatic denial. When he placed his hand on her waist and gave the skirt a shake, it caused an audible jingle of bottles. "What's that, Mama?" he asked. "Whisth! Sergeant, dear, shure it's sody-wather for the boys!" she said, laughing.

As to the sutlers, reminisced this sergeant, "we got to know many of the[m] on sight. Their wagons bore the regimental designation to which they belonged and as we knew they had passes, we did not always halt them. Occasionally some of them tossed a package to the guards containing cigars, tobacco, crackers and cheese or a can of preserved fruit."[47]

In the minds of some soldiers, when a pass could be obtained, a few hours at a Washington bar was better than "sneaking a few hookers of tanglefoot smuggled into quarters from some rule-breaking sutler."[48] Nonetheless, the majority of the liquor in the volunteer army was obtained from the sutlers. When all other means failed, the contraband was conveyed in their pies.[49]

The sutler "pie" was unanimously voted to be far more troublesome than whiskey. They were generally as large as a common saucer and a "little too thick to read fine print through." One soldier described it as "moist and indigestible below, tough and indestructible above, with untold horrors within."[50] Camp surgeons viewed this handmade comestible with alarm because it often produced camp diarrhea and dysentery, "with all their concomitant evils." It was as though the item had been "fried in condemned lard a week before."[51] The Sanitary Commission reports said the doctors' fears were justified. Men died of chronic diarrhea during the Civil War. A medical report that listed the causes of 27,500 cases of illnesses attributed 7,000 cases (26 percent) to a single contributor—diarrhea.[52] As one narrator of the war said, "easy-goers spent their money quickly and often ate things that made them sick," but in every regiment more than one death was attributable to articles that came from the sutler's tent.[53]

The majority of comestibles found in a sutler's camp tent, including pies, could be found in prisoner-of-war camps. Prison sutlers carried a lot of food because prisoner rations were meager. The diary of a Confederate prisoner, Captain Robert E. Park of the Twelfth Alabama Regiment, mentioned breads, apples, pies, cakes, onions, as well as tobacco, matches, oil for cooking, lamps, and stationery. Park said the quality of the goods offered by his prison sutler was uniformly poor.

The problem for the soldier was that it might take five dollars for a fellow to get a pretty good dinner.[54] (Complainers thought five dollars would hardly whet the appetite of a wealthy man.)[55] Soldiers complained most frequently about the prices of the items they loved best— butter, canned fruits, cheese, and tobacco.[56] The higher the prices, the worse the complaints. The butter, they said, was always expensive and was guaranteed to be rancid, and the navy tobacco was "of the blackest sort."[57]

Captain Park wrote that his sutler peddled everything at prices ranging from "between five hundred to one thousand percent profit." His prices were "very candidly and freely complained of and objected to by the needy customer, but while they grumble[d], stern necessity force[d] them to buy."[58] He suggested that his own regimental sutler, "Jolly Sam Brewer, the clever 12th Alabama sutler," would have rejoiced at one-twelfth of Emory's profits; and he would have done well to stop and look at the prices he wrote in his diary before making that suggestion. His "Jolly" Sam Brewer asked and received one dollar per pound for salt; two dollars per pound for common-size apples; five dollars per pound for soda; one dollar per quart for ground peas (goobers); three dollars per pound for lard; six dollars per quart for syrup (made of Chinese sugar cane); one dollar for three porous ginger cakes; one dollar per dozen for smaller, tougher sugar cakes; and a dollar per pound for Confederate coffee made of rye.

Depreciation of the Confederate dollar made bad prices worse. After noting that tobacco cost one dollar per pound, Captain Park wrote that "depreciation in our currency is trying for men who only get eleven dollars per month. One dollar formerly bought more than even eleven does now."[59] And when shortages developed, it was usual for prices to climb after the fashion of supply and demand. When paper supplies were scarce in the South after 1861, inflation and lack of supplies drove prices to a point almost outside a soldier's reach. Sutlers charged five dollars for a quire of paper (twenty-five sheets) and three dollars for a bunch of envelopes. In 1864, a soldier wrote home that ink was nearly impossible to get, but a sutler had some small bottles, each of which held about three thimblefuls. The price per bottle was three dollars.[60]

To the Confederate prisoner Park, his sutler (Emory) and his clerk were "vulgar, impertinent grasping Yankees and ill-bred men." He suggested that his opinion was that of every Confederate prisoner in the camp. Had the Union and Confederate soldiers viewed their sutler's offerings as luxuries instead of necessary supplements, most of the consternation about quality and price would have evaporated. But the peddler's wares provided a change from army rations. The human need for variety drove almost every soldier to the sutler's tent, and over time, those little luxuries became necessities regardless of the price.

A wealthier, more sympathetic minority thought they better understood the sutler and his situation. The sutler was not the conniving, profit-driven miscreant he appeared to be. "When one carefully considers the expense of transporting his goods to the army, the wastage of the same from exposure to the weather, the cost of frequent

Prices of Civil War Sutler Foodstuffs [61]

Butter–60¢ to $1 per pound	Sweet potatoes–15¢ per pound
Cheese–50¢ to 75c per pound	Onions–15¢ per pound
Sutler pies–25¢	Apples–5¢ each
Condensed milk–75¢ per can	Sweet crackers–25¢ per cup
Navy tobacco–$1.00 to $1.25 per plug	Pint of oysters–50¢
	Little bottle of brandied cherries–75¢
Molasses cookies–25¢ for six	Jar of preserved peaches–$1.25
Canned fruit–$1.00 to $1.25 per can	Sausage–50¢ each

removals, and the risk he carried of losing his stock of goods in case of a disaster to the army," wrote one officer, "I do not believe that the sutlers as a class can be justly accused of overcharging."[62]

To the list of a sutler's problems, this well-meaning witness added "the constant increase in the cost of the necessaries of life," but he forgot to include wartime inflation and the occasional reverse in the pattern of supply and demand. For example, before the fall of Atlanta, sutlers had been hawking a plug of tobacco for one dollar and getting fifteen cents for each cigar. When the secessionists abandoned Atlanta, they left behind tremendous quantities of tobacco, so the day after, a plug of tobacco sold for five cents and cigars for twenty-five cents per hundred.[63]

The above information came from an author of Civil War life who characterized the risks a sutler faced as "formidable." Bad weather, spoilage, and increasingly costly supply lines to his source of supplies, he said, were common problems of any business, but the sutler's clientele were also constantly on the move. Inhibiting regulations and his inability to use government transportation crimped his maneuverability and selling time.[64] The hazards of the sutler's wartime occupation were hardly limited to finding ways to increase spot sales and to turn his perishable inventory at a faster rate. The trader faced three other potentially crippling problems: the loss of sales made on credit, the loss of his business to the enemy, and the loss of inventory to his own troops by theft.

During (and after) the Civil War, the sutler was denied tens of thousands of dollars he claimed were due him from soldiers who had made credit purchases. When a sutler's official claim passed beyond the boundaries of the regiment, it was adjudicated by the Second Auditor's office on the basis of information recorded on the muster rolls. If the muster rolls did not contain evidence of "stoppage" (amounts due the sutler), the peddler was out of luck. When soldiers deserted, died, or were transferred, it took months for sutlers to receive their money, if they received anything at all. Sutlers failed to submit paperwork; papers were taken by the enemy; sutlers had been found guilty of selling liquor and were kicked out of the camp before they were able to collect their bills; and legitimate claims were never transferred to the muster rolls.

A number of claims were rejected because they were for liquor, and because sutlers were not supposed to be at the front on the dates they said they sold wares to the men in question. In more than one instance, the men identified by the sutler were not on the muster rolls. It even happened that military records were not updated for those soldiers who were killed, who were placed on temporary duty, and who were transferred. Assuredly, some sutler claims were bogus, but while it was rare that a bogus claim was paid, many legitimate claims were never paid, either.

G. W. Alexander & Co., attorneys for sutler T. H. Alexander, Sixth U.S. Regular Cavalry, submitted an affidavit to the army on November 2, 1865, stating that while T. H. Alexander had been stationed near Washington, D.C., he extended credit to the men of his regiment. Money was still outstanding from the accounts of men in seven companies. The circumstances under which Alexander had failed to receive his pay were not available in the record, but the details of his claim showed that 370 men of the regiment still owed him $2,103.42.

Ezra B. French of the Second Auditor's office, Washington, D.C., had a long history of dealing with sutlers and post traders from 1861 to well into the 1880s. In the above case, he wrote the Adjutant General's office and asked if the muster rolls of the Sixth U.S. Cavalry exhibited any stoppage in favor of T. H. Alexander from January 1, 1862, to June 1, 1865. The answer was no, so the entire claim was rejected.[65]

Solomon, Emmanuel, and Levi Spiegelberg, partners in Spiegelberg Brothers, a mercantile operation, hold the record for the longest successful pursuit of a Civil War sutler claim. Between the beginning of the war in 1861 and March 19, 1862, the Spiegelbergs were sutlers to the New Mexico militia. During that period, they racked up an incredible bill of particulars on the muster rolls of individual soldiers, which totaled $19,041.09. Their claim adjudication literally took an act of Congress, but it was approved—on February 24, 1905, forty-three years later.[66]

The accountant's pen may be mightier than the sword, but the sutler who lingered near the battlefield was in danger of being captured or shot. When the regiment received orders to move on short notice, he had to pack hurriedly, often throwing everything pell-mell into his wagon. One journalist remembered rebels flanking a Union unit and entering a sutler's shanty before he was awake. They allegedly inquired politely about the price of whiskey and tobacco, then informed him they would take what they liked, took all, and made him a prisoner.[67] In December 1862, near Fairfax Station, rebel guerrillas attacked a long line of sutler wagons as they were moving unguarded to the front. They stole the horses, took what they could carry, and then cut the wheel spokes.[68]

Insult was added to injury when two sutlers showed up on June 9, 1864, after payday, and drove through the lines peddling tobacco. In the process, the enemy opened fire, wounded the horse, and killed one of the sutlers. When the other turned back, the horse panicked and the buggy crashed into a ditch. Soldiers cleaned out the cache of tobacco first, then helped the occupant from his buggy. The peddler, minus partner, horse, buggy, and goods, walked back "a poor and less careless man."[69]

Far more devastation came from major military defeats than from individual encounters. Confederate soldiers wrote about driving back Union soldiers at Walnut Grove, near Richmond, in the first year of the war. The Union retreat was so fast that stores of army supplies and sutlers' stores had been set afire. The rebels found coffee, cheese, canned goods, and a general assortment of eatables. "We appropriated some for personal use and had cheese on toast for dinner. A fire and the hot sun had toasted them thoroughly. This was our first meal at Uncle Sam's expense but not the last for some of us."[70]

True words, for after the battle of Holly Springs, Confederate General Van Dorn put Grant in retreat and forced him to abandon everything he'd accumulated to supply his army. In addition to buildings, stores, and stockpiles of quartermaster and commissary goods, there were numerous well-stocked sutlers' shops. With the exception of a few items his men could use, Van Dorn burned everything.[71] Also, when the Confederates were fighting their way to Winchester, they drove the enemy back between fifty and sixty miles in forty-eight hours. General Stonewall Jackson's report said he'd become heir to one hundred head of cattle and thirty-four thousand pounds of bacon, flour, salt, sugar, coffee, hardbread, and cheese. Among the loot were sutlers' stores valued at twenty-five thousand dollars, which had been abandoned for want of transportation.[72]

But any sutler would have preferred to deal with the parsimonious and rule-bound auditor Mr. French or risk being too close to the battle line rather than cope with the spontaneous (or premeditated) antics of a group of his own unruly soldiers. "Privates are unprincipled and profane," a young Union Army private wrote home. "Robbing a sutler is counted as a meritorious deed. They eat pies and drink cider and walk off without a thought of paying for them."

Robbing the sutler probably started as self-indulgent play or a self-righteous game. All too soon, individual incidents became a pattern, and then it became fashionable to "briz" a sutler, to steal something during the transaction to "even out accounts" because he charged so much. A soldier would buy a pound of cheese and "briz" a sausage or pocket knife.[73]

It didn't take long before the sutler became the object of a "rally." A wagon would stop by a camp to sell cheap cigars. Men would enter the wagon, possess nearly everything there, then start the sutler's horse at a gallop. "Rally!" A favorite trick was to cut the guy ropes that held the sutler's tent, then grab everything within reach, and run, or bring the tent down around the sutler's ears. One enterprising group from an Ohio regiment staged a fight in front of the sutler's tent, during which time they made off with about three thousand dollars worth of merchandise.[74]

Wilbur Fisk's regiment got tired and cold while it waited at Stephenson's station for a train to take the men to Washington, D.C., so they rallied at a sutler's shanty and distributed his goods. When they started on a second sutler, Colonel Forster used his arms and fists to break it up.[75]

"Rallying" was not always so spontaneous. After a skirmish at Brandy Station, Virginia, headquarters ordered all of the sutlers to leave the army. One sutler ignored the order and drove his wagon down side-roads to remain parallel to his troops. He didn't count on running into a whole column of cavalry. When the Provost Marshal saw him, he turned to the cavalry and asked them who they were. They responded, "The First Mass Cavalry." "Well, First Mass Cavalry," he said, "go through that sutler!" And in less than fifteen minutes, the contents of the wagon were distributed throughout the regiment.[76]

After the surrender at Appomattox, hungry and snarling men made camp near Petersburg. The sutler had set up shop and was protected by new black cavalry. The Corn Exchange and the First Michigan crowded around the sutler's wagon and began to eye his stock. The black soldiers ordered the whites to stand back, but the old hands were not about to accept the blacks as equals, so when the corporal of the guard started to make an arrest, he was knocked down by a sergeant of the Corn Exchange. The fight was on and great care was taken in the confusion to upset the sutler's tent. Soldiers went running in all directions with cakes, candies, canned fruit, cheeses, raisins, tobacco, and all other goodies.[77]

It could be a cruel world for the risk takers and the naive, as Wilbur Fisk reported in his homebound letters. Wilbur once stumbled across a sutler whom he described as "openhearted and unpretending," a man who was evidently quite unsophisticated in the ways of the world. The fellow had his goods stacked on the roadside and was slowly being overwhelmed by an increasing mob. He tried to keep pace, for he was afraid that if he fell behind he might be robbed and left destitute. While he served one, a dozen hands moved toward his things. "He implored, entreated, sometimes threatened. His pleadings for comity went unheard; worse, they mocked him as they robbed him. He was earnest and vehement, sincere and truthful; he was unable to earn his living any other way, had seen much pain in the world and had had special permission to bring his load to them. He had two sick daughters at home. They heard him and loved his pies more than they felt for his sick children." In the end, they "rallied" on him and he lost everything. "For some sutlers," said Fisk, "I would have had no pity, but for this man, I felt sorry. If properly sold, his goods might have brought him several hundred dollars."[78]

The popular conception during the Civil War was that the magnitude of a sutler's profits was unwarranted. Certainly a number of easy sutler fortunes were made during the Civil War. Sutler Daniel Shove engaged a private for 15 dollars per month to act as clerk, then left for Manitowoc, Wisconsin for an extended leave. After a week, the lad wrote home that he should have asked for more money. "We sell about $60 a day," he wrote his parents, "of which nearly $40 are profit."[79]

Reports of gross sales of $100 to $150 per day, as recounted by the sutler of the Fifteenth Wisconsin, were not uncommon. One sutler allegedly earned ten thousand dollars after only eight months of business; another reported clearing a rather incredible seventy thousand dollars in one year.[80]

Colonel Marcus Spiegel's regiment beautifully illustrates what could result when protection and limitless profit opportunity were concurrently afforded a sutler. Spiegel was one of a handful of regimental Jewish colonels. It quickly became obvious to him that the sutler's job could be extremely lucrative. He informed his relatives that "besides the sutler there is no position outside of military in a regiment that pays. The sutler must pay [sic] from $50 to $100 per day as they sell from $100 to $300 per day at enormous prices and their money as sure as the State Railroad of Ohio whether the law protects them or not."

To benefit from this golden opportunity, Marcus asked his brother, Joseph, to be the sutler to his regiment. After the colonel had reserved the regimental sutler slot for his brother, he wrote home again as an afterthought. "Tell him not to bring over $1000 worth of stock," he wrote, because "after that is sold, he will have made enough to buy from the profit."

When Joseph Spiegel arrived, he quickly set to work and acquired the assistance of three regimental lieutenants to work behind the counter. In two days he took in fifteen hundred dollars—thirteen hundred in cash and two hundred dollars credit.

After Colonel Spiegel watched his brother bring in $1,500 in three days, he kept an eye on the business, even though he didn't deem it proper that he should sell anything personally. When Joseph sold every hat and shoe he had, Marcus Spiegel said that if he had known before what he knew now, he could have sold $1,000 per day for two weeks. Even when it rained incessantly and Joseph was minus a good many items, the man continued to gross from $150 to $200 per day in cash. That same year, Marcus informed his relatives of his and his brother's hopes to open a dry-goods store in Chicago.[81]

When the war was hot, sutler Joseph stopped well behind the battle line, having decided that prudence was the better part of valor. It apparently did not damage his business, for Marcus heard that his brother was still taking in two thousand dollars per day. "I expect they have cleared four thousand dollars in cash since they started," he wrote. "I think that is as well as he might have done at home."

Joseph had one tent at General Osterhaus's headquarters; Joseph's partner, a man named Sinsheimer, had another with the Second Brigade of Spiegel's division. They continued to have cash transactions of from five hundred to one thousand dollars, and from the replenishment of stock alone they took in seven thousand dollars. Col. Marcus Spiegel expressed his expectation that they would clear four thousand dollars on this last stock. "Josey hopes to make about $20,000 for him and Sinsheimer, and start a dry goods store and have [me] go in as a partner."[82]

Civil War sutlers found time to make a buck in a number of ways other than selling food and wares. One of the easiest was to play postman and deliver packages to officers from the express company on their way back from a visit to their suppliers in Washington, D.C.[83] They also served as bankers in making loans, and they discounted soldiers' paychecks, especially during the first days of the war when soldiers were paid with warrants against the U.S. Treasury that were difficult to cash. Moneylenders, including sutlers, purchased them for six or seven dollars per eleven, which netted them up to 50 percent profit.[84] As one analyst of the Civil War wrote, "grafters, pay discount sharks, gamblers, and sutlers were ever ready to relieve the soldier of any inconvenient burden of money."[85]

Even the depreciation of Confederate money offered a profit opportunity. On February 26, 1865, Captain Wirz, who commanded Camp Sumpter, asked the aide-de-camp and assisting Adjutant General Lieutenant G. W. McPhail whether the sutler was authorized to buy at an advanced price from the government-designated rate. In 1864, the commissary and quartermaster had granted sutlers the privilege of buying greenbacks from prisoners at the rate of $4.50 Confederate to one greenback. All greenbacks so obtained were to be turned over to the government. Since then, Confederate depreciation had raised the price of federal money. The sutler could no longer buy them at the prescribed price, and a black market was being conducted by persons connected with the prison.[86]

That same year, 1864, a wounded captain from West Virginia exchanged some greenbacks with Captain Park at a prison camp outside Washington, D.C., for Confederate money at the rate of twenty to one. "With the pittance obtained," he said, "I patronized the sutler and get something to eat. Most of us recovering from our wounds are constantly suffering from hunger."[87]

The official answer to Wirz's question was that sutlers were the only ones authorized to trade with the prisoners. He was to give them permission to purchase U.S. Treasury notes for the use of the government at the rate established by the quartermaster general, which until further notice was five dollars in Confederate for one dollar in U.S. Treasury. Illegal trafficking, said the response brusquely, "will stop."[88]

Almost uniformly authors and editors have branded the Civil War sutler as unethical. Soldiers and officers who did not like their sutler told others that he was demoralizing, a scurrilous peddler of whiskey and sickness, and an amoral opportunist who bled the army dry. "Gamblers came and gamblers went," said one Civil War editor. "Their trade was a seasonal one, but sutlers were an ever-present evil. . . . The remarkable thing is that, considering the prices charged, there was not more general dissatisfaction than generally existed."[89]

Cases of excessively high prices and pricing by opportunity, even during emergencies, were numerous, and often the troops reacted with vengeance. A newspaperman with Joseph E. Johnston's command in 1861 accused sutlers of making profits of several hundred percent on sales. Because of "excessive charges" for ginger cakes, half-moon pies, dried fruit, and other stock items, he said that the sutler was often driven from camp—minus his provisions. Trooper Marcellus Darling wrote that the soldiers in his regiment, the 154th New York Infantry, often stole from their sutler, a man named Saunders, because of their indignation at his high prices. Darling made it clear that his sympathies were with the men by writing, "Saunders may stick his butter and cheese in his ___ before I will pay $1.00 per lb."[90] One private wrote to *Harper's Weekly* to suggest that the Sanitary Commission take on the "few extra items" that the sutler sold and sell them at "compensating" prices.[91]

Cases of pure greed included the sutler who raised his beer prices from ten to fifty cents a glass as the volume of his reserves diminished. At the fifty-cent level, the boys told him the price was too high. He said, "Tough," so that night the boys pulled his wagon up a hill and scattered fifteen hundred dollars worth of goods. In the process, they delivered a box of soda crackers to the colonel as a gift. The next morning, the sutler discovered the trickery. When he went to the colonel's tent, he saw the crackers and called the colonel a thief as well. The colonel told the sutler his commission was withdrawn and ordered him to get out and stay out.[92]

It is doubtful that any sutler tried to present himself as a member of a philanthropic organization. He took the position of provisioner on terms set by others and presented himself as an entrepreneur without equivocation. He was a peddler who took his wagons to the battlefield to offer soldiers a variety of items they could not get otherwise. He looked out for himself and took his chances. If he made good money, it was because he was the only game in town; and if no one objected, he charged what the market would bear. His willingness to accept the risks of the trade was periodically acknowledged in diaries and historical narratives, but the majority of the time he was presented as a greedy little man who stood near the pay table, hand extended, until his share was counted.

When John Pullen wrote about the Twentieth Maine Regiment, he observed that hundreds of respectable fortunes were made from the war, but in "the minds of those who fought, the act of taking a profit so close to the front lines where men were dying and the wounded lay, seemed immoral."[93] And since the sutler's position was semiofficial and his prices were high, he was the object of suspicion; soldiers thought he might be in cahoots with an officer to defraud the troops and split the profits "with his higher up accomplice." And in the end, he could take a man's money at the end of the month, a procedure that might well lead to real or imagined grievances. "So the sutler had a public relations problem," said Pullen. "He was not a PR expert but just a determined little peddler with money on his mind."[94] Pullen's objective analysis did not prevent him from delivering a "eulogium [*sic*] to the sutler and the army mule," a spoof that ridiculed the sutler for wanting to take all the pay at the pay table and risking his neck for canned fruit and "Scheidam Schnapps."

John C. Gray, Jr., sympathized with the sutler. He thought the government treated the man "in a very absurd way." He said that the laws and government officials "insult, abuse and thwart them so badly that it is enough to prevent any decent man from taking up the business." He favored speedy and severe punishment of those sutlers who broke the rules, instead of "severe and stringent rules as greatly mar their efficiency and bring them into contempt." From his personal experience, he knew of one fellow as "something of a scamp, but two are most excellent and fair-dealing men and I have never heard anything against any of the rest." He thought the only case where a sutler could really do much mischief was when he was in league with the colonel of the regiment.[95]

Gray was not alone in his appraisal. On an individual basis, the letters of quite a few line officers showed respect and friendship with regimental sutlers. "I have had a great deal of comfort in my sutler this winter," wrote Colonel Wainwright. "Not a complaint has reached me either of him from the men or of any of the men from him. At General Patrick's headquarters they speak of him as really an honest and trusty man, most rare qualities in a sutler."[96] General Robert McAllister had a handsome pair of shoulder straps with stars presented to him by Mr. Taylor, the sutler of the 120th New York. McAllister said the sutler presented the gift as a Jersey man to a Jersey general who deserved it.[97] A Civil War journalist suggested that sutlers profited by the teachings of experience; if they had faults, they soon mended them, so that late in the war "they rarely found it necessary to beg deliverance from their friends."[98]

The sutler was "one of the most frequently damned and reviled civilians in Civil War history," wrote historian E. B. Coddington toward the end of his work on the Gettysburg campaign. "I think that the name 'sutler' to-day calls up in the minds of the old soldiers a man who . . . was better satisfied to . . . get his living out of the soldiers who were doing his fighting for him." But, he added, the sutler filled a recognized need. No soldier was compelled to patronize him, yet "I question whether there was a man in the service any great length of time . . . who did not." [99]

If the sutler was half of the problem, the loosely run volunteer regiment was the other half. The Sanitary Commission referred to the unfortunate relation between the sutlers and the undisciplined men in many regiments, by which the sutlers were often induced to expand their earnings for food and drinks "in such a way as to injure both health and morals."[100] One account said soldiers acted as though they had "just been endowed with the gift of eating, and were intoxicated with the novel desire that appetite awakened. No matter what exorbitant price was asked for the most insignificant article, if it was eatable it was bought, and all the quicker for the swindling extortion. If the sutlers don't fill their pockets at such times," added the writer, "it is not the soldier's fault." [101]

Had the sutler not been very important to the soldier's comfort, price and availability would not have been such an irritant, and no one would have written half as much about the sutler in letters sent home. In their journals of the war, nearly every soldier remarked about the sutler of his company or regiment, the condition and prices of his goods, and the antics performed by him as well as upon him. One officer remarked casually that a sutler's wagon being unloaded from a platform railway car "was an important event[,] because sutler's goods had been scarce to be obtained even by officers."[102] Even the acerbic Captain Park once wrote that he was living well "by making purchases from the sutler."[103]

Certainly, some sutlers overcharged. "The trade was not without thieves," admitted Coddington, but more often, he believed the sutler was the victim of "unwarranted contempt on the part of government and army officials."[104] The uncertainties of his business and costs of transportation, in Coddington's judgment, justified the prices he charged for his goods.

The Civil War sutler operated, as he always had, within boundaries established for him by the army. Due to the lack of a more professional posture on the part of the Civil War volunteer units, he had considerable leeway. As the war progressed, however, general officers within the army command did their best to minimize the sutler's nuisance factor and still enable him to provide for the comfort of the troops.

NINE

Controlling a Necessary Evil

Are [sutlers] necessary? If so, they are a necessary evil. They tend, in my opinion, to demoralize the men and take from them the money that should go to their families.—Paymaster General Benjamin F. Learned, Letter to the Honorable Henry Wilson, December 5, 1861

In our regiment, we have the best sutlers in the Potomac; nevertheless, in actual practice they prove an unmitigated curse.—Unidentified Volunteer Regimental Surgeon to the United States Sanitary Commission, 1862

Toward the end of 1861, while Congress wrestled with how to fund the war, Henry Wilson of Massachusetts warned his fellow congressmen that the troops were being demoralized and degraded by the sutler system. After addressing his concern for the well-being of half a million citizens, friends, and volunteers, Wilson declared that the sutler's prices were exorbitant, that his food often caused sickness, and that he dealt illegally in liquors.

Wilson was so incensed that he told the newspapers he intended to recommend the abolishment of the sutler from the volunteer forces of the United States.[1] After a more careful assessment, he altered his stance. Instead of asking for the removal of the sutler, he submitted a resolution to ask the Inspector General, the Quartermaster General, and the Commissary General of Subsistence to inform the Senate which articles should be sold by sutlers.

Wilson, who was chairman of the Senate Military Affairs Committee, was known as the "soldier's friend." He said he had no quarrel with individual sutlers, "many of whom are honorable men," but he believed the system was being "abused most wickedly, shamefully." The information that moved him to examine sutler activities was contained in letters from officers in the field. Privates also warned Wilson against "the wrongs imposed on them" by sutlers. Colonel Blaisdell, Eleventh Massachusetts Volunteers, wrote that "in my experience of twelve years as a soldier I have come to the conclusion that the sutler is a complete nuisance and a curse to any regiment." A surgeon with New York's Fortieth Regiment recommended that for sanitary, moral, and religious reasons, the sutler be excised from the army.

Wilson visited regimental camps of the Army of the Potomac and discovered enlisted men who, although they earned but thirteen dollars per month, owed the sutler as much as nineteen dollars for a two-month period. He saw and heard of other bills that ran from twelve to fifteen dollars, all in violation of current regulations that limited indebtedness to a sutler to one-third of a soldier's pay.[2] When Wilson discussed a case where a sutler had taken nineteen of twenty-six dollars of a soldier's pay, an officer told Wilson of a soldier who was still in debt after the sutler took all twenty-six dollars for two months.[3]

In half the regiments, price regulation was totally absent. Articles retailing in New York for $0.75 were sold by sutlers for $2.25. Sutlers also sold liquors in 178 regiments with and without the consent of officers. Only twenty-three regiments of the Army of the Potomac enforced the banishment of liquors. Wilson heard that soldiers suffered illness from sutler food. G. W. Stipp of Jefferson City, Missouri, advised Wilson that sutlers sold "strychnine whiskey, rancid nuts and putrid animal food like sausages and pies." When Stipp had canvassed camps and hospitals in the vicinity of St. Joseph and Kansas City, Missouri, doctors he questioned said that 10 percent of the major illnesses could be charged to sutlers. Stipp thought that figure was too low. "As a class of men," he wrote, "rascal, swindler, and robber are stamped on their features."[4]

From December 10, 1861, to March 21, 1862, Congress debated the problem of how to regulate the business of the volunteer army sutler.[5] One of the examples Wilson produced to illustrate his concern was the case of sutler Silas Seymour. Seymour was attached to the brigade of General Daniel E. Sickles, which had five regiments. Although army regulations required a council of officers to recommend a sutler for each regiment, Seymour was recommended as brigade (rather than regimental) sutler. After the commanding general and the Secretary of War approved his nomination, [6] Seymour casually turned around and sold five regimental sutler slots for $250 per month apiece. His take amounted to a cool twenty thousand dollars per year, whose purchasing power was equivalent to $250,000 in 1989.[7] Wilson thought Burnside's expedition and Sherman's expedition might also have brigade-level sutlers. To further underline the lure of the sutler's slot, Wilson shared with his associates the tale of a man who paid eighteen hundred of two thousand dollars toward a sutlership, only to have his money refunded the following day because another person was willing to pay five thousand dollars. He also showed them advertisements placed in the New York *Herald* by persons who were offering money for sutlerships. "It is beyond dispute," said Wilson, "that persons have received sealed proposals for these places."

Comments from those congressmen who had prior military service confirmed that the militiaman had been a sutler junky since the days of the War of 1812, but when Wilson was asked by a fellow congressman by what authority the sutler was appointed to a regiment, he confessed that although he had looked through all the laws and army regulations he had found nothing. Nonetheless, he calculated that regimental sutlers were raking in one thousand to two thousand dollars a month, and that sutler sales to the Army of the Potomac alone exceeded ten million dollars per year. Half that sum, he added, was profit.[8]

Wilson's initial diatribe against sutlers in December 1861 caused a rapid and focused reaction by members of the sutlering profession. They hired a lobbying organization that circulated a letter and petition to all regimental sutlers. The petition said the army was content with its currently assigned sutlers and did not want any changes to the system. It was to be signed by officers and privates of the regiment and then sent to Congress. In the cover letter, the banker and treasurer of the Sutler Defense Fund called on each sutler to contribute twenty-five dollars to pay for costs associated with blocking the passage of laws inimical to their position. The solicitation caused the New York *Tribune* to add that "to men who charge five cents apiece for a postage stamp, and two cents apiece for the commonest envelopes, this sum is a mere bagatelle."[9]

In response to Wilson's opening diatribe, Congress rallied to repeal the act that had allowed sutlers a lien on the soldiers' pay. [10] Then, on January 2, 1962, Wilson introduced a bill "to provide for the appointment of sutlers in the volunteer service and to define their duties." At the same time, a contingent within Congress pressed to abolish the sutler's position altogether. No regulation, they said, would prevent continued harm to the men by sutlers. Congressman Carlisle argued that the Regular Army post sutler was watched by an officer and thus made useful; the volunteer army regimental sutler was injurious to the service. In those cases where the regimental colonel was a partner of the sutler, there was no way that a congressional law would effectively change anything. In support of abolishment, the Ohio legislature passed a joint resolution on February 12 to protect their soldiers "from the imposition of sutlers":

> The privileges allowed the sutlers by the general government have been greatly abused and so soldiers have been cheated and defrauded of their money, and have paid large sums without any adequate consideration thereof.
>
> The Ohio legislature is urging its senators to try to abolish the office of sutler in the army and use commissaries.
>
>
>
> James R. Hubbell
> Speaker of House
> B. Stanton
> President of Senate [11]
>
>

Abolishment of the sutler was the position that Wilson had abandoned after reflection. Although he agreed in principle, he told his fellow congressmen that he was governed by public considerations. The sheer quantity of army supplies, the logistics involved in moving food and materials in the field, and the risk involved in loss negated the government's ability to do away with the sutler's office. Then, too, even if sutlers were removed they would be replaced by "the 'harpies' who dogged the camps outside the system and sell liquor."[12]

As the Sanitary Commission so ably observed, the sutler system would not have been half so objectionable if army regulations had been carried out, but proper control and supervision were scarcely ever maintained in the volunteer regiments. Congressman Wilson emphasized that the individual sutler was not the source of the problem. His proposal, Senate Bill no. 136, which Congress passed into law on March 21, 1862, addressed the system, not the individual; and its particulars addressed only the sutler of volunteer units. The Regular Army sutler, who was properly supervised, remained unaffected.[13]

Senate Bill no. 136 was an honest attempt to correct widespread abuse. The final bill, which survived the often debilitating House–Senate compromise system, required a board of regimental officers (essentially a Council of Administration) to appoint and oversee the sutler, for example, to set his prices and periodically review them. Senator Wilson, who had identified more than 150 items in the sutler's portable commissary, read into the bill a list of 52 articles that he thought sutlers should be allowed to sell.

Wilson's approved list included apples, dried apples, oranges, figs, lemons, butter, cheese, milk, syrup, molasses, wallets, brooms, comforters, boots, pocket looking glasses, pins, leather gloves, tin wash basins, shirt buttons, short and horn buttons, newspapers, books, tobacco, cigars, pipes, matches, blacking and blacking brushes, clothes brushes, toothbrushes, hairbrushes, coarse and fine combs, emery, crocus, pocket handkerchiefs, stationery, armor oil, sweet oil, rotten-stone, razors, razor strops, shaving soap, soap, suspenders, scissors, shoestrings, needles, threads, knives, pencils, and bristol brick.[14]

No liquor.

Earlier regulations that described restrictions on the sutler were reinvoked: he was not allowed to farm out his business; he could not sell liquor; and he was denied personal use of army conveyances. The sutler's lien on the soldier's pay was reinstated, but limited to one-fourth of that monthly pay. If he violated regulations, he could lose his license and forfeit his goods; and since he was under the articles of war, he was liable to court-martial. As an incentive, Congress allowed the sutler to retain his monopoly over one (and only one) regiment. And finally, to repress the casual manner in which some senior officers had shared in the sutler profits, the bill forbade officers to receive moneys from the suttling business or to receive presents.

At camp, where it counted, the bill was ignored. According to one editor of Civil War history, the board of officers, individually and as a group, had little experience in judging the correctness of suggested prices, or they were willing to split profits with the sutler. In consequence, even though the colonel and board of officers jointly could revoke the sutler's license, the sutler often did what he wanted, which meant that prices stayed high. The attitude toward the situation appeared to be that "if prices got too bad, the soldiers would go elsewhere or do without."[15]

The Wilson bill wasn't the only legal control over the sutler. Under the articles of war, sutlers could be tried, along with other civilian suppliers, for willful neglect and fraud. Sutlers in the Confederate Army were regulated and treated in similar fashion. Article 25 of Confederate Army regulations was identical to sutler regulations used in 1857 by the Union, [16] and both Union Army and Confederate Army sutlers were made eligible for the draft in 1863. [17]

Sutlers of both armies also could be taken prisoner and exchanged like soldiers. The detainment of Union Army noncombatants, including sutlers and their clerks, at Libby Prison in Richmond in 1862 became a congressional concern. An exchange was arranged during February, March, and April 1863.[18] It may not have been much of an issue for the Confederate Army, because at the end of the war, out of five hundred pages of names of paroles of the Army of Northern Virginia only three men were listed as sutlers.[19]

During the early part of the war, Congress and the Secretary of War were more concerned about the impact the sutlers' wagons were having on army logistics. Sutlers had been using military supply routes, and through the use of bribes they had gained unauthorized use of army transportation facilities to move their merchandise. There were too many wagons on the front as it was. Each was a liability to the army's mobility. The Army of the Cumberland had three thousand alone; in the spring of 1864, before the Wilderness campaign, Grant had four thousand wagons. In the opinion of Quartermaster General M. C. Meigs "it was hard enough to get necessities to the troops without giving space to their candies, pies, soft drinks, and gewgaws."[20] Most generals acknowledged the benefit of sutler goods for their men, but few were willing to see their supply lines clogged with another three to four hundred sutler wagons.[21] In September 1862, the Adjutant General's office issued a notice that because sutlers were allowed to use regimental and quartermaster wagons under the guise of quartermaster stores, wagon trains had increased in size. "Hereafter, any officer who permits this abuse will be punished, and the sutler will be placed outside the lines of the army and his appointment revoked."[22]

Thereafter—at least for a few months—the movement of sutler goods in the Army of the Potomac was strictly controlled by regulations. When a sutler wanted to replenish his stock, he was required to make up an invoice that itemized merchandise and comestibles and that conformed to the Wilson bill. The invoice, which was good for only one month's supply, needed approval by the commandant of the regiment and brigade and the Provost Marshal General. Three sutlers could then go to Washington, D.C. There, the quartermaster general would clear a vessel upon which sutler goods could be loaded and shipped to Belle Plain or Aquia Creek, Virginia.

In January 1863, a special investigating agent wrote Quartermaster General Meigs that confiscations of sutler goods were numerous at Aquia Creek because parties had tried to smuggle liquor and contraband goods into the army. It was discovered that sutlers had been paying large fees to officials to ferry goods from Liverpool Point to Aquia Creek on government transport. The practice had become "notorious and universal." They not only lost their goods, but were sent away and told not to return.[23]

Collusion between the Army of the Potomac Quartermaster Corps and sutlers resulted not only in bribes, but in the granting of permits to sutlers to sell goods at Aquia Creek. Seized or stolen property had been allowed to pass to Washington on government transport, and permits had been issued to nonsutlers to sell goods to soldiers.[24] Meigs wrote Secretary of War Stanton that he thought detectives could control this illegal traffic; officers could not. "The followers of an army," he added, "are ingenious, enterprising, often unscrupulous, and it requires police officers of much experience to detect attempts to smuggle improper articles and persons within the lines."[25]

The following year, Assistant Adjutant General James A. Hardie informed George G. Meade, commanding, Army of the Potomac, of a proposal by the Secretary of War. Sutlers who needed additional supplies would fill out a manifest; all goods not covered by passes would be confiscated; and after goods were purchased and permit to ship was given by the quartermaster general, transportation facilities would exclude railroads and other means of government conveyance. He wanted sutlers to hold a valid sutler certificate, and he suggested that certificates be issued only to American citizens.[26] Further, to keep sutler goods from falling into the hands of guerrillas, a regiment of mounted cavalry would leave Warrenton Junction each Thursday for Washington, D.C., and return the following Monday. Employees (clerks) could represent their employers, but a certificate with written evidence of the agency would be needed for approval. Any sutler who failed to comply with regulations would lose his goods.[27]

Local problems with sutlers included the illegal sale of goods across the lines to soldiers and civilians, which amounted to lending "aid and comfort" to the enemy. When General Rosecrans heard of the practice in November 1862, he authorized the arrest and seizure of goods from all parties who broke the following regulations:[28]

I. Sutlers shall not sell to anyone other than members of the army.

II. Sutlers are not permitted to ship shoes or articles of clothing to the regiment without having obtained clearance from the C.O. and get a permit from the Colonel approved by Brigade and Division Commanders for the shipment.

III. No one other than the sutlers are allowed to follow the army.

IV. No one shall sell goods for the need of resident citizens unless he is a resident trader.

Also, by virtue of the circumstances surrounding the sutler's job—his need to move in and out of the army, to transport goods, and to move freely throughout the camps as a salesman—his profession was perfect for anyone who wanted to collect intelligence information. In 1861, spies often disguised themselves as sutlers; in essence, all one needed was a pass, a wagon, and some food. One audacious Confederate spy named Shadburne even went into the sutler meat-pie-making business. He sold his wares directly to Union soldiers. Shadburne knew, as European agents had known as early as the turn of the century, that on the eve of a campaign or eve of retreat, the baggage, women, and sutlers would be removed to the rear of the army. The event was a sure sign that the army was about to move.[29]

One time during the conduct of the war, an entire class of sutlers was prevented from plying its trade. It began in December 1863, when Secretary of War Stanton suddenly prohibited trade between sutlers and Confederate prisoners of war. There were sutlers placed at each prison camp in the winter of 1861–62. Confederate prisoners either possessed or were able to obtain enough money to create a brisk trade.[30] In June 1862, when control of prisoners of war was placed in the hands of the Secretary of War, he regulated the sutlers' prison trade. All of the merchandise that army regulations permitted the sutler to keep could also be sold to prisoners, except for firearms and an excess of clothing, but regulations stated that no sales were to be made directly to prisoners. The commanding officer would pay for the article out of the prisoner's money on deposit. In that way, he could stay informed about what was sold.[31]

About the time Stanton halted all sutler trade with prisoners, he informed the president of the United States that the Confederates had maltreated many Union soldiers through exposure and starvation. He believed the situation resulted from "savage barbarity that could only have been practiced in the hopes that the government would be compelled to yield to exchange all prisoners of war" which would "give them another forty thousand men." As to Confederate prisoners of war held in the North, Stanton believed they had been treated "with the utmost humanity and tenderness consistent with security." As a result of the "barbarity practiced against our prisoners," he had decided to cut the North's indulgence of friendly visits and supplies.[32]

Prisoner-of-war life anywhere was difficult enough without having the only source of decent supplies denied to the men. Less than a week went by before Lieutenant Colonel Pierson in charge of prisoners at Sandusky, Ohio, wrote to Colonel William Hoffman, Commissary General of Prisoners, to complain that many of the prisoners, especially late arrivals, were in need of shoes, stockings, and "other clothing to be suited for the climate and season." There was also a great call for tobacco, paper, stamps, and vegetables. He wanted to know whether it was "the design that they should be prohibited under my present orders to issue no clothing and there being no sutler to buy of, it amounts to a prohibition. If, on the other hand, they can have the items, how can they be supplied?"[33]

The halt in sutler sales was seen by one Confederate intern as simply one more move to pressure prisoners to sign an oath of allegiance to the North. Another Confederate soldier wrote that he and his comrades first were insulted when the Union Army had assigned black soldiers from North Carolina to control the Confederate camp. Then the sutler's privilege of selling provisions in unlimited quantities to those who had money had been abolished. Men were thus forced to rely upon government rations. Since rations were often insufficient to keep the men alive, the prisoner concluded that the United States officers were using every means available to induce prisoners to take the oath. "[I]t is fair to presume," he concluded, "that the 'best government the sun ever shone upon' was now reduced to the policy of starving men into allegiance to it."[34]

Before the end of the month, the Commissioner of Prisoner Exchange issued a notice to say the Secretary of War believed that the treatment of Union Army prisoners had materially improved, and that he desired that prisoners held by the Union be allowed to purchase items of comfort from sutlers. By March 1864, only three months later, the sutlers were again selling an expanded list of items to prisoners of war—sundries: tobacco, cigars, snuff, steel pens, paper, envelopes, lead pencils, penknives, postage stamps, buttons, tape and thread, sewing cotton, pins and needles, handkerchiefs, suspenders, socks, under-clothes, caps, shoes, towels, looking glasses, brushes, combs, clothes brooms, pocketknives, and scissors.

And groceries: crushed sugar, syrup, family soap, butter, lard, smoked beef, beef tongue, bologna sausage, cornmeal, nutmeg, pepper, mustard, table salt, salt fish, crackers, cheese, pickles, sauces and fish in cans, vegetables, dried fruits, syrups, lemons, nuts, apples, matches, and yeast powders.

Even table furnishings to include crockery, glassware, and tinware.

Vegetables, which were originally considered to be a luxury that prisoners were not to have, were eventually seen as beneficial because of their "antiscorbutic" properties. As of February 1865, the Secretary of War allowed sutlers to sell prisoners potatoes, onions, and vegeta-bles "in such quantities as may be necessary to their health."[35]

The sutler was more than an ancillary element of the daily Civil War camp scene; he was a necessary ingredient. Without him, the quality of life for the average soldier would have been much more unpleasant. The trooper would have gone without those little "luxuries" which re-minded him that he was not a barbarian, forever lost in war. Life in prison also would have been that much more difficult. Perhaps the regi-mental commanding officer might have been less frequently vexed, and many of his men might have been more sober more of the time, but in the end, the energy that the commanding officer spent in coping with his sutler would have been spent in coping with the increased volume of complaints from his men if a sutler had not been around.

The degree to which the sutler was "evil" appears to have been di-rectly proportional to three environmental conditions: the background and character of the officers, the discipline of the soldiers in the regi-ment, and the degree to which troops partook of what was offered as a distraction—such as whiskey—instead of items properly supplied for his comfort. The Civil War sutler was no agent of the devil; he was a small economic reflection of the mood of his time: struggle, chaos, weariness, and brief opportunity.

PART IV

THE MILITARY POST TRADER

1867–1893

TEN

Doing without the Army Sutler

In accordance with the provision of this act, the warrants of all sutlers to the army will terminate July 1, 1867. After that date, no sutler will be allowed to keep or sell any goods inside a military post, station or reserve.—Adjutant General's Office, Order no. 6, 1867

One of Congress's many post–Civil War tasks was to tear down an oversized army. On July 28, 1866, the House and Senate passed "an Act to Increase and Fix the Military Peace Establishment of the United States," which defined an organization of approximately twenty-five thousand soldiers that included ten regiments of cavalry.[1] Section no. 25 of the statute abolished the office of sutler in the army and at military posts. General Sherman said the trader had proved unmanageable; he thought the Commissary Department could do the sutler's job. As the Adjutant General of the Army said twenty-five years later:

The demoralizing influences of the sutler's store which had been an appendage of almost every part of our army from the time of its organization, were brought so strikingly before the public eye during the late Civil War that at its close, Congress abolished the system and directed that such articles as were needed by officers and soldiers and were not supplied gratuitously should be kept for sale at cost by the Subsistence Department.[2]

141

The Subsistence Department was thus authorized and required to furnish articles designated by the Inspector General of the Army and to sell those articles to officers and enlisted men "at cost prices and if not paid when purchased, to use payroll deductions." The change, made effective on July 1, 1867, provided a liberal lead time to enable sutlers to close out their establishments, and it gave the Subsistence Department time to obtain and train additional staff and to increase its inventories.[3] To underscore the section of the order that pertained to sutlers, the Secretary of War issued Order no. 6 to all posts: "In accordance with the provision of this act, the warrants of all sutlers to the army will terminate July 1, 1867. After that date, no sutler will be allowed to keep or sell any goods inside a military post, station or reserve."[4]

The army picked a poor time to remove the major source of personal comfort to its troops. The newly reorganized army had been given a major new assignment in the western frontier territories. The country was sparsely settled by whites; each territory had Indian tribes that were actively resisting white encroachment; and because the territories were distant from white settlements, there were few civilized conveniences or facilities other than those in scattered settlements and others provided by the army. Conditions for the average soldier were less than comfortable, and no quick remedy was eminent.

Immediately after the Civil War, the military was told to maintain order in the South and to push back the western frontier. General Philip H. Sheridan, who shouldered the brunt of both tasks, believed that the army's foremost responsibility was to keep the paths to western settlement open and safe. To accomplish that mission, the army's western-based cavalry units discouraged nonreservation Indians from harassing white settlers. They also pursued, corralled, and held both hostile and peaceful Indians on reservations, trying to keep Indians of one tribe from killing those of another tribe, and protecting the property of government officials and reservation officials. In addition, the army acted to protect Indian reservations against the encroachment of whites and made attempts to enforce United States law.[5] Infantry units were assigned to keep open operating lines of communications and protect those under development, including the transcontinental line of the Union Pacific–Western Pacific Railroad.

The combined tasks required the army to monitor major rivers and emigrant, freight, and stage lines from their eastern terminuses to California, Oregon, and Montana. The army therefore concentrated its troops where they would do the most good. To protect the increasing number of emigrant trains headed toward or beyond the Continental Divide, small numbers of troops were stationed at points of preemigration assembly: Forts Ridgely and Abercrombie in Minnesota for diverse points west; Forts Riley and Larned, trailheads for Denver and New Mexico; and Fort Kearny in Nebraska, a jumping-off spot for Denver.[6] Farther west, troops built and then garrisoned new posts. The majority were situated hundreds of miles from any beaten path. Once the army determined that a permanent show of military strength was needed to maintain the peace in a new town, mining development, or reservation, the post site was decided on the basis of the availability of water, fuel, and browse for horses.[7]

According to Professor Raymond Welty, who undertook a detailed examination of the frontier army from 1860 to 1870, the average frontier soldier led a rather harsh, monotonous existence, devoid of most personal comforts and many simple pleasures. The soldier went without sufficient basic food and was at the mercy of the elements without adequate protection. Historians Robert M. Utley and Don Rickey, Jr., would probably agree, especially concurring that the soldier was forced to perform a variety of duties he had never anticipated, much less agreed to perform.[8] Indeed, the picture that Welty drew was reminiscent of the image one had of frontier army posts in 1812. As a result, desertion from western posts during the 1860s broke all records. In his 1870 annual report, the Secretary of War admitted that soldiers deserted because they were asked to work all the time. They were ordered to quarry stone, make adobe, operate sawmills, burn brick and lime, drive wagons, and cut wood. When time allowed, the soldier escorted, patrolled, and scouted, but he was seldom "off on campaigns or expeditions against large forces of hostile Indians."[9]

At no other time in American military history might the sutler have provided a more stabilizing influence on his military clientele, but he had been placed on notice to vacate. The Commissary Department, in response to its new charge to take over for the sutler, informed the Secretary of War that it needed an appropriation of approximately three million dollars to purchase stock to replace what the sutler had carried. If the Secretary of War was sympathetic, Congress was not. The government was in a postwar-economy-conservation mood, and refused to pass a special appropriation for the Subsistence Department to absorb the sutler's duties. The army was told to solve its problems in some other way.[10]

Thus, across the country, sutler stores were being closed or their owners given deadlines by which they had to sell out their remaining stock. Doing without a sutler meant doing without many goods and conveniences, because no one was prepared to replace him. The new regulations to replace his services with the commissary had not been activated. Yet since the 1850s (except during the early war years) the nation had been expanding at an unprecedented pace. Private and government-backed explorations resulted in new roads, new towns, and new military posts. The few major arteries that crossed the continent were punctuated with military posts that not only served as a source of escort through hostile Indian country, but also functioned as critical way stations for emigrant rest, repairs, and refurbishment of necessary supplies. The westbound settler counted heavily on being able to swap tired horses and worn-out cattle, to replenish depleted supplies of flour and gunpowder, and to find boots for sore feet and new cloth goods for his lady. Most of these needs had been filled by the army post sutler.

It is no surprise, therefore, that shortly after the sutler was put on alert to close down, Congress and the army received pleas from a number of travelers and freighters for some kind of merchandise store at frontier posts, at least at those located on major trails across the country. At the same time, members of the endangered sutler profession sought ways to reverse the decision. One influential sutler, Judge William Alexander Carter from Fort Bridger, traveled to Washington to ask the president and Congress to revoke the order that would put him out of business.

Although he acted on his own, Judge Carter was an ideal representative for the suttling profession. He was a Virginia gentleman whose family lines extended back to American settlement in 1649.[11] Born in April 1818, Carter had joined the United States Army at an early age and had seen action with General Harney in Florida during the Seminole War. After his discharge, he became a sutler at Fort St. Augustine, and may have had branch stores in Georgia and Tennessee.

He left the suttling business, married in 1848, and located his family in Missouri. For a short period, he and his brother, Richard, tried their hand in the gold fields of California. In 1857, some years after his return to Missouri, General Harney contacted him. The general had been assigned the task of putting down the Mormon Rebellion. Part of his long-range plan was to erect three new posts in the environs of Utah. He wanted Carter to serve as sutler.

Harney was reassigned that summer, so Carter ended up as sutler to

General Albert Sidney Johnson. Due to delays, they crossed the Territory of Wyoming late in the fall of 1857. South Pass blizzard struck them in early November and froze all but a handful of their horses and mules. Carter's diary recorded the hideous sounds of their braying as the winds swept through the willow of their thinly sheltered camp along the Sweetwater River. Although Carter was initially designated to serve as the sutler for three new military posts in the vicinity of Salt Lake City, the settlement of the confrontation resulted in only one post being purchased and rebuilt—Fort Bridger.

Fort Bridger was located on the Oregon Trail, about sixty miles east of Salt Lake City. It was an ideal location for a sutler because the late 1850s was a period of heavy migration, exploration, and settlement. Carter was the only civilian trader allowed on the military reservation, a huge tract that measured twenty-five miles on each side.

As soon as he was established, Carter arranged for a two-hundred-thousand-dollar line of credit with Robert Campbell—the same Robert Campbell who bankrolled sutlers John Dougherty, Seth Ward, and John B. Todd. To remain as independent as possible, Carter built three sawmills, a limestone quarry, and a kiln. He brought all of his own tools and equipment in from St. Louis, and he advertised as far as London for good workers to join his payroll.

In a short time, Carter became a wholesaler, retailer, farmer, merchant, banker, freighter, contractor, cattleman, speculator, and, according to accounts from his guests, a marvelous host, renowned throughout the Rocky Mountains. He operated a monopoly over most military contracts and services, and until 1870 leased all the reservation farming land. Carter delivered his products and services to the military community, travelers, and tourists; to wagonmasters and their men; to miners and speculators; to government agents, natural scientists, and emigrants; and to local settlers and Indians.

The following chronology of Carter's enterprises indicates the breadth of his talents and energies:

> 1860s–1870s: Carter had army contracts for beef, pork, vegetables, beans, flour, hay, wood, grain, beef, lumber, coal, and lime.
> 1863–1868: He carried on trade with the Shoshone and Bannock tribes, and sold the army more than twenty thousand dollars in trade gifts for the Shoshone and Bannock Indian treaties of 1863 and 1868.

1867–1868: He grubstaked miners and owned an interest in mining claims at South Pass, Wyoming, which netted him twelve thousand dollars. He sold one claim in the fall of 1868 to John Casement, track-laying boss of the Union Pacific Railroad. During this time he improved the road between South Pass and Fort Bridger.

1869: He financed the construction of the "Carter and Brother" warehouse at Carter station, the Union Pacific Railroad depot (and hamlet) that served Fort Bridger. The building served as the railroad and telegraph station, local retail store, and storage facility. Carter used it to store annuities for the Shoshones, army supplies for Fort Bridger, and supplies that Carter's men freighted over the mountains.

From 1869 through the 1880s: Carter developed a herd of cattle that his brother-in-law, Richard A. Hamilton, managed for him. He started with three hundred head from Omaha in 1869 and formed the Carter Cattle Company in 1871. He had the exclusive right to sell beef to the army at Fort Bridger, and he also had a complete stockyards assembly near the railroad line at Carter Station.

Carter's family enjoyed all the amenities of life. In 1864, the judge had his brother bring the family piano across the plains from St. Louis. His four children had a tutor and a music teacher, and the family had Shoshone Indian servants.

It was said that Carter's home was open to all, and that he loved to entertain and did so frequently. Distinguished visitors included Generals Sheridan, Harney, and Augur; scientists Dr. Joseph Leidy of the Academy of Natural Sciences of Philadelphia, paleontologist O. C. Marsh of Yale, and Ferdinand V. Hayden, leader of the U.S. Geological and Geographical Surveys—all well-known scientific dignitaries who stopped or even headquartered their base of operations at Fort Bridger while they conducted local research. Chief Washakie was an occasional guest for dinner. Also, the Carters threw an annual open-house Christmas party.[12]

And like other well-established sutlers, Judge Carter knew that his long-range economic well-being depended on political connections, so he took the time and the trouble to nuture his supporters. He knew the president of the United States, the Secretary of War, the congressmen who affected his region of the world, Judges Gould and Dillon, Union Pacific Railroad directors, and John and Robert Garrett of the Baltimore and Ohio Railroad. He also established cordial and long-lasting relations with the Indian Bureau, the U.S. Post Office, members of the Zion Cooperative Mercantile Institute, and an assortment of army generals.

When Carter went to Washington in 1867 to make his appeal, he stressed that he had been the sutler at Fort Bridger for ten years. His home and all of his property, including a steam sawmill, blacksmith shop, carpenter shop, and house, were located on the military reservation. Every building had been approved by the commanding officer. It was impracticable for him to remove his goods by the July 1 deadline he had received. He referred to his long service as a soldier, underlined his service as a sutler to miners, emigrants, and civilians as well as to the military, and stressed his functionary roles as the local postmaster and U.S. commissioner.

Carter pleaded his case with individual congressmen and submitted a written appeal. Not content with his effort to date, he persuaded Senator Pomeroy of Kansas to introduce a joint legislative bill to authorize the Commanding General of the Army to permit trading establishments on isolated frontier military posts.

Between the time that President Grant received Carter's appeal and the time he responded, he'd decided that it was desirable to encourage settlement and cultivation on the line of travel through Indian country.[13] His decision may have been partly influenced by a report of the inspection of Fort Bridger written by Brevet Brigadier General Babcock. Babcock reported that the reserve was very large and that settlement on the reservation was not encouraged. The situation provided sutler Carter with a monopoly on virtually all civilian services needed by the post and its personnel. Babcock thought the situation was unhealthy and recommended that civilian settlement near the post would be encouraged if the 625-square-mile military reservation at Fort Bridger was reduced to 40 square miles.[14]

Babcock's recommendation was acted upon a few years later, but Carter also achieved his goals. Although President Grant responded, on an official level, that the sutler's post had to be discontinued, he recommended that Carter be allowed to continue milling and farming on the military reservation. In addition, Pomeroy's bill was passed in the form of a resolution to authorize the Commanding General of the Army to permit traders to remain at military posts located between 100 degrees longitude and the eastern boundary of California:

Resolved by the Senate and the House of Representatives of the United States of America in Congress assembled that the Commanding General of the army shall be authorized to permit a trading establishment to be maintained after the first day of July 1867 at any military post on the frontier, not in the vicinity of any city or town, and situated at any point between the 100th meridian of longitude, west from Grenwich and the eastern boundary of the state of California when, in his judgement, such establishment is needed for the accommodation of emigrants, freighters, and other citizens: provided, that after the Commissary departments shall be prepared to supply stores to soldiers as required by law, no trader permitted to remain at such post shall sell any goods kept by the Commissary department to any enlisted men.[15]

Two months later, the Commissary General of Subsistence was relieved of having to carry out Section no. 25 of the July 28, 1866, statute, and was informed that sutlers at posts between 100 degrees west longitude and the eastern border of California would, "after July 1, 1867, be retained until further orders, as traders under resolution of Congress March 30, 1867." To complete the reversal of the order banning post sutlers, the Adjutant General authorized General Order no. 58 on May 30, 1867, which permitted sutlers to continue to trade until further orders.[16]

Commissary General Thomas Eaton saw sutlers as an embarrassment to the efficiency of his regime. A few months after the July 1867 deadline for sutlers to vacate the premises of military posts, his annual report said that the issue of supplying the men of the service had been settled. The army had been well supplied with food, and all posts now kept "supplies of articles not embraced in the ration, sold at a price sufficient to reimburse the department." In addition, line officers acting as commissaries of subsistence for extra pay were making issues to troops. Eaton was satisfied that the system obviated the need for sutlers—which, he reminded his audience, were then prohibited by law, except as mere traders.

Before the summer of 1867 was out, General Grant modified General Order no. 58 to read that any number of traders could practice their trade at military posts, subject only to regulations imposed by the commanding officer. His intent here was to encourage further settlement on military reservations by giving unlimited persons permission to open trading establishments.[17] The post commander, however, retained the right to restrict licensing to one person if circumstances seemed appropriate.

The president's order created a brief period when post traders competed for trade at the same military post. A few posts like Fort Davis, Texas, used multiple authorized traders in the late 1860s. At Fort Stockton, "Don Pedro" Gallagher, Thomas Johnson, George B. Lyles, and Joseph Friedlander all served as authorized traders.[18] General Philip Sheridan, commanding, Department of the Missouri, supported the concept of competition. On November 4, 1868, when Captain Clous at Fort Hays asked him to revoke the appointment of Mr. Warren, the current trader, so that the representative of the parties conducting the store, Mr. Hill Wilson, might be appointed in his place, Sheridan refused. He said he could not revoke Warren's license, "as there must be some fixed system adopted so that there may be some security for Traders," in accordance with the new regulations. He had no objection, however, to appointing several traders on the request of the majority of the officers and the commanding officer.[19]

The reinstatement of the army sutler in 1867, almost immediately after the order for his removal, created pockets of confusion, concern, and dismay among the troops. Several officers addressed letters to their men to explain the ruling of the Adjutant General on the status and function of these new post traders. In his letter of April 17, 1868, Major Buchannan of the Fifth Military District underlined the rule that the new trader, unlike the sutler of old, would not possess a lien on pay or sit at the pay table. He relayed the Judge Advocate General's opinion that "in the present state of the law, no military order, and nothing short of legislation of Congress will invest sutlers with a lien on the pay of regular soldiers, or authorize them to appear at the pay table and receive any part of such soldier's pay from the paymaster." Then he described the trader's new status as solely that of a regular merchant, except that he worked on the military reservation. As such, he was allowed to sell for cash or on credit, as he might find to his advantage.[20]

Brevet Major General Christopher C. Augur, commanding officer for the Department of the Platte, published his explanatory letter in the *United States Army and Navy Journal.* He too explained that the sutler, now called post trader, held a monopoly on the post where he was stationed, but was not permitted to place a lien on the soldier's pay.[21] Buchannan thought the sutler was required to pay a per-head tax to the post fund for the privilege of operating a store at the post, but Augur's letter clearly stated that there is no tax on sutlers or traders. It had been wholly abolished by July 28, 1866 law established by joint resolution of Congress March 30, 1867. It is not deemed so far analogous to that of sutler as to permit the imposition upon the trader of any such tax as that formerly under the regulations of sutlers.

Not only is the trader not appointed by the authority who was empowered to make Army Regulations—the Secretary of War: that he is not appointed for the special use or convenience of troops, but for the accommodation of emigrants, freighters, and other citizens. Moreover, instead of being the sole or chief vendor of miscellaneous goods, he is generally restricted to the sale of certain articles. It is held that he cannot be legally or equitably subjected to a tax therefore.[22]

Sutler or trader, reinstatement of the civilian trader appears to have been justified. While sutlers in the narrow longitudinal corridor (like William Carter) were extending their economic networks, Commissary General Eaton was pleading for assistance. Under Section no. 25 of the act of July 28, 1866, which still applied to the majority of posts, his Subsistence Department was required to maintain an inventory of certain goods formerly supplied by sutlers for sale to officers and enlisted men. Department operations depended on details (work assignments) from the ranks of noncommissioned officers or privates to act as storekeepers to assist officers responsible for stores. There was little personal incentive for efficiency. In his 1869 annual report, Eaton obliquely confessed that the Subsistence Department was experiencing difficulties, stating that

> there cannot usually be obtained from the ranks of the army for this service, a class of the proper requirements. This defect is not the greatest evil this department labors under. Some measure should be adopted which gives the officers who are made responsible for the commissary supplies at each post more reliable assistance than they are usually able to obtain by detail from the ranks of the army. I recommend that the Secretary of War select non-coms with five years of service or civilians and make them commissary sergeants."[23]

The army's attempt to do without the sutler was not working.

The situation remained unchanged until the spring of 1870. Now the army had more than a hundred military posts west of the Missouri,

Post Traderships in the West, ca. 1870.[24]

Texas	16
Dakota	9
Wyoming	8
Kansas	7
Colorado	4
New Mexico	9
Nevada	2
Montana	4
Minnesota	3
Utah	2
Indian Territory	4
Oregon	4
Nebraska	6
Arizona	11
California	4
Washington	1
Idaho	2
Washington Territory	4
Dakota Territory	2
TOTAL	102

and still only those posts located within the corridor between the 100th meridian and the eastern border of California were allowed one or more post traders on the military reservation. Officers and men at army installations east and west of this favored zone complained loudly and at length about being unfairly deprived of a trader's establishment.[25]

President Grant's new Secretary of War, William Belknap, forwarded a proposal to the House of Representatives' Committee on Military Affairs on April 20, 1870, titled "Sales to Enlisted Men by Post Traders." He pointed out that the Subsistence Department of the army had unsuccessfully requested a special three-million-dollar appropriation for articles to meet the reasonable needs of officers and soldiers. Since that appropriation seemed unlikely, military servicemen would continue to be deprived by law "of the convenience of a sutler's establishments." He then recommended repealing the March 30, 1867, resolution that prohibited post traders from "selling to enlisted men of the army goods kept for sale by the commissary dept."[26]

Belknap suggested that the current ruling smacked of favoritism. In its place, Congress should uniformly legitimize the post-trader establishment. And since post traders were to be "entirely subject to military authorities," he did not believe that "the benefit and convenience resulting from such an engagement of their privileges would be offset by any detriment to the public service or the army."[27] Belknap was saying that the new army post-trader position would not be filled by the rule-breaking, whiskey-peddling sutler who had given the Civil War volunteer regiments so many headaches. Belknap was also acknowledging that the sutler still filled a definite need—one that the army had been either unable or unwilling to fill. At least for the nonce, he was indispensable.

Congress gave Belknap his way. The final statute, which was passed on July 15, 1870, read, in part, that "the Secretary of War is authorized to permit one or more trading establishments to be maintained at any military post on the frontier not in the vicinity of any city or town when he believes such an establishment is needed for the accommodation of emigrants, freighters or other citizens."[28]

To persons associated with the army, the term *sutler* had always evoked the image of a very specialized profession. The term *post trader*, however, was a generic term used throughout the 1800s, that included independent fur traders, managers of government factories, employees of large trading companies and associations, and Indian traders. A military post trader might hold a license to trade with the Indians, but his primary license and general behavior was controlled by army approval.

The Indian Bureau (part of the Interior Department), not the War Department, controlled the issuance of Indian trading licenses. A June 7, 1871, army circular from Adjutant General E. D. Townsend reiterated the status of the new military post trader: he was appointed by the act of July 15, 1870, under the authority of the Secretary of War, who furnished him with a letter of appointment that identified the post to which he was appointed. The trader was not subject to the rules prescribed by Article no. 25 or paragraphs 196 or 197, Army Regulations of 1863, in regard to sutlers, because that office had been abolished. No tax or burden could be imposed on him, nor was he allowed "the privilege of the pay table." He was, however, permitted to erect buildings and conduct business "on that part of the military post to which he may be assigned as the C.O. may direct," and which was expected to be "within convenient reach of the garrison."[29]

More important to men interested in applying for future vacancies, the post trader had an "exclusive privilege" to trade upon the military reserve to which he was appointed. No other person was allowed to peddle or trade goods within the limits of the reserve.[30]

An 1872 circular then defined the manner in which rates and prices were to be fixed for the sutler's goods:

> (1) The Council of Administration, where there is a Post Trader, will examine, from time to time, his goods and invoices for goods of sale, and will, subject to the approval of the post C.O., establish the rates and prices (which should be fair and reasonable) and which specific items will be sold. A copy of the list will be posted in the traders store. (2) In determining the rate of profit, the Council will consider the prime cost, freight, other charges and the fact that while the trader pays no tax or contribution to the post fund for his exclusive privileges, he has no lien on the soldiers' pay and is without security once enjoyed by the sutlers of the army. (3) The trader will carry on the business himself, and habitually reside at the station at which he is appointed. He will not transfer, sublet, sell or assign his business to others. (4) He will be allowed 90 days to comply with the circular. (5) Post Commanders will report to the War Department any failure of the post trader to comply with the circular."[31]

The new post trader, who in this manner was placed under the control and protection of the military, was officially reclassified as a camp follower. The army sutler's profession had come full circle. Until 1822, he had been a lowly, scrambling camp follower, a peddler who was forced to fend for himself beyond the protective walls of the post, yet subject to the whim of his unit or post commander. During the following four decades, the sutler's reputation improved, the value of his services to the army was recognized, and his business evolved into a profession. The army gave him social status equal to that of an officer and backed him with regulations. At the end of the Civil War, the Regular Army sutler had been lumped together with his unprincipled cousin who had served with the militia, and he was extirpated from the army. Now, although his functions once again were receiving official sanction, the army had plucked his personal perquisites and he had been downgraded to his pre-1822 status.

He was a camp follower once again.

ELEVEN

Patronage and the Military Post Trader

> As Post Trader establishments are entirely subject to military authorities it is not believed that the benefit and convenience resulting from such an engagement of their privileges would be offset by any detriment to the public service or the army.—William W. Belknap, Secretary of War, Letter to House of Representatives, March 1870

When Congress passed the 1870 statute to authorize one or more post traders at each military installation, it unwittingly gave Secretary of War William Belknap total control over the lucrative world of post trading. The bill, as passed, specified that each post should have but one trader, and it relocated post-trader-appointment authority (both to hire and fire) from military post officers to the Secretary of War.

The post-trader bill, attached to a congressional appropriations bill, was objected to by Senator Nye of Nevada on the grounds that it would created a monopoly for traders, but the statute was backed by Senator Wilson, the chairman of the Military Committee—the same Wilson who had led the fight to control sutlers during the Civil War— so it passed without amendment.[1] Although the post-trader slot allegedly was created to serve emigrants and local settlers, an Adjutant General observed much later that the army ended up with substantially the same system that previously operated under the name of sutler.[2]

If the centralization of power tends to encourage graft, Secretary of War William Belknap proved the age-old adage that power corrupts and absolute power corrupts absolutely. No sooner was the ink dry on the statute than Belknap's wife promised the post tradership at Fort Sill to a friend of the family, Caleb P. Marsh. If this transaction had been an isolated incident in an otherwise untarnished record, Belknap might have gotten away with a slapped wrist, but the Secretary of War doled out this kind of patronage to a number of select associates—comrades who profited financially from the middleman game of matching post-tradership slots with those seeking to acquire either a new license or one up for renewal.

Patronage, the use of one's position and political power to benefit or reward friends and relatives, was an accepted management principle of the day. And patronage was the rule rather than the exception during the administration of President Grant. During the first half of the 1870s, while the Tweed political machine took millions of dollars from taxpayers in New York City, eager antiadministration politicians uncovered a series of scams, including the DeGolyer or "District of Columbia Ring," the Credit Mobilier of America scandal, and the "Whiskey Ring." This last flimflam funneled sales dollars from distillers and distributors into a campaign fund to support Grant for a second term. General John McDonald, a Grant appointee who served several years in prison for his role in the scandal, said that Grant had been a "god-father to its christening," and that Grant's private secretary, General Babcock, had taken an active role in the direction of the affair.[3]

Stories of irregularities in the appointments of military post traders reached Washington ears in 1872, but a pro-Grant congressional investigating committee obfuscated the issue until public interest waned. As a result, Belknap's covert role in peddling post traderships was not revealed. Three years later, a newspaper exposé on the sale of post-trader licenses pointed the finger at President Grant's brother, Orvil, and Secretary of War William Belknap. When Belknap's role was eventually revealed to the public, Democrats and anti-Grant newspapers lined both sides of the gauntlet and called for his resignation.[4]

One of the first men who worked to expose influence peddling in the assignment of post traders was Lieutenent Colonel William B. Hazen. A maverick army officer who had a surfeit of integrity and honesty as well as a great capacity for righteous indignation, Hazen had been an instructor of military tactics who made brevet brigadier general in the Civil War.

While Hazen was at Fort Hays, Kansas, in 1871, he assembled information about the sale of post traderships and passed it to his friend, Congressman James Garfield. Garfield was a major general of volunteers during the Civil War, a one-time chairman of the House Military Affairs Committee, and eventually the twentieth president of the United States. In February 1871, Hazen told Garfield that the system of exclusive sutlers was evil, leading the sutler to bribe the officer and rob the soldier, "selling at cost to the former and overcharging the latter."[5] Traders were also allowed to farm out their privileges, which formerly they could not do.[6] And as the Secretary of War had refused to appoint but one trader per post, the 1870 law recreated the "exclusive sutler of olden times without any of the checks we formerly held over him."

Hazen alleged that he knew of one trader who had paid five thousand dollars per year for the privilege of an exclusive license, and the Fort Sill trader, John S. Evans, was paying C. P. Marsh of New York City twelve thousand dollars per year to trade. Evans was to pay Marsh as long as Belknap was Secretary of War.[7] These sums would have to be made up by overcharging the troops.

The year Hazen wrote Garfield about the sutler, he authored a book titled *The School and the Army in Germany and France,* in which he examined military schools and the character of the German and French officers. He used the opportunity to bluntly critique the United States Army for its imbalance in line-staff ratios, its inadequate military education system, and its practice of retaining officers with undesirable character traits.

Hazen also voiced his complaint against the army's "inept handling" of the post–Civil War post trader, leveling charges at the army's Subsistence Department for its deliberate intention of not shouldering the responsibilities of the sutler's enterprise. Officers of that department, he charged, viewed the additional tasks as degrading. He further accused that department of using the excuse that the Congress had not made a special appropriation. The Adjutant General excused them, said Hazen, even though "the appropriation for the Subsistence Department was so large, that none was asked for the following year."[8]

Garfield responded to Hazen by saying "there appears to be a ring of Iowa men, either relatives or intimate friends of the Secretary, who are concerned in the business of Post trading, and Colburn [chairman, Committee on Military Expenditures] is apprehensive that it will appear that the Secretary is seriously implicated in the matter."[9] He said he thought they should proceed to expose the group, then promptly gave Hazen's letter to a New York *Tribune* reporter.

The *Tribune* published Hazen's letter on February 16, 1872, with an editorial that said the War Department was involved in influence peddling. When, as a result, Hazen was called to testify before the Army Military Affairs Committee, he said that in his opinion, the purpose of the 1870 law was to place post traders outside the control of officers and to give control to the Secretary of War, who made the appointments.

When Belknap heard the news, he ordered General Irwin McDowell, commander of the Military Department of the East, to draft a circular to require post traders to take charge of their own business and to reside at the post where they traded. No longer were they to farm out, sublet, transfer, or assign the business to others. Belknap also required the Council of Administration of each post to oversee trader prices and activities.[10]

Four years later, when Colonel Hazen testified a second time before the Military Affairs Committee on irregularities in the appointments of post sutlers, he alleged that John Colburn, who chaired the 1872 investigating committee inquiry, had covered up Belknap's misdoings. After Colburn screamed "foul," the New York *Times* said that Colburn had been given all details and his committee had been invited to probe, but never did.[11]

So in 1872, a partisan Military Affairs Committee let the incipient scandal subside. To prevent other officers from staging a repeat of Hazen's performance, Belknap issued what Lieutenant Colonel George Armstrong Custer called a "gag order." Custer—who also testified during the 1876 sutler probe—said that, according to Belknap's order, no officer after March 15, 1873, was to "directly or indirectly, suggest or recommend action by members of Congress for or against military affairs." All petitions to Congress relative to subjects of military character were to be forwarded through the General of the Army and Belknap's office for action. In addition, any officer visiting the seat of government during a congressional session was to register his name at the Adjutant General's office upon his arrival, as well as address a letter to the Adjutant General of the Army "reciting the purpose of and the time that will be embraced by his visit and the authority under which he is absent from his command or station."[12]

In 1873, Colonel Hazen was transferred to an obscure post in the Dakota Territory. In the absence of any public outcry, newspaper headlines turned to other matters, and the issue was soon forgotten.

Three years later in the fall of 1875, the issue of selling post-trader slots reappeared when reporter for the New York *Herald* Ralph Meeker wrote a series of articles on western military-post scandals. His investigation indicted the War Department for being directly involved in the sale of post traderships. When details that implicated William Belknap were published in February 1876, both the *Herald* and the New York *Times* called for a full investigation.

In the first week of March 1876, the Secretary of War was called to testify before the Committee on Military Affairs. When confronted with information that Mr. Marsh had paid Mrs. Belknap for the privilege of becoming a post trader, Belknap refused to deny the truth. The following day, the New York *Times* called for Belknap's resignation.[13]

In a frightful hurry, Belknap rushed apologetically to ask President Grant to accept his resignation. The following day, the entire first page of the New York *Times* examined the world of the military post trader. In addition to loading its front page with reviews, interviews, hypotheses, and hearsay, all in equal proportions, the *Times* suggested that Belknap be impeached in spite of his resignation.[14]

Caleb P. Marsh advised the *Times* that initially he paid the Belknap household ten thousand dollars per year in quarterly payments. After two years, he reduced payments to six thousand dollars per year because profits at the post had dropped. By 1876 the Belknaps had accepted payments totaling twenty thousand dollars.[15]

At the very least, Belknap was liable for a fine of three times the amount he had received and possible imprisonment of up to three years. On the basis of what Congress had learned to date, it voted unanimously to impeach Belknap, but since he had already resigned, the Senate questioned its impeachment authority.

Through March and April, the New York *Times* became the voice for information about post traderships. The paper printed every incoming missive that shed any light on the scope, substance, or personalities involved in influence peddling. As the case proceeded, the paper printed stories about a variety of allegedly nefarious activities by post traders. Interviews made particularly interesting reading. Post trader Evans told the *Times* he had issued charges against Belknap to the Military Committee more than a year before. With the backing of officers at Fort Sill, he had furnished a list of witnesses to his claims. He said he had also written the president (a claim later verified by the *Times*). Evans believed the only event that resulted from his attack was that he was cashiered from the army.[16]

Follow-up articles alleged that trader Evans and his partner, Smith, had paid five thousand dollars for the Cheyenne agency, and that Evans & Co. had paid ten thousand dollars for the Fort Sill post tradership. Evans and Smith claimed they had obtained their tradership licenses from the president's brother, Orvil Grant, and that Orvil represented Belknap. They said that when Orvil could not get the price he wanted, he accepted merchandise. He knew the market value of each post tradership and made the post traders come to his terms.[17]

March 7, 1876, was a busy day in the bubbling post-trader scandal. A warrant was issued for William Belknap; Orvil Grant was indicted; Caleb P. Marsh fled to Canada; and by direction of the president, the Adjutant General's office sent a letter to all military post commanding officers asking them to report whether they believed the appointment of the current trader should be revoked. If such was the case, the commanding officer was to convene the Council of Administration and select a suitable replacement. All paperwork was to be sent to the office of the Secretary of War.[18]

At first Orvil Grant denied everything, but a reporter's interview with two traders contradicted him. Post traders Bonnofon and Casselberry reported that they paid Orvil Grant 33 percent of their profits on all sales.[19] The March 16 issue of *The Nation* branded Orvil Grant as a man "entirely devoid of a sense of honor," and a good illustration of the "moral tone of 'administration circles.'"

The following month, Congress sent a true bill against Belknap for accepting bribes, and in May 1876 the Senate confirmed they had jurisdiction against Belknap, so this particular scandal became common newspaper reading throughout the summer. Congress eventually tried Belknap, but it couldn't muster sufficient votes to impeach him, nor did it pursue him with a civil indictment. Belknap was acquitted because twenty-three members of Congress insisted it had no jurisdiction.[20]

While Congress conducted its farcical exercise, the House Committee on Expenditures in the War Department, under the direction of Chairman Clymer, took testimony from officers, post traders, territorial governors, congressmen, Indian agents, and those accused of improprieties in the appointment of post traderships. The committee's report, "Management of the War Department," left no doubts about the pervasiveness of graft and corruption in this War Department function. The committee documented partnerships, mutually profitable arrangements, paybacks, and bribes at ten posts on the Upper Missouri: Fort

Benton, Fort Peck, Fort Buford, Fort Stevenson, Fort Abraham Lincoln, Fort Rice, Standing Rock, Fort Sully, Lower Brule, and Fort Randall. Outside of the Missouri River Valley, the committee learned that post traderships had been obtained, purchased, leased, and retained through political influence, cash payments, or both at seven forts in Texas, Oklahoma, and Wyoming, including Fort Griffin, Fort Clark, Fort Concho, Fort Supply, Fort Fetterman, Fort D. A. Russell, and Fort Laramie.

The record was clear, the case simple: once again corruption had followed opportunity and profit. The number of post-trader slots was limited, and it was said that a good sutler could gross twenty-five hundred dollars per year for each military company on post. The most lucrative posts had four or more companies.[21] Belknap, who possessed the authority to hire and fire and to change army regulations, made everything possible. He provided information to a number of men he knew planned to manipulate military post traderships (and Indian traderships) for money. Of all those involved, two of the three most active individuals were retired army generals, J. M. Hedrick of Ottumwa, Iowa, and E. W. Rice of Washington, D.C. The third person was Orvil Grant, the unemployed brother of President Grant.[22]

According to figures published by the investigating committee, General Hedrick earned a minimum of $20,750 between 1871 and 1875 as a broker of post traderships. General Rice, an intimate friend of Belknap, who had been a "same town resident" and had served with him in the Civil War, received no less than $15,250.[23] Hedrick offered his broker's services for two to five thousand dollars per post tradership. He also received a share (usually one-third) of the profits from several post-trader operations. Rice's most lucrative partnership was with three brothers from Ottumwa, Iowa—Joseph, James, and Alvin C. Leighton.[24] They furnished the capital and did all the fieldwork; Rice had only to furnish the information and the political clout. In addition, Rice extracted $10,775 from eleven other post traders as "assessments for political purposes."[25]

Generals Hedrick and Rice fared well because the garrisons of the Missouri River posts they had selected were large, and only one trader was allowed at each post. The trader's profits, therefore, were considerable. George C. Cook, post trader at Fort Wingate from October 1870 to June 1872, earned an estimated profit of fifteen thousand dollars per year, of which he paid General Rice 50 percent. George C. Bennet, supported by the officers at Fort Griffin, applied for the vacant sutlership there, but he lost out to A. C. Leighton. Leighton turned around and offered it to Bennet for $37.50 for each quarter of the year per company of troops. Bennet eventually paid $2,400 per year to Leighton, then he sold out to a man named Hicks for $6,000.[26]

The committee judged that Orvil Grant had used his brother's name and connections to peddle post-trader licenses. By Orvil's own later admission, he had no profession, yet on notice from the president he knew of post-trader openings, "a number from which he drew money from [*sic*] but put none in." The committee's report said that after causing many extant trading licenses to be revoked (military post-trader and Indian-trader licenses), Orvil "appeared on the scene," met with traders, and "haggled over the price to stay in business." Those who paid his price stayed; those who refused lost their post to Orvil's man and had to sell their merchandise at a loss. By 1874, Orvil's team had run the largest supplier of posts along the Missouri, Durfee & Peck, out of business.[27]

Durfee & Peck, described by congressional investigators as a large and responsible firm, had operated on the Missouri River since the mid-1860s. The partners had considerable capital in the transporting of goods, and held military post-trader licenses (some of which were appointed before 1870 and were approved by Councils of Administration) and Indian-trader licenses to conduct business at Fort Sully, Fort Rice, Fort Richardson, and Fort Buford, as well as at the Cheyenne agency and Standing Rock. When Peck had applied to renew his existing licenses, he was refused, and the slots were reassigned to Orvil Grant's men. Even his applications for Indian-trading licenses were refused, at least in those cases where a license would have enabled the individual to compete directly with Orvil Grant. These refusals were in direct violation of existing statutes, but by 1874 Durfee & Peck were without one trading license.[28]

As for President Grant, the committee charged him with having "fixed" everything for his brother, Orvil. He'd informed him when there were vacancies in post traderships at Standing Rock, Fort Peck, and Fort Belknap (and possibly Cheyenne), and cleared the way to oust incumbents.

A number of additional politicians were tarred with the scandal's broad brush: the brother-in-law of the Secretary of War, John Tomlinson, and W. D. W. Bernard, brother-in-law of John C. Dent, who, in turn, was the eldest brother-in-law of President Grant; John F. Athey, a clerk to General W. C. Babcock, Surveyor General of Kansas and

brother of General Orvil E. Babcock, President Grant's private secretary; and General Frederick T. Dent, who served at the White House.
Dent was allegedly responsible for post-trader appointments at Fort
D. A. Russell, Fort Lyons, and several other posts up and down the Rio
Grande, as far as El Paso.[29] Outside Washington, D.C., the name of
Nebraska Senator Thayer appeared several times. He was accused of
having taken more than one thousand dollars in bribes in exchange for
his "support" in post-tradership matters. His subsequent manipulation
of appointments in the post tradership at Fort Washakie (see chapter
13) indicates that bad habits are hard to change.[30]

The manner in which John S. Collins acquired his appointment as
post trader at Fort Laramie is typical of what a man with connections
could do during Grant's administration. It also demonstrates the extent
of President Grant's cronyism.

John Collins and his brother, Gilbert H., were the sons of Eli
Collins, a tanner and leather craftsman who ran a saddlery shop in
Galena, Illinois. Eli Collins and Ulysses S. Grant had been business
partners from 1841 to 1853. Nine years later, in 1864, Eli sold his
business to Orvil Grant. The year their father sold the business, John
and Gilbert moved to Omaha, Nebraska, where they established their
own saddlery and leather-goods shop. Gilbert minded the store while
John made a marketing trip into the western territories. Always based
in Omaha, the brothers successfully developed retail and wholesale
branch stores in the Montana Territory towns of Miles City, Billings,
and Great Falls, and in the Wyoming Territory town of Cheyenne.

On his 1864 tour, John Collins had stopped at Fort Laramie. He
could not have failed to note the density of traffic along the Oregon
Trail or the urgent demands placed upon the post trader by emigrants,
local Indians, and the garrison. When he heard, in 1871, that the post
tradership would soon be available, he decided he would try to get
President Grant to give it to him. To open the door to the White
House, Collins got Orvil Grant to write a letter to White House usher
Frederick T. Dent. Since the 1876 congressional committee revealed
that Dent had taken money for his role in the sale of post traderships, it
is not impossible that Collins's letter to Orvil included a promise of
money.

In his interview with the president on December 28, 1872, John
Collins was up front about his needs: he was a Democrat (a blow
against him) and had no other connections in Washington, but was

hopeful of an appointment as post trader to replace R. S. McCormick and George Arnold at Fort Laramie. President Grant wrote a note that Collins was to take to Secretary of War Belknap. The secretary told Collins that he had a lot of competition, so Collins saw President Grant once more. Grant wrote a second note, which said that if the secretary saw no special reason why Collins should not receive the appointment, or if he had no appointment he especially wanted to make himself, he should give it to Collins, for E. A. Collins and his sons were strong Grant supporters.[31] Upon reading the second letter, Belknap (according to Collins) said that he was sorry that the president had not ordered him to make the appointment. Collins's party affiliation notwithstanding, he received his appointment.[32]

Rumors of influence peddling in the western portion of Wyoming Territory forced its governor, John A. Campbell, to appear before the committee. On March 17, 1876, he denied New York *Herald* accusations that he controlled the appointment and the sale of Wyoming post traderships through his brother, Ian Campbell, and had received one-third of all the profits.

Campbell had a clean administrative record, and he swore that he had never been concerned about post traderships. He said he had heard general rumors about men paying for post traderships, but no one ever complained to him. He added that he had made recommendations for Wyoming posts, but some were accepted and others rejected. Under the old general order of April 11, 1870, he had recommended his brother, Ian, for the post tradership at Fort Fetterman, but that appointment had been revoked before he came to hold the office of territorial governor (he was appointed in June 1870). Campbell readily admitted that he had recommended E. D. Lane at Fort Sanders to General Augur, in October of 1870, and J. D. Wooley for Fort D. A. Russell, as well as recommending the retention of Judge William A. Carter at Fort Bridger. Each of those recommendations had been accepted.[33]

As in most scandals, the hubbub over peddling of post traderships flared and died, taking with it a number of those prominently involved. Aside from assisting the Democrats in their goal of embarrassing President Grant's administration, the scandal added a lasting sour note to the image of the post-trader profession. It was bad enough that the Regular Army post trader had been ejected from the army a decade earlier because of the uncontrolled behavior of a number of volunteer-unit sutlers during the Civil War; now he suffered the additional stain to his reputation because of those who had to pay squeeze to hold their position.

Whether Secretary of War William Belknap originally planned to establish a new field of patronage may be debatable. California State Archivist and Historian William C. Davis believed Belknap was not involved in anything other than the Evans scandal. He said that because twenty to thirty names were submitted for each post in the country, and he was the only one who could make appointments, Belknap was swamped. The "rush" came during a period of record-breaking profits.[34]

But if Mr. Belknap's only character flaw was moral weakness, his behavior between 1871 and 1875 leaves little doubt about his attitude toward patronage. Whatever his reasons, he supported the status quo in which patronage ruled, and he took full and long advantage of his control over the best of the post-trader slots—at least those with enough profit to be handled like a commodity.

TWELVE

The Military Post Trader as Entrepreneur

WAKE UP! NEW MEXICO!
Post Trader's Store
FORT UNION, N.M.
We have, this day opened at Fort Union, an excellent assortment of DRY GOODS, CLOTHING, BOOTS, SHOES, HATS, CAPS, GROCERIES, HARDWARE, QUEENSWARE, ETC. especially adapted to the needs of CITIZENS AND SOLDIERS. We shall endeavor at all times to keep a complete list and sell at reasonable prices. Orders from the different Military Posts and Towns in the territory RESPECTFULLY SOLICITED.—Advertisement by J.E. Barrow & Co., Santa Fe Weekly Gazette, *May 2, 1868*

The post trader's heyday in America—that is, his period of greatest profitability—occurred between 1867 and 1880.[1] During what Robert G. Athearn called a "war-boom-rich" period,[2] the western territories of the continent were rapidly explored and settled. Vacant sections of maps acquired lines indicating new trading routes, the names of new mining complexes, and symbols depicting new frontier posts. Risk takers, who believed that "where there's a will, there's a way," made (and lost) fortunes by driving cattle from Texas to Kansas or Colorado and by freighting tons of equipment, supplies, and food to mining towns and new settlements a thousand miles or more across the plains. The character of the times permitted individuals like Alexander Toponce to make a fortune from hauling flour to a fledgling mining camp where, in a three-month period, supply and demand sent prices soaring from $3.50 to $35.00 per hundredweight.[3]

During this expansive period, the influence of the U.S. Army pervaded all phases of frontier life. Twenty-five thousand troopers garrisoned 116 army posts, more than 100 of which lay west of the Missouri River. The forts not only provided protection; they were sources of jobs, money, and information. They served as a market for goods and services, and their presence signified stability, an important psychological factor for investors. These combined roles placed the army snugly into "the vanguard of western economic development."[4]

Posts like Fort Bridger and Fort Laramie in Wyoming, Fort Union in New Mexico, and Fort Leavenworth in Kansas were oases for cattlemen, freighters, and emigrants. At these posts, at any time of day and on any day of the year, one might find a blacksmith, leather worker, wheelwright, cooper, carpenter, hunter, scout, or guide. The post was a true microcosm of life on the frontier, and within its perimeter the most stellar attraction was the post trader's store.

His emporium was the center of social interaction. Everyone was welcome and everyone's money was good. He offered a cornucopia of necessities from dry goods to plows, and from needles to pickle barrels, trading with transients, settlers, soldiers, and Indians. Messages to assist emigrants were posted to his door—if he had one. At temporary camps, he normally worked from a tent. At permanent posts, his store, post office, and home complex might be carefully crafted from adobe or handhewn stone. At Fort Bowie, the complex of post trader Sidney R. Delong consisted of a clean adobe brick building sixty-five feet by sixty-five feet. A corral, to which an old stone house was attached, was in the rear. The interior of the building was divided into an office, a sales room, several warehouse rooms, a sleeping chamber, an enlisted man's and an officers' bar, a billiards room for officers, and a restaurant and kitchen. Fort Hays, Kansas, boasted one of the finest post-trader stores in the West. Officers had their own clubroom for card playing, drinking, and billiards. Enlisted men, too, had a separate room in which to drink beer and liquor, to gamble, and to relax. The Fort Fetterman, Wyoming, store had a large browsing area and two bars, and officers had one of their own, which irritated bullwhackers and other civilian men at the post who were not allowed entry. At Fort Sill, post trader John Evans maintained a large officers' clubroom that was equipped with a billiards table, card table, and reading material. Under some administrations, Evans was permitted to sell the men wine and whiskey.[5]

Merrill Mattes, former historian at Fort Laramie National Monument, called the post trader's store a shrine of western American history, and compared it to the missions of California and the Alamo of

Texas. "Here the harsh, heroic, kaleido-scopic life of the frontier came into sharp focus," he said. "For over forty exciting years it was a favorite rendezvous for the restless folk who followed the Oregon-California Trail, or who loosely inhabited the Central Plains—soldiers, Indians, traders, travelers, emigrants, bull-whackers, Pony Express riders, stagedrivers, cowboys and ranchers. . . . To all these, the sutler at Fort Laramie was host."[6]

When Colonel Carrington rode west in 1866 to establish posts along the Bozeman Trail, his wife visited the Fort Laramie post-trader's store and wrote:

> The long counter of Messrs. [William] Bullock and [Seth] Ward was a scene of seeming confusion not surpassed in any popular, overcrowded store of Omaha itself. Indians, dressed and half dressed and undressed; squaws, dressed to the same degree of completeness as their noble lords; papooses, absolutely nude, slightly not nude, or wrapped in calico, buckskin, or furs, mingled with soldiers of the garrison, teamsters, emigrants, speculators, half-breeds, and interpreters. Here, cups of rice, sugar, coffee, or flour were being emptied into the looped-up skirts or blanket of a squaw; and there, some tall warrior was grimacing delightedly as he grasped and sucked his long sticks of peppermint candy. Bright shawls, red squaw cloth, brilliant calicoes, and flashing ribbons passed over the same counter with knives and tobacco, brass nails and glass beads, and that endless catalogue of articles which belong to the legitimate border traffic.[7]

Nearly every post trader's store across the West had a bar, a separate saloon where at least beer and wine, if not "high spirits," were served. The options available to customers depended on the attitude of the commanding officer. The saloon at Fort Laramie was visited by Jim Bridger, Kit Carson, and William Cody as well as by Mark Twain, Horace Greeley, Jack Slade, veteran "mountain men," and pale-faced easterners, gentlemen, and desperadoes. "Here, the whole of the fantastic social strata of the frontier assembled and tossed coins at the bartender, blew clouds of foam, gurgled barrels of whiskey, engaged in occasional knifings and shooting scrapes, plotted robberies and assassinations, boasted of Indian scalps and gold nuggets; and dreamed of (or dreaded) a time when this vast, wild land would be tamed and civilized." [8]

According to Fort Laramie's post trader John Collins, the soldiers were a "rough, devil-may-care assortment." Many were refugees from justice, some were former convicts, and nearly all were as tough a lot "as could be sifted through the mesh." The bad ones appeared "with a colt revolver in one bootleg, hunting knife in the other," and if the clerk in his store did not come in contact with them "at the height of their ragge" [sic] it was considered a quiet day.[9]

On paydays, one early Wyoming resident and his friends "used to watch with glee" as soldiers and cowboys got into fights. The guardhouse was usually full of drunks on paydays and there were a lot of desertions.[10] At the extreme, when tempers were fueled on alcohol, someone got shot. On Christmas Day 1872, Peter and William Janis entered the sutler's bar at Fort Laramie. The brothers were progeny of a Cheyenne mother and a respected French scout. Words were exchanged, and both brothers came to a violent end when they were outdrawn by a little-known man named Montrose.[11] In the establishment run by Fort McKavett's (Texas) post trader Sam Wallick, Corporal Ed Coyle shot Private Anton Rosenberger to death on February 9, 1874. No one ever discovered why.[12]

The personality of the post trader was an extension of the rustic atmosphere of his establishment. A newspaper for the Fort Riley community said that "words could never accurately portray [post trader] Moses Waters." It advised that as an antidote to depression or calamity, when "clouds and fog shut one in on every side," the reader should hunt out Moses Waters. "He will cut out the *cheavaux-de-frize* [sic] with melancholy, unloose the dregs of disquiet, eliminate the unrest and cause geniality, bonhomie and content to flow placidly in copious streams."[13]

With considerably less affection, officials at Fort Concho demanded that the post trader evict five prostitutes who resided near his store. The women had already been evicted from the fort's premises. Twenty years earlier, at nearby Fort Clark, a Scotsman named Shaw was chief clerk. This "fat old man who had deserted his wife and family in England" was remembered for proving himself to be an amiable companion, as he enjoyed a few drinks and reading Robert Burns; but he was remembered also for having owned a pet bear named Jacob, which he kept drunk.[14]

More often, as Merrill Mattes reminded his readers, the post trader was a dignified and highly respected individual. He was also a man with a purpose. "Adventurous, shrewd, imaginative, highly capable business man of his time," was a descriptive profile given to John Collins of Fort Laramie, but it also fits successful traders such as William A. Carter of Fort Bridger, James K. Moore of Fort Brown/Washakie, Seth Ward of Fort Laramie, John Evans of Fort Sill, and Robert L. Wilson of Fort Riley. Each was out to make a fortune and to live as he chose. Each took advantage of the unlimited opportunities that existed during the opening of the West during the last third of the nineteenth century.[15]

These energetic traders had a number of traits in common: simple integrity leavened with understanding, humor, and courage. They listened well, in part because news was a worthy commodity; indeed, no one within the post knew more about what was happening than the post trader. They made an effort to be bilingual and to know military policy changes. Each expected to serve, at one time or another, as banker, advisor, father confessor, and even as peacemaker and counselor for the Indians.

Honesty went a long way. When Sergeant Ostrander at Fort Reno, Wyoming, received a field promotion to lieutenant, he was transferred to another post. Before he left, he wanted to settle his debts. He had but part of a month's salary to pay for a horse, a small store account, and two-thirds of a month's board bill. He was due about $385 plus a travel allowance of 10 cents per mile from Reno to his place of enlistment. The post trader credited him with $450 against his forthcoming pay and gave Ostrander a bill of sale for a horse named Billy and $250 in cash. Nine months later at his home in New York, Ostrander got a letter from the sutler that enclosed a draft for $58 on Kountz Brothers, bankers in Omaha. The letter stated that the U.S. paymaster had paid $508.05, not $450.00 on Ostrander's papers.[16]

Courtesy, diplomacy, and fairness also ranked high as desirable traits. These words were often the first in the journals of those who had pleasant dealings with post traders. "The wives were received courteously by the traders, W. G. Bullock and Seth Ward," wrote Mrs. Carrington, "both of whom had lived in the Platte country for years. They assured their visitors that they had nothing to fear from the Indians around the fort."[17] She noted that "whether white man, half-breed, or Indian, Mr. Bullock, a Virginia gentleman of the old school . . . gave kind and patient attention, and his clerks seemed equally ready and capable, talking Sioux, Cheyenne, or English just as each case came to hand."[18]

Dudes from the East came to the West to trade for the fast dollar. The majority quickly discovered there was a shortage of hard cash and that the Indians had seen their kind before and were no longer easy marks.[19] So the run-of-the-mill post trader quit or was removed after a year or two. Few were remembered; they came and went and contributed little. Those who remained, who avoided corruption and graft, and who made an effort to be of service, left their mark. It was this breed to whom one chronicler referred when he wrote that "although troops and commanders came and went, the post trader remained. He was maligned by some, but oldtimers testify that he was usually charming, and admitted to the best social circles."[20]

Mr. William H. Quinette at Camp Supply is a good example. He arrived on the scene as a clerk in 1878 and remained forty-eight years, twenty-one as post trader. After he became the trader, he was admitted to the officer's circle in their "ride to the hounds, lawn croquet and tennis, whist clubs and dances." He offered prizes for baseball games played in front of his store and sponsored field day on the Fourth of July. The Indians attended and Mr. Quinette provided them with fresh beef, and donated cash and prizes.[21]

Fort Laramie had a number of memorable sutlers during the post–Civil War period. The two better known are Seth Ward and John (and his brother Gilbert) Collins. Frontier trader Seth Ward, tagged by some as the Horatio Alger of the fur trade, was born in Virginia on March 14, 1820. At the age of fourteen, he journeyed to Indiana and then to St. Louis. In St. Louis he worked along the river, eventually joining the Lupton Fur Company. By age eighteen he had been introduced to the South Platte River and had found his way into Wyoming and Colorado as a trapper and trader. He made his headquarters at Bent's Fort on the Arkansas, where he trapped for Bent and St. Vrain, and freighted along the Santa Fe Trail between Westport (Kansas City) and Bent's Fort.

In 1845, with financial backing from John Campbell and a partner named William Le Guerrier, Ward set up a trading post at Sandy Point, nine miles west of Laramie on the south side of the river. By 1857 his Indian-trader's license (backed by a five-thousand-dollar bond) authorized him to trade with the Sioux, Cheyenne, Arapahoes, and other Indians visiting his trading posts, all within the upper boundaries of the Upper Plate agency. Working for him were B. B. Mills, William Le Guerrier, Antoine Janis, Joseph Emond, and Charles Guru.

THE TEXT OF SETH WARD'S SUTLER'S LICENSE [22]

To Whom It May Concern:

Know ye that reposing special trust and confidence in the patriotism, fidelity and abilities of Seth E. Ward I do hereby constitute and appoint him Sutler to Fort Laramie, Nebraska Territory in the service of the United States, with all the privileges and immunities appertaining to said situation. He has therefore carefully and diligently to discharge the duties of Sutler, in conformity with the rules established for the government the Army of the States; and he is to be subject to such laws and regulations having reference to Sutlers as now are or, hereafter may be, established. This warrant to continue in force; and to be valid to the fourth day of March in the year one thousand eight hundred and sixty . . . unless sooner revoked by competent authority. Given under my hand at the city of Washington this thirtieth day of April, 1857.

Secretary of War John B. Floyd

Ward became Fort Laramie's second sutler when he bought out Dougherty and Tutt on May 4, 1857. At the end of the first year, his partner, Le Guerrier, died, and William Bullock took his place to become the storekeeper. During his early years at Fort Laramie, Seth Ward built the Laramie toll bridge, under contract with the U.S. government; he controlled hay contracts, at five dollars per ton, and sold dry goods, for which he charged his St. Louis cost plus 25 percent, plus an additional ten cents per pound for transportation; and he sold groceries at St. Louis prices plus 10 percent as well as additional cents per pound for transportation. Ward also sold ponies for $15.00 worth of goods, oxen for $70.00 per yoke, buffalo calf robes for $3.50 each, and beaver skins for $1.00 per pound.[23]

Ward's goods were all transported from St. Louis. Material moved first by river barge or steamer to Nebraska City, where it was put on wagons. Ward's wagon trains in the 1860s consisted of between eighteen and twenty-four wagons, each of which hauled at least five thousand pounds of goods.

Ward was observed as one who gave little personal attention to his business, but who had made a lot of money from it. He had a great deal of stock and no competitors. On some days, he sold one thousand dollars worth of merchandise. Under the management of his capable partner and store manager, William Bullock, Ward moved thousands of bales of furs and robes, brought tons of freight into the West, and became the unofficial supply officer for the surrounding territory. When the Indian Peace Commission came through in 1866 to pacify the Sioux and Cheyenne, his gross trade was twenty-nine thousand dollars.

On May 13, 1868, when he thought the fort was to be closed, Ward listed everything he was willing to sell after ten years as sutler: goods on hand, 3,000 bushels of corn, 136 mules (at $400 per span), 20 mule wagons, 130 yoke of oxen (at $1,020 per team of five yoke of oxen and one wagon), 26 ox wagons, mowing machine, pay press, a house ($8,000 for this comfortable dwelling house, with four rooms, a kitchen, a storeroom, and other conveniences), and a store with two warehouses and a sitting room and sleeping room for the clerk.[24]

Ward acted as an intermediary for S. F. Nuckolls, a western merchant who developed a string of stores. He also acted as an intermediary for some of his less-educated customers, often to pursue claims, by writing letters to Washington, D.C., officials.

Ward developed a cattle herd from about four hundred head in 1868 to four thousand head by 1871, and sold beef to the Indian agent. One transaction brought him $20,700. When he retired in 1871, he sold his local cattle herd for $12,000, and returned to his home in Westport, Missouri, where he raised Durhams on his 485-acre ranch. In his final years, Ward was active in real estate and civic affairs. He was a trustee for William Jewel College, Liberty, Missouri; a member of the Board of Regents; and president of Mastin Bank of Kansas City for eight years. Missouri's prominent Ward Parkway was named after him.[25]

John Collins followed Seth Ward. (The story of how he acquired his license was told in the previous chapter.) In the summer of 1874, he accompanied the army's Sioux expedition into the Black Hills, and when the army established Camp Robinson, Collins became the acting post trader. The following year, President Grant made Collins the secretary for the Sioux Peace Commission, what the editor of Collins's biography referred to as "the formal attempt of the government to renege on treaties with the Sioux" in order to steal the Black Hills.

While negotiating with Indian Chiefs Red Cloud and Spotted Tail, Collins took time to profit from the Black Hills gold-rush business by erecting the Rustic Hotel near Fort Laramie. It opened March 15, 1876, and was used as the headquarters for the Cheyenne and Black

Hills Stage Company. The stage line ran from Laramie, Wyoming, to the notorious gold-mining and gambling town of Deadwood, South Dakota.

Collins opened a branch saddlery shop in Cheyenne that same year. The top of his line, the $130 Collins saddle, was used by Buffalo Bill Cody in his Wild West Show until 1913, and Theodore Roosevelt reportedly used one on his Dakota ranch in the 1880s. When Collins retired, he was able to boast that from Cheyenne to Omaha, leather goods with the name *Collins* would pass as current as gold coin on the range.

Collins operated his Cheyenne store alone until 1886, then formed a partnership with longtime employee John Morrison. During his stay at Fort Laramie, he also became an incorporator of the Nebraska National Bank (in 1882) and developed a ranch on LaBonte Creek (in 1886). He freighted supplies and hired out teams of horses to the army. (Two four-horse teams for a three-week period went for $252.)

As a keen politican and avid hunter, Collins made a fast friend of General Crook. Both he and Crook were hunting enthusiasts, and traveled the mountains and plains of Colorado, Montana, and Wyoming together for twelve years. Collins also knew Webb Hayes, the son of President Hayes, well enough to correspond with him, make saddles for him, and ask him for favors. In 1880, he wrote Webb to ask about the availability of the new post tradership at Fort Niobrara. When he decided his bid was a lost cause, he asked Webb not to mention his interest to the Secretary of War.

John Collins's sutler license was revoked on September 20, 1877. No reason was provided, but if the absence of criticism is indicative of his integrity, John Collins had a good record. His only problem appeared to have been that the commanding officer considered Collins's pet elk, which had the run of the post, to be a nuisance.

The post-sutler appointment went to John's brother, Gilbert, who contributed to the family business income as the head of Collins and Petty, a wholesale establishment for guns, ammunition, and sportsman's gear. When Gilbert died in 1880, John reassumed the position of post trader as interim trader from July 1880 to February 1, 1881.

In 1890, John Collins returned to Omaha, where he helped found a saddle store, the "Collins and Morrison Company." At the age of sixty-one, which he reached in 1900, he retired. At the urging of a publisher friend, he wrote *Across the Plains in 1864.* At his death in 1910, John Collins's estate was worth $187,000.

Seth Ward and John Collins were the counterparts of frontier merchants who had stores in surrounding frontier towns. Merchants were working managers, with a small staff, who spent far more time on business than they did on pleasure. The military post headquarters, on which the post trader was required to reside after 1872, provided some direct and indirect resources and a sense of security. What made some post-trader posts so lucrative was the monopoly over the military reservation, plus the chance to serve all personnel who conducted business with the post.

Forts Randall, Sully, Rice, Stevenson, and Buford, all along the banks of the Missouri River, had reservations of thirty square miles upon which no one was allowed to remain except troops, one sutler, and one contractor. Indian trader Charles Larpenteur wrote bitterly, in 1870, that "on these large military reservations no licensed Indian traders are allowed; but the sutler is allowed to trade with Indians, and they are permitted to come on the reservation. If a licensed trader wishes to establish a post, he cannot do so nearer than 125 miles from the garrison, much too far to receive any protection, and this gives the sutler the monopoly of the Indian trade."[26]

The ruling that kept Indian traders away from the army reservation may have been a holdover from the Civil War. During the war's last years, the army tightened controls to minimize Confederate influence in the West. The American Fur Company was specifically forbidden to trade at Fort Berthold, and probably at other posts along the Upper Missouri. Only the sutler was allowed to trade with the Indians.[27]

Larpenteur also lost his post trader's license. He'd been appointed by General Hancock at St. Paul, Minnesota, but the July 1870 congressional bill allowed only one trader per post, and the new post tradership was given to Alvin C. Leighton, a confidant of license-peddling General Rice.[28]

A monopoly per se, however, did little for a sutler if his post was suddenly closed. After the Civil War, the military shifted its attention and its personnel from the South and Southwest to the Great Plains. As new posts were raised, a number of pre–Civil War posts were abandoned, including fifteen of the thirty posts built in Texas between 1848 and 1861. By 1867, forty-two posts were strewn across the Great Plains. Five years earlier, no military posts had existed in what are now Montana and Idaho, and Fort Randall had been the only permanent post on the riverbanks of the Upper Missouri.[29] The number of military installations accompanying new Indian reservations on or near the Missouri River, above Fort Leavenworth, jumped from one to seven, and the number of troops rose in proportion, from 110 in 1861 to 1,940 in 1870.[30] Forts Rice, Union, Sully, and Berthold were created in 1864. Fort Stevens was added in 1867; then Fort Shaw, and in 1870, Fort Logan. Wyoming Territory, which had only Forts Bridger and Laramie in 1860, now had 3,570 soldiers at seven posts on major routes and near endangered settlements.[31]

Nor was a monopoly particularly advantageous if business was poor because of location or size. In the post–Civil War scramble to position troops where the army thought they were needed, western military posts were situated "in the most improbable parts of the continent," isolated localities to which all food, forage, clothing, and ammunition had to be hauled in wagons and at great cost.[32] Depending on the season, roughness of the terrain, and the quantity of goods, it cost the army from one to four dollars to haul one hundred pounds of freight one hundred miles.[33]

When the cost of maintaining posts became a consideration, the army closed a number of marginal and difficult-to-reach locations. Fort Stanton, New Mexico, for example, was established in 1855 to protect and encourage development along the Rio Grande, but settlement was slow and sparse. The sutlership at this post turned over six times in one year, in part because the garrison was the sutler's only major market.[34]

If an applicant for a post tradership received an assignment to Fort Sill (regardless of the year), or to Fort McPherson, Nebraska (during the 1860s), the size of the post would assure him of a lucrative opportunity. Having a monopoly over Fort Fred Steele, a supply post, was more of a hit-or-miss proposition. The post was designed for a garrison of 3,300 men and 225 officers, but when the troops were away—a condition that lasted from late spring through early fall—the garrison strength was less than 100 men. In the winter, the post might contain 600 to 700 men.[35] And holding the post trader's license at Fort Fetterman was more often than not a marginal proposition, because the post was small and business suffered from a lack of civilians in the area. Between 1870 and 1876, the Fort Fetterman license was shunted from Wilson and Cobb to Coffee and Campbell, then to Tillotson and Cobb. Cobb sold out to Tillotson, who then sold out to another partner in 1881.[36] The majority of traders resided at posts the size of Fort Stevenson, where J. S. Winston kept his license from 1874 to 1881. Stevenson was a two-company post built for a maximum of 238 men, yet from 1869 until it was abandoned, the garrison averaged only 110 men.[37] If Winston was lucky, he had a cooperative Council of Administration, like the one at Fort Concho that allegedly "sampled the sutler's wares, drank his whiskey, smoked his cigars, and winked at the prices he charged."[38] A strict council had the clout to take the wind from a trader's profits.

Because the jurisdiction of the post trader's monopoly was limited to the edge of the military reservation, it did little to eliminate competition. Civilian whiskey traders appeared outside all the posts, hoping to realize the same gain they had received from Indian trade, and off-post merchants made competition lively in the sale of dry goods. At Fort Richardson, post trader J. L. Oldham advertised "Staple and Fancy Dry Goods, Groceries, Boots, Shoes, Hats, and Caps . . . everything required to fill up a General Assortment of Goods suited to the necessities of frontier life." His counterpart in town, S. W. Eastin, countered by advertising that he promised to pay particular attention to military orders.[39] And when Charles Larpenteur took charge of a trading post near Fort Union, he competed against a military sutler and the Northwest Company, which dealt in furs and Indian goods. Larpenteur nonetheless made five thousand dollars for the year from the sale of hides: two thousand buffalo, nine hundred elk, eighteen hundred deer, and one hundred wolves.[40]

Because of the rapid redeployment of the army after the Civil War, and because so many new posts offered the sutler marginal profit, only 20 percent of the 108 sutlers who were post traders in 1870 still held their licenses in 1876.[41]

The sutler's monopoly became a major factor in profitability when his market began to expand. Before the Civil War, the post trader's primary customers were the garrison troops. By the mid-1870s, although the average garrison had more than doubled from under 100 men to 205 men since the 1830s, military business became the successful sutler's secondary market. Now he sold to emigrants, freighters, explorers, government parties, miners, settlers, and military troops passing through as well as to the garrison. He stocked barrels of staples, sold agricultural hardware and tools, and offered clothing for the whole family. He sold livestock. What he didn't have on hand he mail ordered through a network of wholesalers and retailers from coast to coast.

The 1877 order book of Fort Washakie's post trader, James K. Moore, listed more than 650 different items—everything from nursing bottles, knit jackets, and axle grease to nippers, copper rivets, candlesticks, and hats. Moore did business with wholesalers in New York, Boston, San Francisco, Chicago, and St. Louis.[42] His liquor, which came from Denver Brewing, was shipped to Bryan, Wyoming, and then freight-forwarded to the post.

Peck of Durfee & Peck told an 1876 congressional investigating committee that the gross value of goods sold to soldiers at Fort Sully came to between $50,000 and $75,000 per year—$250 per man. When it was pointed out that the per-man amount was more than twice what a soldier made, Peck said he meant sales to everyone at the post.

An aggressive post trader stabilized his economic position by trading with local Indian tribes. A number of the post traders who became sutlers prior to the Civil War started out as Indian agents or Indian traders, including Captain George Kennerly (Jefferson Barracks), Benjamin O'Fallon, John Kinzie (Fort Dearborn), Samuel C. Stambaugh (Fort Snelling), Hiram Rich (Fort Leavenworth), John Dougherty (Forts Kearny and Laramie), John Tutt (Fort Laramie), Charles E. Galpin (Fort Rice, North Dakota), and Seth Ward (Fort Laramie). By 1870 the military post that was not accessible to at least one local Indian tribe was in the minority. Besides, trade with the Indians was more lucrative than post business, because there was no price control over goods sold to the Indians. Prices were regulated by supply and demand, and by the number of traders in the area.[43]

At James K. Moore's post–trader establishment at Fort Washakie, furs were a lucrative business until the early 1880s. Every year as creditor for the Shoshones' annual fall hunt, he doled out dry goods, soap, matches, tobacco, cloth, ammunition, and lead. In 1879 he spent twenty-five thousand dollars on inventory to service two thousand Indians for the year. When the Indians returned in the spring, he paid them according to market prices. He bundled furs in one of his two presses: one for buffalo robes that created a three-hundred to four-hundred-pound bale about four feet square, and a smaller one for pelts.

Each Indian bought and paid for one item at a time. To avoid congestion in the store, Moore gave each Indian his own account and used Indian trade tokens, after the practice of William Carter at Fort Bridger. The brass coins, similar to the sutler tokens of Civil War days, served as change. Moore also issued them as credit chits to pay Indians for services rendered, such as livestock recovery, sawing logs, and freighting materials. The Shoshones called them *Boha-boo-u-way*, yellow money.[44] In 1878, Moore shipped a railroad car full of buffalo hides to Boston, and as late as 1881, the Shoshones sold him two thousand buffalo robes. By 1885, however, the buffalo had disappeared, and the Shoshone hunting range was restricted by a treaty stipulation.

Indian peace treaties were also occasions for considerable profit for the post trader. A visitor to Fort Laramie in the mid-1860s observed that it was "manifestly to the advantage of the sutler and agents that some treaty be made, for the reason that every Indian treaty involves the giving of many presents and other valuable considerations. Whatever the Indians may finally receive become articles of exchange in trade. In this the astute sutler profits largely, as the Indian has little knowledge of the intrinsic value of manufactured goods and the sutler enjoyed exclusive rights of traffic with them at the posts."[45] The last treaties were conducted in 1869, and the the treaty system was abolished in 1871.

Second in line to the Indian trade was the army contract. The average soldier loathed the effort involved in building, cutting, and gathering hay and wood, and making adobe brick. The Secretary of War sided with the private. He believed that supplies were considerably cheaper if they could be obtained locally, and he thought contracting with civilians was a far superior use of time, money, and materials.[46] Local civilian services were most often obtained by offering contracts for bid.

In 1870, the army used 125,762 cords of wood. Prices per cord, which ranged from $111 at Fort Sedgewick in 1865 (but only $67 per cord in 1867) to a low of $8 at Forts Fetterman and Washakie, Wyoming Territory, in 1880, reflected the cost of transportation.[47] Although local settlers always bid on such contracts, they often went to the post trader. At Fort Washakie, post trader James K. Moore won the contract several years in a row; post traders Lee and Reynolds, William Carter, and John Hunton all successfully sought wood contracts at their respective posts, and normally hay contracts as well.

When Seth Ward secured his first hay contract in 1859, he subcontracted the work to Charles Harvey. Harvey agreed to cut, cure, and stack fifty tons for Ward for five dollars per ton. Ward provided the tools and paid him two-thirds of the contract during the process, and the last third after all was tallied.[48] John Hunton, the post trader at

Fort Laramie in the 1880s, also landed wood contracts (among other supply contracts) for Fort Fetterman between 1871 and 1881. In 1880, after paying Nick Janis thirteen dollars per ton for wood, he paid to have it freighted across one hundred miles of wild terrain, and sold it to the quartermaster at Fort Fetterman for sixty dollars per ton. In contrast, the price of hay at Fort Shaw (Montana) between 1874 and 1880, where it was available locally, remained in the neighborhood of twelve dollars per ton.[49]

Some traders, like William A. Carter, post trader at Fort Bridger, maintained a corner on army contracts. Before the military reservation was severely reduced in 1870 to twenty-five square miles, Carter had more than four hundred square miles of land that he alone could lease from the army. As a result, he had a competitive edge on contracts for nearly everything the army required. According to a clerk named Adams, with Leighton and Jordan at Fort Buford, contracts with the U.S. Army, for supplies and transportation to posts strung along the Upper Missouri River, were rigged. They were let by bids, but there was no competition. He said that the traders colluded to make sure each secured his proper share of the business without a reduction of rates.

Post traders were required to freight in their own supplies. A number of them turned this required cost of operations into a profitable enterprise by offering freighting services to the army and local settlers. John Dougherty saw the advantage in the late 1840s, a full decade before the days of the large army freighting firm of Majors and Waddell. Sidney Delong's freighting operation between Kansas and Santa Fe consisted of twenty-five ten-mule and ten ox teams. Three to four teams, which represented an investment of between $50,000 and one hundred thousand dollars, were always on the road. And because a round trip in 1870 took three to four months, Delong always maintained three sets of stock: one out on credit to miners, soldiers, and settlers; a second on the road, and a third on his shelves.[50]

Among the more unusual, yet logical and profitable freighting enterprises, were the steamboats owned by Alvin C. Leighton, who held the post tradership at Fort Buford. Like Franklin Steele of the 1850s, Leighton shipped his supplies upriver from St. Louis. He owned at least two steamboats—the *F. Y. Bachellor*, named after Joseph Leighton's wife Fanny Bachellor, and the *Eclipse*.[51]

Leighton's firm, Leighton & Jordan, exemplified another profitable sideline—the frontier banking institution. The bank nearest to Fort Buford was located at Miles City. Leighton and Jordan usually kept their deposits in St. Paul. When a soldier or hunter received a check or draft or currency for wages, he deposited it with Leighton's firm. He could then obtain goods or cash from his account. Large deposits provided Leighton & Jordan with its working capital. The same practice was followed by Leighton's store at Williston.[52]

Financial affairs for the army in the early years were conducted through the assistant treasurer's office in New York City. To transmit papers to New York and return them to Fort Laramie took four months.[53] Under the management of Bullock and Ward (1858–1871), the Fort Laramie sutler's store served as a chief supply house and the chief banking institution for hundreds of miles around. Promissory notes amounting to thousands of dollars each and checks and deposits of credit "to be paid from Utah to Ireland and from Montana to Virginia" passed through the hands of the sutler and his agents.[54]

F. E. Conrad, who had been appointed post trader at Fort McKavett, Texas, until 1870, linked up with Indian trader Charles Rath in a sutler store at Fort Griffin. In addition to his military market, Rath grubstaked buffalo hunters with guns, ammunition, cash, and provisions. He was the town banker, so he purchased a large safe in which patrons could keep money.[55] The trader at Fort Sill provided complete banking services, including loans at interest rates comparable to banking institutions. In 1878, when Congress failed to appropriate money for troops, he gave credit to everyone and continued to cash pay vouchers.[56] His counterpart at Fort Laramie, William Bullock, occasionally arranged to receive thousands in cash so he could pay off the troops at the post.[57]

Cattle and horse ranches were favorite and successful post-trader enterprises, particularly where horses could be sold to the army and the beef to the local Indian agent. In addition to Ward's cattle operations (mentioned previously), William Carter built a substantial herd in southwest Wyoming. When he had twenty-five hundred, he decided, on the advice of Shoshone Chief Washakie, to move them to the vicinity of Cody, Wyoming. There, the herd eventually exceeded twenty thousand head.[58] In the Wind River Valley, not far away, post trader James Moore formed a cattle company in 1876 in partnership with Fort Washakie's commanding officer, Robert A. Torrey. They ran cattle north of the Shoshone reservation and sold cattle to the Indian agency to meet treaty annuity requirements. Moore also had his own JK-brand horse ranch. Leighton also dealt heavily in horses and cattle in the

1880s. While Sioux Indians were held as prisoners of war at Camp Buford, their employees hauled beef to the camp every day.[59]

Financial enterprises like road building, which indirectly increased the wealth of the more energetic post traders, also contributed to the development of the local economy. Lee and Reynolds of Fort Supply, who eventually owned several ranches near the Texas–New Mexico line, built the first stage road to Fort Elliott. It improved trade and made it easier to supply the tradership they had established there. William Carter built and improved roads in three directions from the Fort Bridger vicinity: a direct cutoff from his Carter Station warehouse to the freighting road between Salt Lake City and Montana; a road to Camp Supply that he supplied (with forty drivers); and a road between Fort Bridger and South Pass, which he helped to build in 1868 after the gold strike.[60]

Within Carter's multifaceted business (see chapter 10), he found a variety of lucrative opportunities with the Union Pacific Railroad. First, he had a contract to supply the company with 100,000 ties; then he sold the Union Pacific Railroad oil from an oil seep that he owned. After the railroad was operating, he arranged for special prices to ship his cattle to market and obtained the right for his brother Richard to feed the passengers on the westbound express.[61] Carter even sold a South Pass gold-mining claim he owned to John Casement, the Pacific Railroad track-laying boss.

Mining opportunities frequently were exciting affairs. They came and went quickly, and left wiser men in their wake. In the summer of 1881 at Fort Sill, Oklahoma, a prospector from Colorado named Snyder reportedly found silver on the nearby reservation. A formal company was formed, but a group of men, including the post trader, William Quinette, having heard the news, quickly rode west and staked out claims. Before the week was out, the landscape was dotted with piles of rocks with names like the "Lucky Strike" and "Old Dominion." Men used dynamite to blast samples free and send them to Denver. Soon, a horde of civilians arrived on the scene. They dug up the Indian land and drove off stock. An officer finally put a stop to the illegal ruckus. As to silver, none was located.[62] Then there was Andrew Snider, the 1870 sutler at Camp Warner, Oregon, who, like John Collins of Fort Laramie, used to hunt with General Crook. Snider became president of a Nevada mining concern—the Murchie—in which Crook, Phil Sheridan, and other officers held shares. The mine never paid off.[63]

In his role as tavern- or innkeeper, the post trader was expected to provide care and concern for his clientele. John Evans put Indian interpreter Horace Jones to bed in his own home the night Horace was too drunk to walk home. In the morning, he invited the old gentleman for breakfast and served steak and fried mushrooms. Jones took one look and pushed the latter to one side. When Evans asked the older man what was wrong, he said that it was bad enough that Evans had charged him five dollars for a bottle of champagne, without also serving him fried cork for breakfast.[64] When the Yale University paleontological expedition of 1870 outfitted at Fort Bridger, the hospitality and logistical support provided paleontologist O. C. Marsh by William A. Carter must have been outstanding. Marsh's biographer, after praising Carter's contributions, described the post trader as a soft-spoken Virginian, a capitalist generally, and the "local genius."[65]

In addition to serving as host, part-time intermediary, banker, and creditor, many post traders became the local postmaster and accepted county jobs, such as notary public, probate judge, county commissioner, and territorial representative. In a few instances, the post trader went on to become mayor of a local town, as did Sidney Delong in Arizona, and even territorial governor, as did John Todd (cousin to Mary Todd Lincoln), who became governor of Dakota Territory in the late 1860s.

Historian Don Rickey, Jr., termed the military post trader's occupation a "coveted plum."[66] The post trader had some distinctly lucrative opportunities and advantages, but the job was no sinecure. John J. Fisher, partner of post trader John Evans at Fort Sill, said: "Our profits were the result of keeping a large amount of money invested in the country, and taking advantage of contracts in everything outside, things that all the world could bid upon; and the vending of goods to the soldiers entrepreneurial was a mere drop in the bucket."[67] The post trader entrepreneurial enjoyed the fruits of his trade, but he earned his profits.

When C. K. Peck of Durfee & Peck testified before Congress in 1876, he said that the profits of a trading post could be estimated on the basis of twenty-five hundred dollars per year per company of men. When he managed his business carefully, his profits at Standing Rock, for example, were about ten thousand dollars per year. Staples were generally marked up 15 to 25 percent; fancy items were marked up by perhaps 50 percent; and tobacco and liquor were the most expensive because they were luxury items. Customarily, officers normally received lower prices than the enlisted men.[68]

In 1876, John Collins said he thought his annual profits for the first years at Fort Laramie may have run between eight thousand and fifteen thousand dollars. When his license was passed to John London in 1880, Collins sold him all the fixtures and stock for nine thousand dollars. Two months later, London tried to entice his North Carolina wife to Fort Laramie by saying: "This place is very profitable, and I can surround you with the comforts and luxuries of life."[69]

Edward Welch, an old soldier who was post trader at Fort McPherson from 1871 to at least 1876, invested four thousand dollars into his business. His partner, R. W. Bowers (Secretary of War Belknap's brother-in-law) invested another twenty-two hundred dollars. He told the 1876 congressional investigating committee that profits at the post were eight thousand dollars per year. They should have been closer to ten thousand dollars, he added, but the Fifth Cavalry had left owing him about two thousand dollars, and profits had been dropping off because the garrison at the post was being steadily reduced. A Mr. Seip, who held the post trader's license at Fort Lincoln in the early 1870s, invested thirty-two hundred dollars in his business. So had his partner, Alvin Leighton. Seip intimated that his annual profits reached forty thousand dollars but said that Leighton's share was 75 percent.

It is unlikely that post traders brought their ledgers to the 1876 congressional hearings, but testimony revealed that profits at Fort McPherson and at Fort Randall also should have been about ten thousand dollars per year. Profits had been falling at Fort Randall, because companies of troops, originally one hundred men each, were being reduced to half strength.[70]

With profit potential so high, it is no coincidence that the wealthiest sutlers were those who had more than twenty years of experience in the business. These career traders maintained a long-range perspective.

Historian-archivist William Davis estimated that Judge William A. Carter took in close to two hundred thousand dollars in one year.[71] Alvin C. Leighton of Fort Buford was estimated to have been worth one million dollars at his death. Seth Ward, upon retirement, built a twenty-thousand–dollar home that was touted by newspapers as the finest brick house west of the Missouri. His predecessor, John Dougherty, reportedly had a buffalo herd that roamed his private reserve.

SOME HIGHLY SUCCESSFUL SUTLERS AND POST TRADERS

Name	Post and Location		Years	Duration
James Kennerly	Council Bluffs,	Mo.	1822–1827	6
	Jefferson Barracks,	Mo.	1827–1836	9
Hiram Rich	Ft. Leavenworth,	Kans.	1840–1860	20
Franklin Steele	Ft Snelling,	Minn.	1837–1857	20
John Dougherty	Ft. Kearny,	Neb.	1847–1857	10
	Ft. Laramie,	Wy. T.		
Seth E. Ward	Ft. Laramie,	Wy. T.	1857–1871	15
William A. Carter	Ft. Bridger,	Wy. T.	1857–1882	26
Alvin C. Leighton	Ft. Buford,	Mt. T.	1866–188?	20
Sidney Delong	Ft. Bowie,	Az.	1869–1890	20
James K. Moore	Ft. Washakie,	Wy. T.	1869–1906	35+
J. H. McKnight	Ft. Shaw,	Mt. T.	1871–1887	16
John Collins	Ft. Laramie,	Wy. T.	1872–1882	10

The most successful post traders were dedicated to their careers, and they used their ingenuity to expand their business. They worked long hours, and they paid attention to detail to provide consistent service. Most of the men who did well befriended those in positions of power to help them fend off the uncertainties of the times. In return, they made good money. Those who persevered deserved their reward.

THIRTEEN

The Beginning of Hard Times

Probably as many men lost their lives by the use of alcoholic liquors as were killed by Indians. Several of my men dropped dead in going from a saloon to the camp but I never knew until afterwards that one of the traders had brought several barrels of what was known as "high wines."—Personal Recollections of General Miles

A fter having earned record profits during the 1870s, the ranks of the military post trader began to experience hard times. Traders suffered a number of setbacks throughout the 1880s from government rulings that, in toto, presaged the demise of the post-trading profession. The first blow was an 1881 presidential decree that prohibited the sale of liquor on the military reservation. The second financial disaster was a ruling that prevented the sutler from holding both a military post trader's license and a license to trade with the Indians. Less obvious, but more debilitating to his financial security, was the inchoate development of the American urban West, the onset of a transition that signaled the passing of the frontier.

Once the soldier, through his own labor, had erected his frontier post, life became a bore; and in the atmosphere of relative inactivity and tedium, the bored soldier drank heavily. An enlisted man in 1867 wrote to the *United States Army and Navy Journal* that the soldier, en masse, lacked stability of character, and when there was a "tacit invitation" before him, he became enslaved by a "desire for dissipation."[1]

William B. Gaddis, post trader at Fort Baker, a small post high in the mountains east of Helena, Montana, sold drinks to his captive audience at the rate of fifteen cents each. It was not unusual for a customer of his to incur a bill of three dollars (twenty drinks) for one evening's entertainment. Not surprisingly, liquor became a source of dereliction of duty, and an indirect contributor to the high rate of desertion.

The author of the above letter also related the anxiety he said he experienced when he watched a post trader measure out glass after glass "for a man who he knows is beggaring his family and degrading himself." He considered it an awful thing to see with what composure the trader "scrape[d] together his ill-gotten gain while the poor wretch who fill[ed] his coffers can scarcely totter out of his shop."[2] For that reason, and to ensure "the perfection of natural social order in the army," the writer considered it mandatory that the post trader be forever abolished.[3]

Intoxication in the military service in the 1870s was said to have been five or six times the norm in society, but whiskey was still condoned by most army officers, in part because they believed that it promoted good health and good morale. The majority of post traders were permitted, even encouraged, to carry spirits for the men. In June 1873, when the Seventh Cavalry escorted surveyors for the Northern Pacific Railroad in Dakota territory, General George A. Custer brought along a trader named Balarian out of Fort Rice. Balarian brought two wagonloads of goods and liquor. Although Custer did not drink, he thought some liquor would be good for morale. Custer's commanding officer, General Stanley, was not of the same opinion. In fact, it had been Stanley who ordered Balarian out of Fort Rice for selling whiskey to the soldiers. When he discovered Balarian was with Custer, he sent a trusted man back to search the trader's wagons. Custer got word to the trader first, and Balarian cached his kegs with temperate officers.[4]

Post traders who decided to ignore or bypass regulations to sell liquor to soldiers could become quite enterprising. Fort Buford's post trader, A. C. Leighton, set up shop on one of his steamboats, headed upriver, and sold booze to men of the Seventh Cavalry just before Custer's last campaign. And when soldiers were paid off at Fort Peck in Montana in the summer of 1879, traders came from all over the country with beer in their wagons.[5]

Fort Riley's post trader, Moses Waters, made windfall profits from the sale of liquor in the summer of 1888, when the entire Seventh Cavalry came to Kansas and the Eighth Cavalry was passing through on its way northeast. While at the post, all these men received pay for the first time in several months. Waters established a branch store and a bar in a tent near camp. His employees hauled beer to the camp in wagons. A man in the rear sold drinks as the wagon rolled through camp. Sometimes the keg would be emptied before the wagon reached the far end. In about three days, Waters grossed fifteen thousand dollars.[6] Waters secured his supply of beer from a fellow townsman, Theodore Weichselbaum, who had a brewery in Ogden, Utah. Weichselbaum developed a financial interest in sutlers' stores at Forts Larned, Dodge, Harker, Wallace, and Camp Supply by hauling beer around the country to saloons and post-trader stores.[7]

The sutler at Fort Hays, Kansas, owned a pet buffalo that acquired the beer habit by the age of two and knew only the limit imposed by the generosity of officers and enlisted men. The beast frequented the officer's club. When he got drunk, he often cleared the room with a charging lunge, sending "bluecoats flying out the windows and doors." On occasion he would follow someone upstairs, then was afraid to go back down and had to be pushed backward, blindfolded, with ropes and planks. As his horns grew, this sport became dangerous, but he still served as a drawing card for people who wanted to view this "monarch of the plains."[8]

Beer was a small problem in comparison to distilled whiskey. In his *Recollections*, General Nelson Miles wrote that an increase in distilled spirits resulted in a decrease in discipline and health.[9]

At the cantonment there were two or three traders who would come up the river in the autumn with a stock of goods. They had many things for sale that the officers required, fur caps, woolen underclothing, and other useful articles were among their stores and at the same time they brought up a stock of liquors. I tried to regulate this liquor traffic in different ways, such as confining the soldiers to malted liquors, beer and wine, allowing only a certain number of drinks per day and by various other methods, but during the short time we spend in cantonment we always had more or less trouble. The effects upon the commands were injurious and there were disturbances and breeches of discipline. When we out in the field where liquors were not allowed to be carried we had the best discipline and not the least trouble.[10]

Whenever his regiment returned from the field to a town, village, or military post where there was a saloon, said Miles, trouble was sure to follow. He permitted three traders to operate at his cantonment: an old frontiersman, one who had been an army contractor, and a third fellow, who belonged to a good family in the East. The last mentioned was the only one to sell the men a concoction of high wines and drugs.[11]

From documentation about the life of more than one hundred military post traders, examples of unscrupulous behavior are certainly not difficult to locate. One sutler on the march with the Army of the West wrote a letter back home of his intentions to sell increasingly watered-down whiskey, at increasingly higher prices, to men in his unit. He related that whiskey in St. Louis when he left in 1846 cost nineteen cents per gallon; in Albuquerque, it sold for six dollars per gallon. The trader bragged that he planned to double his stock by diluting it with water and, as the troops moved farther south, to dilute it further and jack the prices to nine dollars per gallon.[12]

There was also Sam Mellison, the Fort Hays, Kansas, post trader from 1882 to 1889, who may have exemplified the hardened whiskey seller. It was said he sold drinks to men who were already drunk. According to Captain E. R. Kellog, commanding officer for Company A, the amount of drunkenness at the fort during the spring of 1885 had been "fearfully on the increase," in spite of the fact that the Department of the Missouri 1881 regulations prohibited the sale of intoxicating liquors to military men stationed in Kansas. On July 2, 1885, he wrote the post adjutant:

Lieutenant,

It is now not quite nineteen days since my company arrived at this post, but since its arrival there has been more drunkenness in it than there had been for many months before. This is probably due in my opinion to the apparently unrestricted sale of liquors by the post trader. There appears to be no limit to the quantity which a man can obtain at the post traders except that imposed by the amount of money at his command. [13]

The Indian agent at Standing Rock in the mid-1870s complained that the Indians regularly went to Fort Rice, where they obtained liquor, and soldiers bought liquor in unlimited quantities there from the post trader. When the commanding officer closed the post bar, however, "whiskey ranches" sprang up around the post.[14]

The relationship between the military post trader and the off-post whiskey trader was comparable to the relationship between the "regular trader" and the "coureur de bois" of earlier days. Captain John Fremont explained the difference in his 1842 report of his explorations:

> The difference between the regular trader and the coureur de bois, with respect to the sale of spirits, is here, as it always has been, fixed and permanent, and growing out of the nature of their trade. The regular trader looks ahead, and has an interest in the preser-vation of the Indians, and in the regular pursuit of their business, and the preservation of their arms, horses, and everything necessary to their future and permanent success in hunting: the coureur de bois has no permanent interest, and gets what he can, and for what he can, from every Indian he meets, even at the risk of disabling him from doing anything more at hunting. [15]

The post–Civil War whiskey trader, more often than not referred to in a deprecating manner as a "half-breed," was much more dangerous than the post trader because he was uncontrolled and unprincipled, and the liquor he sold was often poisonous. He was called every conceivable name by congressmen, army officers, and Indian agents alike because he was so disruptive and impossible to stop. Regardless of how much of a rascal he might be, he was a civilian and thus not subject to military code. Even when he was caught red-handed, most western juries failed to prosecute him. The pioneers on the frontier were an aggressive, land-hungry lot who saw little or no justification in preserving the Indian's rights, and in court it often came down to a white man's word against that of an Indian.[16] Allan Axe, a trader situated just outside the Shoshone Indian reservation boundary near Lander, Wyoming, was caught selling whiskey to the Indians, but the U.S. district attorney said white juries in Wyoming Territory would never convict a white man in an offense against an Indian. There were too many bad memories. In spite of the testimony of two Indians, one of whom was Shoshone Chief Washakie's son, Axe was found not guilty.[17]

In 1876, with approval of the post commander, the Secretary of War issued licenses to post traders who wanted to sell liquor on the military reservation to soldiers and officers.[18] The logic behind licensing liquor sales on the post was the same as that behind the idea of legalizing prostitution: when a basic appetite is outlawed by an act of a legislature, it does not disappear, it merely goes underground. Not only does the trade become more difficult to regulate, it becomes a source of danger to the health of its clientele. By legalizing the purchase of alcohol and offering it on post, the army believed it could control consumption. The arrangement negated the soldier's need to indulge in off-post drinking. The run-of-the-mill whiskey ranch near the post offered very low-grade liquor. It also offered an atmosphere that often led to brawls, shooting scrapes, and accidental deaths. In the winter of 1873, a soldier stationed at Camp Stambaugh, Wyoming, got drunk in an off-post saloon and froze to death in a snow squall on the way back.[19]

Drinking regulations, however, were tailored to individual posts, so they lacked the official, uniform character of those printed in army regulations. On February 1, 1876, James K. Moore received authorization from the Adjutant General's office to trade liquor only to the soldiers and officers at Camp Brown, if he sold in such quantities and under such restrictions as were prescribed by the post commandant. The order was signed by the Secretary of War and endorsed by Lieutenant General Philip H. Sheridan and Robert Torrey, the commanding officer of Camp Brown.[20] At Fort Bowie, also, the sale of intoxicants was permitted. The hours the bar remained open were regulated. Fort Bowie's post trader, Sidney Delong, was admonished only not to let the enlisted men drink too much. He was also forbidden to sell liquor by the bottle. Elsewhere, a soldier might be placed on a "black list" for drinking too much and lose his privileges, or an employee at the trader's store might be fired if he broke the rules.[21]

No matter how honest or well intentioned the trader, there was always trouble. The sutler at Fort Randall in the late 1850s constructed a roomy facility, stocked it with goods for both soldiers and Indians, and kept his prices lower than at neighboring Fort Pierre. He kept ale on draught that, with some restrictions, he was allowed to sell to the soldiers. But while the trader was careful to toe the mark, whiskey was smuggled in from Sioux City and sold to the troops by more daring parties. An enterprising soldier's wife fixed up a small still in her quarters and made a little corn whiskey, which she sold to the soldiers secretly. (After a while, she was informed on and her plant was destroyed.)[22]

Trader Moore, who went out of his way to maintain good relations with his superiors at Fort Washakie, was threatened with closure of his saloon if men on the black list were served one more time at his facility. At Fort Robinson, because the majority of courts-martial originated from inebriation, the post trader was obliged to maintain a list of all the enlisted men who bought drinks at his bar. Each man was allowed two drinks per day, and those drinks had to be separated by a three-hour interval.[23] At Fort Winfield Scott, Nevada, the commanding officer forbade the men to enter the trader's store.

Controlling the source appears to have been the key to controlling the rate of consumption. Colonel Kearny, the epitome of discipline and restraint, marched to New Mexico from Fort Leavenworth in the spring of 1846 with the First Dragoons and fifteen hundred volunteers. On July 4, he allowed his men to buy whiskey from the accompanying sutler to celebrate the country's birthday.[24] The same year, Colonel Mason, who was also in the Southwest, allowed his sutlers to sell whiskey to his soldiers under his regulations, and he was able to report that disorderly houses were abandoned and drunkenness was much reduced.[25]

No substantial change was made to the theme of "condone but control" until the spring of 1881, when temperance reformers convinced the president of the United States to halt the sale of all liquor on military reservations and posts. On February 22, 1881, the Adjutant General's office issued General Order no. 24, which, by direction of the president and by command of General Sherman, prohibited the sale of all intoxicating liquor at all posts and stations. At Fort Laramie, the order arrived less than a month after a newly appointed post trader named John London assumed his position. London was a lawyer from North Carolina who had gone west for his health. He acquired the post trader's appointment with the assistance of his brother, who was an officer at Fort Laramie. As soon as he read the order prohibiting the sale of liquor, he wrote to his wife:

All the officers here from General M. [Merritt] down, say that the order can't stand, that it would be destruction of all discipline if it did not break up the army; the soldiers will have liquor, and will desert to get it. The restriction will seriously affect the profits of my business and I am much concerned about it.[27]

One factor that may have helped the passage of the "no-whiskey" rule was the government's increasing desire to quash the whiskey traffic on the Indian reservations. During the second half of the administration of President Rutherford B. Hayes (1876–1880), Congress addressed the need to control the sale of alcoholic beverages, guns, and ammunition to reservation Indians. As a result, the Indian Bureau forbade military post traders to trade with Indians.

The policy change opened the door to a few political opportunists, and one of the first post traders to get burned was James K. Moore, sutler at Camp Brown, Wyoming Territory. Moore had held a license to trade with the Shoshone Indians since 1870 and a license as military post trader since January of 1871. Less than three months after his annual Indian trader's license had been renewed in the fall of 1878, Moore was informed by the Shoshone agency Indian agent that as of December 1, he would no longer be able to trade with the Indians. Moore had just paid out twenty thousand dollars for supplies; loss of the license would mean ruin. Baffled and understandably panic-stricken, he made every effort to discover the reason and reverse the decision. He had no way of knowing that he was a casualty in a game of power politics.

The previous summer, Wyoming Territory Governor John Hoyt had visited the Indian reservation, where he listened to complaints voiced by Chief Washakie of the Shoshones and Black Coal, the chief of the Northern Arapahoes who had recently been placed on the reservation. Black Coal complained that his people had been promised a separate agency, farmer, and trader. Hoyt reported his conversation to the Indian Commissioner and recommended that a second trader license be granted. Instead of adding a second trader, the Indian Bureau terminated Moore's Indian-trader license and awarded it to another person. The acting Indian Commissioner told Hoyt that the Bureau was concerned about liquor and guns. He said that his office had "experienced a great amount of trouble and embarrassment from Post Traders who have a license to trade with the Indians, and to quell all further difficulties, this office has adopted the policy to grant no licenses to persons who have permission to trade at military posts."[27]

Moore was perhaps the man least likely to provide an embarrassment to anyone. He held the title of military post trader from 1871 to 1906, longer than any other man in his profession in American history, and the record supports him as one of the most ethical, diligent, and sensitive military post traders in America.

Moore walked across the country as a bullwhacker at age twenty-one, then he wrangled a position with the Ben Halliday Stage Line and

Express Company in Virginia City, Montana. A few years, later he ran a merchandising store in Bear River City, a small town in the path of the proposed Union Pacific Railroad line; but after a riot that took the lives of fifteen people, the railroad bypassed this "hell on wheels" town, so Bear River City perished.[28]

At Fort Bridger, Moore worked as a clerk with post sutler Judge William Carter, and received the position of sutler for Camp Brown in the Wind River Valley in the summer of 1870. His clientele consisted of a command of 53 men of the Fourth Infantry, plus 1,200 Shoshone and 475 Bannock Indians. When the post was relocated fifteen miles north in 1873, Moore placed his new store and home west of the cluster of post buildings, but within the one-square-mile military reservation. He married Nevada Cornell of Missouri, raised a family, and remained at Camp Brown–Fort Washakie for thirty-five years.

Moore made good money as a post trader. He put his profits to work by purchasing an interest in a ranch and buying a building in Lander (the only town of any size near the post), which he turned into a branch store. Ten years later, that store ledger listed 475 accounts. By 1880, Moore bankrolled Justus Thacher, the new post trader at Fort Niobrara, Nebraska. Moore invested eleven thousand dollars and paid the salary of one store employee, in return for which he received half the store profits. That year, he also acquired the Double Diamond brand (and any cattle "wandering about" with that brand) for one dollar. By the late 1880s he also owned a thriving horse ranch. His property at Fort Washakie then consisted of a home, stable and barn, the store and a storehouse, a cabin for his hired man, and the JK Moore Hotel, an imposing structure that had its own barn and stable.

Until the early 1880s, furs had been a lucrative business. Moore shipped a railroad car full of buffalo robes to Boston in 1878, and as late as 1881 the Shoshones sold him two thousand buffalo robes. But the eighties was a decade of loss for Moore. He lost his liquor license and his saloon in the spring of 1881, when the sale of liquor at military posts was prohibited, and he lost cattle during the great blizzard of 1886–87. His clerk, Edgar A. Carter, wrote his family at Fort Bridger that he didn't think Moore's store would pay for itself without the Indian trade. Forewarned that the sutler's profession might be shut down at any time, Moore acquired 240 acres of land in California, and relocated there in 1906.

Moore died in 1920, two weeks short of his seventy-seventh birthday.

Obituaries spoke about kindness and generosity, and his having been one of the "red blooded energetic bunch who opened the way to civilization, giving to coming generations, the great and glorious west."[29]

To those in power in 1878, Moore's local reputation meant nothing, nor did it make any difference that Moore sold no firearms nor liquor at his off-post store. He sold alcohol at his saloon on the military reservation, but only under supervision of the post commander. Wyoming Territorial Governor John Hoyt sent several letters to the Indian Commissioner on Moore's behalf, and finally he wrote to Secretary of the Interior Carl Schurz. Moore had a record of dealing fairly with the Indians, said Hoyt, and was highly esteemed throughout the territory. "The opinion prevails," wrote Hoyt to Schurz on January 7, 1879, "that the accusation of his license had been brought about by Senator Saunders [of Nebraska] as a means of providing for one of his friends." He added that Nebraska had always sought to control the politics and political patronage of Wyoming and that the deal "smited of the old hand in the till," which for so long had disgraced that Indian office.[30]

Former territorial representative Judge Joseph M. Carey, who also requested that Schurz suspend the order to remove Moore, added his own smear to Nebraska by asserting that Senator Saunders's state had been a past source of "dishonor and disgrace" that "caused the world to think that we were without honor and virtue."[31]

Indeed, Senator Saunders had used the opening at Fort Brown to obtain an Indian license for a personal friend named Seth Cole. Two months after Cole was installed, however, the Shoshone agency Indian agent wrote the Indian Commissioner that Cole had no capital, could find no backing, and spent his whole time gambling at Camp Brown and Lander. He requested that Cole's license be revoked.[32]

Moore remained without his Indian trader's license for four years. It was reinstated in 1885, through the efforts of Senator Vest of Missouri, who wrote the Indian Commissioner that the Indians wanted to trade with Moore again and that the man's character alone was sufficient to ensure that no liquor would be sold to the Indians.[33]

In the mid-1880s, the military post trader became the pigeon for the Indian Bureau after a congressional investigation showed that Indian traders and Indian agents often colluded to cheat the Indians of annuities and natural resources. They also sold the Indians contraband—rifles and whiskey. Since a military post existed near or on each reservation, and the military post trader was almost always an Indian trader, too, Indian Commissioner J. J. Atkins chose to tighten controls on the military post trader. If a military post trader and a local Indian trader were close together, competition between them would be allowed to continue; however, while the Indian trader may trade with the soldiers, the post trader can no longer trade with the Indians. "The object of the [Bureau of Indian Affairs] office," wrote Atkins on July 29, 1886, "has been to forbid [double licensing of post traders] for the reasons that the Post trader will sell contraband articles" to the Indians.[34]

As a measure to suppress the sale of contraband, the ruling was ineffective. The regulation did not touch the trade of the independent, off-post trader, the Indian trader, or the renegade whiskey trader, all of whom were the most frequent sources of contraband goods to reservation Indians. As George Croghan had pointed out in the 1830s, the military post trader was the only trader under constant administrative review, and he was accountable on almost a daily basis to a higher authority. He was not the source of the problems associated with controlling the flow of liquor. To focus on him was misspent effort.

If Congress wanted to put a dent into the post trader's profits, however, it had found the way. The Indian trade had always been the post trader's most profitable business. Henry Hastings Sibley, a manager of western posts of the American Fur Company in the 1830s, was so concerned about the sutler as a competitor that he tried to get the Secretary of War to prohibit sutlers from carrying on intercourse with the Indians. Sutlers, he said, had an "undue influence in the trade with the Indians," because the Indians were "impressed with the belief that by trading with [the sutlers], they are securing the favor of the officers of the Government."[35] When Sibley failed in his endeavor, he became a sutler himself.

And if the presidential ruling of 1881, plus the subsequent loss of the post trader's Indian license, were not sufficient to put the sutlers' business into steep decline, the profession was seriously undermined by the growth of competition in nearby towns. The country west of the Missouri was fast being settled. Between 1880 and 1900, the population of the eleven states and territories of the Far West increased by 125 percent. By the mid-1880s the population of most of the western territories was sufficient to enable them to apply for statehood, and by 1890 all but Oklahoma, Arizona, and New Mexico had received statehood.

Job opportunities, mineral wealth, land, space, and adventure had drawn people west. Improved transportation and communication facilities helped keep them there. Those improvements also reduced the isolation of western posts and placed them within the reach of competitors in nearby towns. The sutlers at posts located on or near railroads, rivers, and overland stage routes were first to be affected, but even traders at remote posts were affected. By 1885 the time between taking an order and taking delivery at Fort Washakie, Wyoming Territory, was less than two weeks. The post trader's leverage was gone. He was now on even terms with civilian merchants.

Archivist William Davis suggested that the post traders became small-time storekeepers again in the 1880s because economic opportunities and investment were falling away; and that men of large enterprise were no longer interested in the office of sutler.[36] It is more likely, as Professor Atherton observed in the late 1930s, that the decline of retail and wholesale general merchandise business—which included the sutler—resulted from growing specialization, backed by improved transportation.[37] It is also likely that the average military post trader saw only one more immediate threat to his profession: the establishment and rapid growth of the army canteen, a clubhouse where goods could be purchased at cost and which offered soldiers gymnastic exercises, billiards, and other games. The rapid spread of the canteen concept not only took trade from the old sutler, it highlighted the prominence of his liquor sales. It was the kind of spotlight he no longer wanted.

Fast profits from liquor sales was one of the more attractive aspects that attracted peddlers to the suttling business in the early part of the century. And there was perhaps no issue larger than the control over the access to, and the flow of, liquor that consumed the attention of the army almost as much as it did the attention of the sutler and military post trader.

Like any controversial issue, the importance of liquor sales to the post trader was probably overinflated. His financial stability depended on maintaining a balanced business with diverse markets. Yet the loss of the post trader's license to sell alcohol came at a time when a number of major changes were in the wind: patronage was on the run; stiffer government controls were being set in place; and the army was drying out and settling in.

In retrospect, the canteen foreshadowed an idea that was right for the time and that augured the demise of the sutler's store. That idea was temperance. In the decade that followed, the military post trader faded fast while the canteen grew into a multimillion-dollar operation known today as the post exchange, also known as the "PX."[38]

FOURTEEN

The End of an Era

The abolition of the post trader was through no antagonism to the trader, but because it was believed that the army would be more temperate if the use of intoxicating drinks was under the more immediate control of post administration. If this proves a mistake, the trader will have his day again.—*"The Canteen On Trial,"* Army and Navy Journal, *July 12, 1890*

In 1893, at the end of a five-year period of examination and debate, an official spokesman for the U.S. Army announced that the military post trader was no longer necessary. The West was filling in, settling down, and growing up. Army posts were being shut down and the army's troops were being consolidated. The conditions that had necessitated and sustained the suttling profession no longer existed, and the sutler now stood out as a privileged citizen. The army planned to replace him with an amusement room called the canteen, to benefit enlisted men.

The concept of the canteen arose not long after the Civil War, in response to the nondrinking soldiers' need to find a nonalcoholic environment on post where they could spend leisure time. Those who sought support for their objectives found little outside assistance. Formal support from the army general staff was out of the question, and the frontier post was beyond the reach of the Temperance League, which fought the evils of alcohol. The post trader's clubhouse was out of the question. A new place was needed.

At Camp Baker, Montana, in 1873, Lieutenant William B. Nelson or-

197

ganized a Lodge of the Order of Good Templars Society. Good Templars was an international organization started in Utica, New York, in 1851, whose purpose was to fight "King Alcohol."[1] Another branch of this organization was founded at Fort Randall, Dakota Territory, to combat the "fearful influence of the saloon and gambling den." Eighteen men showed up for the first meeting.[2] General Nelson Miles advanced the cause of temperance when he wrote the Honorable H. B. Banning, chairman of the House of Representatives Committee on Military Affairs, in 1876, to recommend that the sale of liquor on all military establishments and posts be prohibited. He pointed the finger at the post trader's establishment, and said that most court-martial offenses originated there.[3]

The idea of the canteen, according to an *Army and Navy Journal* article authored by Chaplain T. G. Steward, Twenty-fifth Infantry, had originated at the Vancouver Barracks in Oregon. The facility, supported by the Department of the Platte commander, General A. H. Terry, was opened November 29, 1880.[4] Captain and Assistant Surgeon A. C. Girard, who started a canteen in March 1880 at Fort Keogh, Montana Territory, said his idea for a canteen came from General Morrow's account of the Fort Vancouver canteen, and from what he had read about the movement in the British army.[5] Girard's canteen offered coffee and a ham sandwich to the soldier for five cents. Credit was also available. Soldiers began to frequent Girard's canteen instead of the trader's store, but he continued to lose money on the operation, so he closed the business on April 30, 1881. Girard subsequently pointed out to those who might be interested that a half-pint of coffee with sugar and a small sandwich cost three and a half cents, and he emphasized that the key to a successful canteen was to place it under the control of a reliable noncommissioned officer. Soon thereafter his canteen reopened under the aegis of the librarian to avoid problems of private speculation. Sales for the month of December 1881 amounted to $5,065.[6]

Vancouver, however, was not the U.S. Army's first canteen experience. An Inspector General's report from Fort Sullivan revealed that when the post sutler had died, the commanding officer had allowed the orderly sergeant to suttle for the men. The sergeant received eight dollars a month for his trouble; and the remaining profits went to the company fund, where they were used to purchase sugar and coffee each morning and night for the troops. After a short time, the commanding officer liked and perpetuated the arrangement. That was 1828—fifty years before the Vancouver experiment.[7]

The 1881 presidential decree prohibiting the sale of whiskey hastened the spread of the canteen concept, but the degree to which his policy change was implemented varied in proportion to the isolation of each frontier post and the temperament of the commanding officer: the more isolated the post and the more tolerant the officer in charge, the less local regulations over alcohol were changed. On the one hand, trader James Moore at Camp Brown, Wyoming Territory, simply closed his saloon when he received the order; on the other, trader Sidney Delong at Fort Bowie, New Mexico, did business as usual. The order to halt the sale of hard liquor was usually ignored there, and beer was always sold.[8]

Yet the 1881 message was clear, and its intent was unmistakable: "King" alcohol was being dethroned. If the more conservative congressmen had had their way that year, the post trader probably would have been thrown out with the liquor, but for the nonce, cooler heads prevailed and he was left unscathed.[9] In fact, the first canteens of the 1870s were required to operate in such a way as not to interfere with the rights of the post trader.

A judicial test case arose after it had become legal to sell alcohol in the canteen. It appeared that the army had finally settled its century-long debate of whether to regulate or abolish alcoholic beverages. The army said it now recognized the advantages of openly trying to control a habit that was impossible to eradicate. Regulation of the sale of wine and beer, where properly conducted, would result in less drunkenness and a better attitude in the men.[10] This latest competitive foray into the post trader's market, combined with the rapid spread of the canteen, however, prompted men of the suttling profession to register a formal complaint.[11] In September 1888, the Honorable S. W. T. Lanham of Texas presented objections for the post trader at Fort Bliss, Texas, concerning the sale of wine and beer at the canteen. The traders felt it represented competition on the reservation. Other post traders had complained also, but the Adjutant General of the Army based his decision on the Fort Bliss case.

The ruling after the first review favored the post trader. A letter from the Secretary of War dated October 25, 1888, which resulted in Circular no. 9, dated November 6, 1888, said that a canteen could infringe on the rights of post traders, and that meant canteens could not sell wine or beer. When officers and enlisted men inquired about posts where there was no post trader, including Forts D. A. Russell, Ontario, Omaha, Clark, and Vancouver, the army assigned the entire question to Assistant Adjutant General Major Schwan, who was asked to prepare a comprehensive report on frontier-post needs.

Schwan's report of December 1888 would set a new trail for the future, a direction for army leisure time that left the post trader on a dead-end spur. Schwan recommended the abolishment of all post traders at posts close to towns and communication lines where the trader had held appointment for four or more years. Although he suggested that individual traders be given time to dispose of their goods, he recommended that no new post-trader appointments be made except at remote posts, and then only as a necessity. Lastly, he suggested that the army establish canteens where no post traders were located and allow them to sell wine and beer.

The United States Army regulations for 1889 contained a separate section for the canteen and for the post trader. Article 39 stated that "canteens may be established at military posts where there are no post traders, for supplying the troops, at modest prices, with such articles as may be deemed necessary for their use, entertainment, and comfort; also for affording them the requisite facilities for gymnastic exercises, billiards, and other proper games."[12] Paragraph no. 329 forbid the sale of ardent spirits,

> but the commanding officer is authorized to permit wines and light beer to be sold therein by the drink, on week days, and in a room used for no other purpose whenever he is satisfied that the giving to the men the opportunity of obtaining such beverages within the post limits has the effect of preventing them from resorting for strong intoxicants to places without such limits, and tends to promote temperance and discipline among them.

Paragraphs no. 345–357 of Article 40, which addressed the freedoms and restrictions placed on the post trader, included four new features: his exclusive right to trade on the reservation did not include producers of fresh vegetables, fruits, and dairy products; he was required to pay a tax for the privilege of exclusive trading (up to ten cents per month per man), and he had to purchase at fair value the goods left by the former trader. In addition, the Council of Administration, when setting prices, was asked to consider that the trader sold on credit.[13]

During this eventful year of 1889, the post trader at Fort Supply resigned. The Secretary of War refused to appoint the recommended nominee unless he agreed to refrain from the sale of intoxicants. The nominee refused and was therefore not appointed. Not long thereafter, a trader at Fort Spokane was discovered selling strong liquor. These two incidents led to General Order no. 75, September 27, 1889, which said all sales of alcoholic beverages at the post traders' establishment would cease, and that canteens would be permitted at all posts.[14]

Sutlers organized to oppose General Order no. 75. J. K. McCannon and George B. Williams notified the War Department on June 4, 1889, that they represented a post-traders organization and asked to be heard. On October 23, 1889, they submitted an argument against enforcing General Order no. 75, and they asked for protection for the post trader. The acting Judge Advocate General called for an opinion. On November 1, 1889, the issue was reviewed. The final decision said that restricting the sale of liquor or abolishing the post-trader establishments was not an infringement on the legal rights of post traders.[15]

That decision further prompted the Secretary of War to consider revoking the license of eight post traders. During his deliberations, although only one license was eventually taken, the Secretary of War approved all of Schwan's recommendations on December 31, 1889. General Order no. 10 of 1890 authorized the establishment of a canteen where there was no post trader.[16] The rules and regulations to guide the management of the canteen included permission to sell beer and wine, but only by the drink, not by the bottle.[17]

The army's attitude towards alcohol was a fine line inscribed by the verb *tolerated*. The sale of wine and beer was tolerated in canteens, not encouraged. The army stuck to its guns when it said it believed that it was better to regulate "what cannot be prevented." The canteen was intended to control consumption by keeping drinking in the open, and by prohibiting the sale of bottles or larger packages of beer and wine that might be taken to the barracks or mess rooms.[18]

Reports from the field indicated that the concept was working. Posts that did not have a canteen requested one. In one case, a soldier advertised in the *Army and Navy Journal* to have a canteen established at Fort Totten, North Dakota.[19] At Fort Custer, Montana, First Cavalry Colonel James S. Brisbin emphasized in his January 20, 1890, report that the canteen had improved discipline and decreased drunkenness by almost 50 percent. He said he believed the canteen was less expensive

EDITORIAL—1890 "The Canteen and the Post Trader" *Army and Navy Journal* [20]

It is understood to be the settled policy of the War Department to get rid of all the traders' stores except those at very inaccessible or isolated posts. At present there are less than forty posts at which stores are maintained. The majority may go this year. Canteens now exist at 69 posts.

The gradual extinction of the post trader system will be regretted by no one familiar with its inward working, and in spite of one who has the true interests of the Service at heart, the fact not to be lost sight of that in times gone by the store was in some respects a great convenience on the frontier, especially to the officers, nor the further fact that the tax paid by the trader has always been put to excellent use.

---

and of greater comfort to the men. A subsequent Fort Custer report by Lieutenant Colonel David Perry, Tenth Cavalry, said that drunkenness after payday had almost ceased. A business like the canteen that declares "as it does large monthly dividends," he said, "must be considered a success."[21] Chaplain Steward cited an 1892 letter from General H. A. Morrow to liquor dealers in Sidney, Nebraska, and outside Fort Sidney, that pointed to a drop in arrests for drunkenness—from 193 to 63 in a similar five-month period.

Most officers approved of the new system. It was a good excuse to get rid of the post trader, and it was generally alleged to reduce drunkenness.

A different group of officers thought it was a mistake. They contended that a canteen stimulated even more consumption of alcohol. In the days of the trader, the physical space around the bar was relatively small, so a man purchased a beer and left. Now there was an amusement room next to the bar. Those who never drank before came in, hung around, and got drunk. The notion of some to expand the amusement complex would make things worse, in their opinion. These gainsayers were against the sale of alcoholic beverages in the saloon. They voiced the opinion that the Subsistence Department should take over the canteen.[22]

A soldier (or group of soldiers) submitted to the *Army and Navy Journal* a sarcastic notice about the concept of the new canteen:

Look! Look! Canteen. Saloon. Credit Check System. Wines, Beers, Pies, Cakes, Doughnuts, Pop Corn, Peanuts, Major Honorable Career, U.S. Army. Look at it! Nice business isn't it for the U.S. Army!

The complainer(s), who signed their missive with a "Z," declared that the army had gone overboard, and then suggested that it should consider issuing a new regulation to visit the barracks and lullaby the men to sleep, and to use safety pins on bandages.[23]

As of March 4, 1889, there were eighty-five post traders. During that year, forty-two post traders were put out of business. Some sold their stock to the canteen and abandoned their buildings after the commanding officer told them they were no longer needed.[24] In March 1888, John A. Davis, post trader at Fort Davis, Texas, said the canteen was ruining his business and asked that the government purchase his buildings. He moved his saloon off the reservation after General Order no. 75 became operational.

Others managed to squeeze in an extra year or two of business before they were shut down. In 1888, Fort Riley's post trader, Moses Waters, completed a new three-story stone building (Waters Hall) at a cost of $11,500. It contained a large general store, an enlisted man's bar, dining rooms for enlisted men and officers, and an officers' club upstairs, complete with pool and billiard tables. When Moses Waters died on June 25, 1889, his widow sold Waters Hall to the government for $5,000. On February 1, 1890, the post canteen opened in the basement of the building, and three months later the canteen occupied the entire building.[25]

Benjamin S. Paddock, post trader to Fort Robinson, Wyoming Territory, for six years as of 1889, requested time to dispose of his stock, knowing that his appointment was being revoked as of April 1890. On May 6, 1890, that revocation was suspended. A letter to him dated June 18, 1891, said the revocation of his license had been rescheduled for April 1892. Then, after officers petitioned for his retention, additional political maneuvering extended Paddock's license until June 1, 1893.

In addition, Mr. Norton, the sutler at Fort Grant, Arizona, was allowed to compete with his post canteen until October 1, 1893. Even then, Governor L. C. Hughes (probably at Norton's request) asked for an eighteen-month extension.[26] Charles A. Weidemann of Fort D. A. Russell, who was appointed January 8, 1877, had his license revoked March 21, 1885, on the recommendation of the commanding officer that the store was no longer needed. Those post officers who did not agree with that decision (a number which was not revealed) appealed the decision to the Secretary of War.[27]

Those in favor of retaining the post trader were in the minority, so canteens continued to be installed in posts across the West, and post traders continued to lose their licenses. As of October 7, 1890, sixty-eight canteens had been established, and by the fall of 1892 seventy of the eighty-five post traders had been put out of business.[28] Each time a canteen replaced a post trader, the Secretary of War received flack from the field, but the War Department was determined that the post trader had to go. Standing his ground in his 1891 report, Secretary of War W. C. Endicott justified the decision by saying that the abuses incident to the old sutler system had been "but slightly if at all abated" by the joint resolution enacted by Congress on July 15, 1870. To him, the name *post trader* had simply been a sutler's pseudonym.[29]

While the canteen was replacing the post trader, the army was concentrating its troops. Twenty-eight posts—a quarter of all frontier posts occupied in 1889—were closed by 1891. Contract surgeons were eliminated, the licenses of attendant post traders were revoked, and the respective military reservations were turned over to the Interior Department for public sale.[30]

By General Order no. 11, dated February 8, 1892, the name *canteen* was changed to *post exchange*. Later that year, U.S. Army Commanding Major General J. M. Schofield issued the first official army report to recommend abolishment of the post trader's official slot. His message was that times had changed. "The Post Trader," he wrote, "is no longer necessary. At the beginning of this administration, there were licensed Post traders at most posts. They were a privileged class, exempt from taxation because located on government reservations, and had practically a monopoly of the trade in such articles as were not furnished or sold by the Quartermaster or the commissary."[31]

Schofield reminded Congress that the position of post trader was originally established in part as a substitute for the old sutlership, which had been abolished. The post trader had been a means to supply necessities to immigrants and travelers passing or visiting military posts, "at a period of time when the army and roving Indians were almost the sole inhabitants of the country."

Now the frontier was settled, and frontier posts were no longer isolated. As a result, the post trader had become a "privileged rival" of citizens engaged in legitimate business. In addition, under the "wiser social custom gradually developed in the army," officers and enlisted men had been provided a far better means of social entertainment and recreation. The officers had their post messes or clubs, and the soldiers had the post exchange. Schofield confessed his purpose was to discontinue the trader system as rapidly as possible and to permit the trade at military posts outside the ordinary government supplies "to take its regular channels."

Many post traders had influential congressmen as staunch friends, so Congress was in no hurry to accept the army's recommendation. The War Department, however, was adamant. Schofield and Secretary of War Redfield had devised a phase-out plan, so they poked Congress again. "Parties who held these privileges had large personal and political influence," Schofield acknowledged. Many traders invested considerable capital in their enterprise, "but their profits have been large and I believe no injustice has been done them." He restricted his arguments to the system and avoided names. The system had outlived whatever usefulness it may have had, and its continuance was no longer in the best interest of the service or the public good.[32]

In fact, if the system was continued, said Schofield, it would be "a source of detriment to the army." In some cases, he delayed implementation of his policy to enable the traders to sell what they had on hand—what he called "a just and generous regard for vested interests in the present incumbents." He wanted his phase-out program to remain in effect "until those persons who are now post traders die or retire. When vacancies occur, the position will be abolished."

Congress consented and gave the army fifty thousand dollars to purchase post-trader buildings. Redfield, who said traders had accepted the evaluation set by his office, asked and received an additional thirty-five thousand dollars to care for trader stores that the army planned to maintain.[33]

Thus, the sutler–post trader system disappeared from the frontier—the frontier which, by an act of Congress, had been declared closed in 1890.[34] The sutler–military-post-trader system died slowly, without grace. Against an inexorable wave of change, its members fought to maintain a status quo that offered them security and preferential treatment.

But all the factors that had bound the post trader to the military were swept away as the dust of the frontier West settled. Military posts were no longer isolated: transportation and communication facilities had usurped the post trader's prior advantage. Small-town traders were near-by, here to stay: the post trader was no longer special.

Some post traders cut their losses, quit quickly, and retired; others hung on until the last. The majority of the gentlemen traders—the entrepreneurs who had put down roots, diversified their business, and reinvested their profits in the land—blended into the local scenery. William Hugus of Fort Steele, Wyoming, retired and let the profits from his partner's store in Laramie support him. Sidney Delong, who had served as post trader at Fort Bowie for twenty years, ran a newspaper. James K. Moore, veteran of thirty-six years of trading at Fort Washakie, Wyoming, sold his business to his son in 1906, and relocated to California where he operated an orchard within sight of the San Francisco Bay. John Hunton, the last trader at Fort Laramie, homesteaded the ground on which the fort had stood; for the next forty years, he was "a walking embodiment of the lore of old Fort Laramie."[35]

FIFTEEN

A Niche in American History

The sutler was one of the most important men at a frontier post. "A cruel or exacting commander could be tolerated; hard service was accepted as an inevitable part of life; but an unaccommodating or inefficient sutler was a real calamity."—Edgar Wesley, "The Diary of James Kennerly"

It was a pernicious system and necessity was the only excuse for its existence at any time. It has outlived whatever usefulness it may have had . . .—Adjutant General of the Army, May 14, 1892

S ome will argue that the army would have been better off without the sutler and his post–Civil War counterpart, the military post trader. Without differentiating between the Regular Army sutler, the sutler who served the militia and the volunteers, and the military post trader, detractors can list this purveyor's disruptive role in the illegal whiskey trade, his bent for profit, his disregard of regulations, his privileged position, and his capacity for political mischief. His supporters can point out that he assumed his own risks to provide a broad range of unique and invaluable services and conveniences to the soldier on the frontier, and that he acted as victualler, merchant, postman, banker, and creditor with no guarantee of profit and, often, no guarantee of protection.

As a provider of food to the military in the eighteenth century, the value of the sutler's services might have been characterized as salubrious, although Matthew Prior, a well-known poet of the day, implied that the sutler's role was critical. His ballad, "The Viceroy," written in 1715, satirized the tactics used by the reigning viceroy to acquire money from the populace. In his poem, Nero, the king of Hibernia, tried to force sutlers to pay for licenses and thus brought disaster to the army:[1]

> The suttlers too he did ordain
> For licences should pay,
> Which they refus'd with just disdain,
> And fled the camp away.
>
>   *   *   *
>
> By which provisions were so scant,
> That hundreds there did die,
> The soldiers food and drink did want,
> Nor famine cou'd they fly.

The uncertain methods by which the army acquired its food led France's General Le Tellier to seek state control over the process. In England, the Duke of Marlborough applied strict supervision to the army's food procurement process by naming a commissary-general and by using purveyors, commissaries, munitionaries, and selected sutlers. The commissary provided bread; the rest was scrounged by foraging and collected from local inhabitants or provided by the sutler. Each regiment had a grand sutler; and each troop on horse or company on foot had a petty sutler. As a result, Marlborough's troops were allegedly better fed than any since the time of Oliver Cromwell.[2]

The British soldier who fought in the Crimean War of 1854–55 would have said the services of the sutlers were indispensable, because "in the general ignorance of war, no one knew what to take."[3] Due to the "imperfect working" of the army's commissariat, the Crimean Army found itself destitute of basics, including food, clothing, and items of personal hygiene. An army of local ad hoc sutlers—Greeks, Armenians, and Turks—did a thriving business. One bought a canteen license and supplied the soldiers directly. A few started a subscription (at two guineas per year) to care for personal packages sent from England. One Frenchman made up to thirty pounds a day by selling bread at two shillings a loaf.[4]

The majority of American army sutlers, like their European trader counterparts, were clean, hardworking men. Some, too, were "gentlemen by birth, education, and mental attainments."[5] Their food-procurement business quickly expanded to general merchandise once they arrived on the frontier.

During the Blackhawk War, the Mexican War, and the Civil War, four of five officers and perhaps half the enlisted men might have said the sutler was a pain and more trouble than his luxuries were worth. They might also have advised that the army—if not army life—would have been better without him. The sutler took advantage, they said. True. The wartime sutler did work in a volatile environment of indefinite duration, in which he balanced profits against risk. But, as one British soldier observed, no one stopped to consider that prices were high because the demand was there, and that in the general law of commerce the greater the obstacles thrown in the path of a seller, the higher the price will be to the customer.[6]

The post–Civil War military post trader was in a league by himself. The majority of his class was out to make a killing, but the military reservation he served was a controlled environment and the Council of Administration gave him limited slack. His high prices reflected the costs of doing business: the risk associated with credit sales, vagaries of the country, transportation, spoilage, the interest on borrowed money, competition, and the fact that he held a temporary license.

The post trader who realized that he was in the right place at the right time could channel his energy, diversify his interests, and over time become a wealthy entrepreneur. He had everything going for him, particularly location. At Fort Laramie, the store of the sutler–post trader was the busiest place throughout the post's forty years of military history; it served as a focal point of social intercourse for all classes of men in frontier society and was a vital supply link for travelers on the great transcontinental wagon road to Oregon, California, and Utah. It also functioned as a banking and trading center for Dakota, Nebraska, and Wyoming territories.

In addition, the post trader's headquarters—especially the western frontier post—served as a seed pearl for economic development. The trader, as a leader situated at the hub of local enterprise, had ample opportunity to assist in the development of the urban West. His merchandise offered his nascent community an escape from the need to be totally self-sufficient, and he relieved the western resident from having to be a jack of all trades. Like merchants in nearby towns, the post trader went east once a year, brought back specialized goods, and thus "offered the west the challenge of lifting herself to a higher degree of economic organization."[7]

He was also receptive to shouldering extra responsibilities, because diverse services kept his customers coming back. As one of the more educated men in the area, he often served as banker, postman, and creditor. As someone who traveled east, he became the provider of news; and as a friend with "a barrel of whiskey in the back room, with a tin cup tied at the side," he served as the understanding friend."8

When Professor Lewis E. Atherton addressed the contribution of the early western mercantile class, he might as well have been talking about the military post trader when he said that the merchant made travel easier for others, wrote letters of introduction, and invited travelers to stay at their homes. Frontier merchants, he said, were "courteous, hospitable, supportive," and they "helped to mitigate the bleakness of the western frontier to those who came before community life was fully developed."9 The Regular Army sutler and the military post trader were members of that same merchant class to which Atherton referred, particularly when he observed: "It is because of their leadership during this period of transition that [they deserve] a place in the story of the frontier."10

On an individual level, historical records reveal that like every other profession, the sutler–post trader gang had its knaves and its thieves; it also spawned a number of constructive, creative men who contributed to society and to the improved status of their fellow man. These benefits did not spring from the sutler's philanthropy, but were a normal byproduct of his entrepreneurial activities. Elias Brevoort, once a sutler of Fort Buchanan, Arizona, acquired property and drew emigrants to New Mexico with his book called *New Mexico, Her Natural Resources and Her Attractions*.11 Sutler Goodfellow of Fort Leavenworth built a private school that his daughters operated for officers' children until the early 1900s.12 Others became mayors and territorial governors, and after they retired they gave of their time and wealth as bank and university trustees.

One of the last words written by a contemporary on the American sutler–post trader was a January 1920 eulogy by ex-frontier surgeon Thomas G. Maghee. In his encomium of post trader James Kerr Moore of Fort Washakie, Maghee said that the post traders had been "hospitable, kindly, and big-hearted men, upon whom the garrisons, far from civilization and its conveniences, leaned heavily." They kept their houses open all year around for friends, and assisted many an orphan and widow to return to their homes. He spoke for many when he said, "The Army is indebted to them for innumerable acts of kindness."13

EPILOGUE

The post exchange was a big success. Aggregate receipts of $1.8 million in 1898 yielded profits of $323,500. Profits in 1899 exceeded $400,000. Some of that money went to the post fund, the library, and recreational activities; a portion served as dividends.

Under the roof of the PX, the soldier could find a reading room, a recreation room, a cooperative store, and a restaurant. At most facilities, he could also find a bar. Section no. 10 of army regulations said that on the recommendation of the post exchange council, "the commanding officer may permit light beer and wines to be sold by the drink."[1] The Anti-Saloon League didn't appreciate the sale of beer and wine to soldiers, so it continued to push to outlaw the sale of all alcoholic beverages.

Secretary of War Elihu Root proposed that the canteen stand as it was. He repeated the age-old argument that men will drink, and it's better to have them drink in a stable environment, in the presence of restraint, than to drink outside the confines of the post.[2] Further, he and the Adjutant General warned that if the sale of wine and beer was removed from the canteen, enlistments into the army would be badly damaged.[3] Three senior military officers and one thousand officers wrote the Adjutant General in May 1900 to support his position.[4]

Nonetheless, on December 14, 1900, the House Committee on Military Affairs once again passed a law to prohibit the sale of all alcoholic beverages on the military reservation. Now that the post trader was gone, the target was the post exchange.[5] Congressmen who believed that the United States "should not in any way be part of the liquor traffic" pushed the bill, and the anti-canteen law was enacted February 2, 1901.[6]

Two years later, the acting Secretary of War wrote a letter that called for the revocation of that act. He attached a 525-page report that contained newspaper accounts and reports from officers at 126 posts, 98 of which had canteens while 28 had none. His report (which sounded considerably like the one issued by Inspector General Croghan in the early 1830s), concluded that

> (1) once a post canteen was closed, gin mills around the post perimeter began to open up, and
>
> (2) incidents of courts-martial and drunkenness off-post had increased since alcohol was prohibited in the canteens.[7]

His point was simple and clear: in the long run, the regulation of alcohol remained an improvement over the hopeless attempt to eradicate an irrepressible habit.

Temperance allies fought the secretary's contentions with statistics. Under the canteen law, they argued, courts-martial had increased from 42.0 per thousand in 1898 to 100.5 per thousand in 1900. Since the turn of the century, which included six months of the canteen law and eighteen months of the anti-canteen law, courts-martial had decreased to 61.3 per thousand. There had also been a marked decrease in hospitalization, insanity, and other medical problems related to alcohol.[8]

The editor of the July 12, 1890, *Army and Navy Journal* editorial said the abolition of the post trader was due to the belief that the army would be more temperate if the use of intoxicating drinks was under the control of post administration. He was correct; unfortunately, the benefits of the canteen, as conceived in the 1890s, did not stand the test of time. The ongoing problem of overindulgence was not solved, it simply shifted from the bar of the post trader's club to the bar of the post exchange. And that same editor also suggested that "if [the canteen] proves a mistake, the trader will have his day again." Here, he was wrong. By 1900, the post trader's profession was a distant memory. No one would ever attempt a comeback.

NOTES

Introduction

1. Pierre Ducrey, *Warfare in Ancient Greece* (New York: Schocken Books, 1986), 203.

2. Barton C. Hacker, "Women and Military Institutions in Early Modern Europe: A Reconnaissance," *Signs* 6, no. 4 (1980): 647–48, 655; Philip Mason, *A Matter of Honor* (London: Jonathan Cape, 1974), 223; *Chambers Encyclopedia: Dictionary of Universal Knowledge*, ed. David Patrick and William Geddie (Philadelphia: J. P. Lippincott, 1923), 694; Hans Delbruck, *History of the Art of War*, 3 vols., trans. Walter J. Renfroe, Jr., (Westport: Greenwood Press, 1982), 1:21–22.

3. In early modern Dutch (*soeteler*) the term *sutler* means small vendor or petty tradesman, victualler, or soldier's servant; in French, sutler (*soetelen*) means to be foul or to follow a low occupation. *Oxford English Dictionary*, 2d ed., 20 vols. (Great Britain: Oxford at the Clarendon Press, 1970), 17:331.

4. Myna Trustram, *Women of the Regiment: Marriage and the Victorian Army* (London: Cambridge Press, 1984), 4, 13; Hacker, "Women and Military Institutions," 657.

5. Duffy, *Army of Frederick The Great*, 59.

6. An ancient custom. Ducrey, *Warfare in Ancient Greece*, suggests that the merchants who accompanied the soldiers not only supplied provisions, they also gathered produce by pillaging. By becoming a part of the system to dispose of the booty, the merchants themselves made substantial profit.

7. Christopher Duffy, *The Army of Frederick the Great* (London: David and Charles, Newton Abbott, 1974), 137. The feather was more appealing than the

tin plate with a number scratched that was worn by sutlers in Bonaparte's army, to which Paul Thiebault refers in *An explanation on the duties of the several etat-majors in the French Army* . . . (London: T. Egerton, 1801), 884.

8. Major R. E. Scouller, *The Armies of Queen Anne* (London: Oxford University Press, 1966), 389–90.

1 Early American Camp Followers

1. Donald Kagan, *The Peace of Nicias and the Sicilian Expedition* (Ithaca: University of Cornell Press, 1981), 210.

2. The Journal of Captain James Walker, June 16, 1760–Feb. 26, 1761, in The City of Bedford, *The History of Bedford, New Hampshire* (Concord: Runford Printing Company, 1903), 475–76.

3. July 20, 1759. Lake George, New York. Order of march uplake. "Boats follow belonging to the Quartermaster, Engineers, Surgeons, Hospital, Commissary, and suttlar's [*sic*] large boat." William H. Hill, *Old Fort Edward Before 1800* (Fort Edward: privately printed, 1929), 42.

4. Ibid., 188.

5. "The Orderly Book of Lieutenant William Henshaw," *Transactions of Colonial America*, Antiquity Society 11 (1909), 221.

6. Ibid., 57.

7. Order of July 1, 1757, from "The Orderly Book of General Phineas Lyman," in Hill, *Old Fort Edward*, 45.

8. *Transactions of Colonial America*, 197.

9. Ibid., 185.

10. Part 1 (Philadelphia: 1779), chaps. 16, 79.

11. September 20, 1776, Section 8: Articles no. 1-4. John F. Callan, ed., *Military Laws of the United States Relating to the Army and Volunteers Militia and to Bounty, Lands and Pensions* (Philadelphia: G. W. Childs, 1864).

12. Many sutler rules applied to both British and American sutlers. A 1777 British document called "Rules and Articles for Better Government of his Majesty's Horse and Foot Guards" states that sutler tents which dispensed alcoholic beverages and entertainment of sorts, were ordered closed on Sunday during the hours of devine service on threat of permanent loss of sutler license. Silvia R. Frey, *The British Soldier in America: A Social History of Military Life in the Revolutionary Period* (Austin: University of Texas Press, 1981), 116.

13. Callan, ed., *Military Laws*, Articles no. 1-4.

14. Ibid., 27 (1784), 388–89.

15. Erna Risch, *Quartermaster Support of the Army: A History of the Corps* (Washington, D.C.: War Department, 1962), 9.

16. Frey, *British Soldier in America*, 63. Harry E. Wildes, *Valley Forge* (New York: Macmillan Co., 1938), 172–73. Charles Royster, *A Revolutionary People at War: The Continental Army and American Character, 1775–1783* (Chapel Hill: University of North Carolina Press, 1979), 75.

17. Carl Van Doren, *Mutiny in January* (New York: Viking Press, 1943), 231.

18. Walter H. Blumenthal, *Women Camp Followers of the American Revolution*, (Philadelphia: G. S. MacManus Co., 1952) 22–23; Van Doren, *Mutiny in January*, 32. The author says that women sutlers were usually laundresses and nurses who now and then acted as unofficial sutlers in selling liquor or other commodities.

19. Hacker, "Women and Military Institutions in Early Modern Europe," 650–51.

20. Duffy, *Army of Frederick the Great*, 137.

21. Allen Kemp, *The British Army in the American Revolution* (London: Almark Publishing Co., 1973), 7-9.

22. E. B. O'Callaghan, *Burgoyne Orderly Book* (Albany: n.p., 1860), quoted in Blumenthal, *Women Camp Followers of the American Revolution*, 23–24.

23. United States, Continental Congress, *Journals of the Continental Congress* (Washington, D.C.: Government Printing Office, 1904–1937), 4 (1776), 113, 114, 158.

24. Jared Sparks, *Correspondence of the American Revolution*, 4 vols. (Boston: Little, Brown and Co., 1853) 1:498; United States, Continental Congress, *Journals* 27 (1784), 388–89.

2 With America's Fledgling Frontier Army

1. Francis Paul Prucha, *Broadax and Bayonet: The Role of the United States Army in the Development of the Northwest, 1815–1860* (Madison: State Historical Society of Wisconsin, 1953), 30.

2. For a background account of the battle and how the U.S. Army arrived on the frontier, see Wiley Sword, *President Washington's Indian War* (Norman: University of Oklahoma Press, 1985); or Edgar W. Wesley, *Guarding the Frontier, A Study of Frontier Defense from 1815 to 1825* (Westport: Greenwood Press, 1970). See also "William Clark's Journal of General Wayne's Campaign of 1793–94," *Mississippi Valley Historical Review* 1 (December 1914): 418–44.

3. In addition to Fort Washington (1789), Fort Massac (1794), and Fort Wayne (1794), the army acquired Niagara, Mackinac, and Detroit, forts previously held by the British. Spain yielded Fort St. Stephens, and between 1800 and 1805 the army added Fort Adams, Fort McHenry, Fort Pickering at Chickasaw Bluffs, and Fort Bellefontaine (1805) just below the Mississippi-Missouri fork. See Francis Paul Prucha, *A Guide to Military Posts of the United States, 1789–1895* (Madison: Historical Society of Wisconsin, 1964).

4. Francis Paul Prucha, *The Sword of the Republic: The United States Army on the Frontier, 1783–1846* (Bloomington: Indiana University Press, 1969), xvii, 1, 169.

5. The exception was New Orleans, which was garrisoned by 375 men. Prucha, *Sword of the Republic*, 59, 73.

6. James R. Jacobs, *The Beginning of the U.S. Army, 1780–1812* (Princeton: Princeton University Press, 1947), 89, 298.

7. On January 29, 1786, Captain J. Hart noted that "Provisions will be issued to the women in the garrison at the rate of four to a company." These were laundresses, a tradition that lasted to the Civil War. See Edward M. Coffman, *The Old Army* (New York: Oxford University Press, 1986), 25.

8. Bert J. Griswold, *The Pictorial History of Fort Wayne, Indiana* (Chicago: Robert O. Law Co., 1917), viii.

9. Ibid., 200n.

10. March 21, 1796. Anthony Wayne, "General Wayne's Orderly Book," *Michigan Pioneer and Historical Society Collections* 34 (1900), 686; Griswold, *Pictorial History of Fort Wayne*, 311; Norman W. Caldwell, "Civilian Personnel at the Frontier Military Post (1790–1814)," *Mid-America* 38, no. 2 (October 1955): 114.

11. Bert J. Griswold, ed., *Fort Wayne, Gateway to the West, 1802–1813* (Indianapolis: Indiana Library and Historical Department, 1927), 397–98.

12. General Orders, Greenville, July 6, 1794. Wayne, "Wayne's Orderly Book," 527.

13. Jacobs, *Beginning of the U.S. Army*, 202.

14. Greenville, February 23, 1795. Wayne, "Wayne's Orderly Book," 587–88.

15. Scouller, *Armies of Queen Anne*, 220.

16. Greenville, February 27, 1796. Wayne, "Wayne's Orderly Book," 679–80.

17. The use of grand (regimental-level) sutlers reappeared during the Civil War. See chap. 7.

18. February 27, 1796. Wayne, "Wayne's Orderly Book," 679–80.

19. Ibid., 614–15. The men "who must attend personal on the spot" included David Ziegler, A. Hunt, James Findley, Ormsby and Hamilton, Thomas Gibson, and Levi Munsell.

20. Garrison Orders, April 28, 1808, state that in the future, the noncoms and officers may buy a half-pint and the musicians and privates one gill of liquor each per day except when on guard or on the sick report. General Order of November 29, 1804, read that troops, in the future, will do all their business at Peltier's store between eleven and one o'clock. Griswold, *Pictorial History of Fort Wayne*, 267, 200. On April 10, 1806, Articles of War adapted in 1776 were revised. Under chapter 20, Articles 29–31, sutler shops were to close at 9:00 P.M., open at reveille, and be closed during Sunday services.

21. September 17, 1802. Griswold, *Pictorial History of Fort Wayne*, 97, 98.

22. January 4, 1804. Griswold, *Pictoral History*, 159.

23. December 5, 1804. Griswold, *Pictorial History.*, 201.

3 Risks, Losses, and Retreats

1. See Royal B. Way, "The United States Factory System for Trading with the Indians, 1796–1822," *Mississippi Valley Historical Review* 6, no. 2 (September 1919): 220–35.

2. Information about John Kinzie's life comes from Joseph Kirkland, *The*

Chicago Massacre of 1812 (Chicago: Dibble Press, 1893); J. Seymour Currey, *The Story of Old Fort Dearborn* (Chicago: A. C. McClurg and Co., 1912); Milo M. Quaife, *Checagou: From Indian Wigwam to Modern City, 1673–1835* (Chicago: University of Chicago Press, 1933); Mrs. John Kinzie, *Wau-Bun, The "Early Day" in the Northwest* (Chicago: Lakeside Press, 1932); Clarence Edwin Carter, ed., *Territorial Papers of the United States*, vols. 16 and 17 (Washington, D.C.: Government Printing Office, 1934–), and Caldwell, "Civilian Personnel at the Frontier Military Post."

3. Carter, *Territorial Papers*, 16:68.

4. D. Jackson, "Old Fort Madison—1808–1813," *Palimpsest* 39 (January 1958), 23–24.

5. Information about the Hunt family was extracted from Griswold, *Pictorial History of Fort Wayne*; "Old Fort Madison: Some Source Materials," *Iowa Journal of History and Politics* 11 (1913): 517–26; and Charles E. Slocum, *The History of the Maumee Basin* (Indianapolis: Bowen and Slocum, 1905).

6. Jackson, "Old Fort Madison," 29–30.

7. Ibid., 9–10.

8. "Old Fort Madison: Some Source Materials," 517–26.

9. For details of this story, see Jackson, "Old Fort Madison," 41–42; and "Old Fort Madison: Some Source Materials" 526–32.

10. See Kirkland, *Chicago Massacre of 1812*; and Currey, *Story of Old Fort Dearborn.*

11. See Jackson, "Old Fort Madison."

12. Because of the detail, the article entitled "Old Fort Madison: Some Source Materials" should be attributed to John Hunt. (See n. 5 and 9, above.)

13. *American State Papers*, Military Affairs, 7 vols. (Washington: Gales and Seaton, 1834), 4:680–82. Paper no. 470, "On Claims of a Sutler for Property Destroyed by the U.S. Army to Prevent Being Used by the Enemy."

14. Ibid. Smool was "local," e.g., from Mobile, Alabama, a fact that lends support to the idea that sutlers were brought on by arrangement with regimental field commanders.

15. Ibid., 681.

16. Ibid., 682.

17. The claim, filed on February 4, 1831, included the value of the building and of all the goods he lost because he had sold to the soldiers on credit and had never been paid.

18. Price control was not as sensitive as the sutler's lien. Prices were set by officers as early as 1815. Sutler Symmes at Cantonment Davis on the Missouri was allowed a 100 percent markup (50 percent profit). See Lewis Atherton, "The Merchant Sutler in the Pre–Civil War Period," *Southwestern Social Science Quarterly* 19, no. 2 (September 1938), 146.

4 Suttling on the Mississippi

1. George Croghan, *Army Life on the Western Frontier: Selections from the Official Reports Made Between 1826 and 1845*, ed. Francis Paul Prucha, (Nor-

man: University of Oklahoma Press, 1958), xiii; Wesley, *Guarding the Frontier*, 119; Prucha, *Sword of the Republic*, 136.

2. Bruce E. Mahan, *Old Fort Crawford and the Frontier* (Iowa City: State Historical Society of Iowa,1926), 57; Wesley, *Guarding the Frontier*, 9.

3. Prucha, *Sword of the Republic*, 126.

4. Ibid., 30–31.

5. Marcus Hunton, *Old Fort Snelling, 1819–1858* (Iowa City: State Historical Society of Iowa, 1918), 26 n.75, and 212.

6. Wesley, *Guarding the Frontier*, 133, 137, 171, 174.

7. Most information about John O'Fallon's St. Louis career is from J. T. Scharf, ed., *History of St. Louis City and County*, 3 vols. (Philadelphia: Louis H. Everto and Co., 1883); and from Louis Houck, *History of Missouri*, 3 vols. (Chicago: R. R. Donnelly and Sons Co., 1908).

8. Richard Edwards and M. Hopewell, M.D., *Edward's Great West and Her Commercial Metropolis and a History of St. Louis* (St. Louis: Edward's Monthly, 1860), 79–80.

9. Louise Barry, ed., "William Clark's Diary," *Kansas Historical Quarterly* 16 (February 1948): 17 n.41.

10. Edwards and Hopewell, *Edward's Great West* 80–81.

11. Carter, *Territorial Papers*, 17:406–10; also, see *Wisconsin Historical Society Collections*, 9, 436–39.

12. Benjamin O'Fallon conducted treaties with Indians in 1817 and was made Indian agent of the Upper Missouri in 1819. Leroy Hafen, ed., *Mountain Men and the Fur Trade* (Glendale: Arthur H. Clark Co., 1972), 5:255–81. Also, see L. Houck, *A History of Missouri*, 3:4n; and the *Missouri Gazette*, July 30 and August 6, 1814.

13. W. E. Hemphill, ed., *The Papers of John C. Calhoun*, 10 vols. (Columbia: University of South Carolina Press, 1959–1989), 2:398–99.

14. Louise Barry, *Beginning of the West: Annals of the Kansas Gateway to the American West, 1540–1854* (Lawrence: Kansas Historical Society, 1972), 80.

15. William C. Kennerly, *Persimmon Hill,* ed. Elizabeth Russell (Norman: University of Oklahoma Press, 1948), 41–44, n. 21. Also, see the introduction to Edgar B. Wesley, ed., "The Diary of James Kennerly," *Missouri Historical Society Collections* 6 (1928-1931): 41-46.

16. Roger L. Nichols, ed., *The Missouri Expedition of 1818–1820: The Journal of Surgeon John Gale* (Norman: University of Oklahoma Press, 1969), 8, 29.

17. Ibid., 44.

18. When scurvy also plagued troops that established Fort Snelling in 1821, the sutler allegedly saved the day by arriving at the post with vegetables. See Charlotte O. Van Cleve, *Three Score and Ten: Lifelong Memories of Fort Snelling, Minnesota*, 3d ed. (n.p., 1895).

19. Chicago, Pittsburgh, St. Louis, and New Orleans were major centers of trade and sources of sutlers' supplies.

20. Letter, April 20, 1819. John O'Fallon Papers, Adam Smith Collection;

Joint Collection, University of Missouri Western Historical Manuscript Collection–Columbia State Historical Society of Missouri Manuscripts (JCUM) (hereafter cited as the John O'Fallon Papers).

21. The biography of David Meriwether is found in Robert A. Griffen, ed., *My Life in the Mountains and on the Plains* (Norman: University of Oklahoma Press, 1965).

22. Letter to General Smith, June 28, 1819, John O'Fallon Papers. Captain Bissell arrived at Cantonment Martin with several boats and additional troops of the Sixth Regiment on August 17.

23. Roger B. Nicols, *General Henry Atkinson: A Western Military Career* (Norman: University of Oklahoma Press, 1965), 48.

24. Ibid., 174–75.

25. Edwin C. Bearss and Arrell M. Gibson, *Fort Smith: Little Gibraltar on the Arkansas* (Norman: University of Oklahoma Press, 1969), 3–6.

26. Prucha, *Sword of the Republic*, 176.

27. Alexander McNair's brother, Thomas McNair, was a partner, and John L. Findley was in charge. Mahan, *Old Fort Crawford*, 38.

28. Griffen, *My Life*, 33.

29. Wesley, *Guarding the Frontier*, 142.

30. Letter, July 27, 1820, John O'Fallon Papers.

31. Letter, July 1821, John O'Fallon Papers.

32. Ibid.

33. Dorothy B. Dorsey, "The Panic of 1819 in Missouri," *Missouri Historical Review* 29 (1935): 83.

34. Hemphill, *Papers of John C. Calhoun*, 6:240.

35. Letter, September 28, 1821. Hemphill, *Papers of John C. Calhoun*, 6:240. Also, June 29, 1822, letter from John O'Fallon to Thomas Smith, John O'Fallon Papers.

36. John O'Fallon to Smith, February 13, 1823, John O'Fallon Papers.

37. Ibid.

38. Griffen, *My Life*, 103.

39. Edwards and Hopewell, *Edward's Great West*, 81.

5 Creation of the Army Post Sutler

1. Wesley, *Guarding the Frontier*, 194, 67.

2. Two large contractors were William Duer, who supplied St. Clair and Anthony Wayne between 1786 and 1790, and John Johnson who supplied the Yellowstone expedition in 1818–19. Jacobs, *Beginning of the U.S. Army*, 80, 119–20.

3. *American State Papers*: Military Affairs, 2:199–274; Wesley, *Guarding the Frontier*, 84.

4. *American State Papers*: Military Affairs, 2:217–19

5. "Report of the Surgeon General, November 16, 1818," *American State Papers*: Military Affairs, 2:806.

6. "On Claims of a Sutler," *American State Papers*: Military Affairs, 4:680–82.

7. The rank was defined as cadet level without any direct authority over troops. America State Papers: Military Affairs, 2:218.

8. Register of Post Sutlers, Adjutant General's Office, Record Group 94, National Archives.

9. *American State Papers*: Military Affairs, 2:806.

10. "General Wayne's Orderly Book," February 1, 1796, 668.

11. Minutes and Tariffs of Fort Gibson's Council of Administration, May 8, 1845. National Archives, M1466, Roll no. 6.

12. Rona Ostrowe and Sweetman R. Smith, *The Dictionary of Retailing* (New York: Fairchild Publications, 1985), defines markup as retail price minus cost divided by retail price.

13. "General Wayne's Orderly Book," February 1, 1796, 682.

14. The first mention of this device found by the author was at Fort Dearborn in 1809. See Carter, *Territorial Papers*, 16:122. By the Civil War, these vouchers were critical to the sutler if he wanted to be reimbursed after having extended credit.

15. In the late 1800s, the fund was composed of the sutler's assessment plus money saved by troops baking their own bread. The money was used (in order of priority) for the expense of a bakehouse, garden seeds and utensils, post schools, post library and reading room, gymnasium, a chapel, fruit and shade trees, fruit-bearing vines and shrubs, and a printing press. *Farrow's Military Encyclopedia, A Dictionary of Military Knowledge* (New York: Military-Naval Publishing Co., 1885), 568–69.

16. McNair was a man who, among other things, had been the first sutler to Fort Crawford in 1815.

17. Barry, "William Clark's Diary," *Kansas Historical Quarterly* 16 (May 1948): 1–2.

18. For details of the life of John Kennerly, see Kennerly, *Persimmon Hill*; Houck, *History of Missouri,* vols. 2 and 3; Mrs. Daniel R. Russell, ed., "Early Days in St. Louis from the Memoirs of an Old Citizen," *Missouri Historical Society Collections* 3 (1908–11): 407–22; Hemphill, *Papers of John C. Calhoun* 6; Hafen, *Mountain Men, 5*; Nicols, *General Henry Atkinson*; Carter, *Territorial Papers,* 15; and Barry, "William Clark's Diary," *Kansas Historical Quarterly* 16 (1948), Parts 1–4: February, 1–39; (May), 136–74; August, 274–305; and (November), 384–410.

19. Kennerly's life as sutler at Fort Atkinson is taken from Wesley, "Diary of James Kennerly." A description of life at Fort Atkinson may be obtained from Sally A. Johnson, "The Sixth's Elysian Fields—Ft. Atkinson on the Council Bluff," *Nebraska History* 40 (March 1959):1–38; and from W. H. Ellers, "Old Fort Atkinson," *Transactions and Reports of the Nebraska State Historical Society* 4 (1892): 18–28.

20. Pratte was engaged with Choteaux in the fur trade for years. His firm became the western department of the American Fur Company in 1827.

21. 1826 Inspector General Report, Fort Atkinson, Record Group 624, National Archives, Microfilm Roll no. 2, 89.

22. Ibid., 72, 90.

23. Johnson, "Sixth's Elysian Fields," 19.

24. Kennerly's diary referred, one time or another, to military officers Colonel Henry Atkinson, Colonel Henry Leavenworth and Stephen Watts Kearny; General Ashley, Lucien Fontenelle, Andrew Dipps, and Edward Rose of the fur trade; Charles Bent, first governor of New Mexico; and Indian agents John Dougherty and Thomas Fitzpatrick.

25. On December 21, 1825, Croghan was appointed as Inspector General for the army. Barry, "William Clark's Diary," (May 1948), 14, n. 36., 38.

6 The Evolution of Suttling, 1820–1840

1. Wesley, "Diary of James Kennerly," 83n.

2. Johnson, "Sixth Elysian Fields," 19.

3. New Orleans, 1818, Inspector General Reports.

4. Ibid., no. 3: 155.

5. General Order of Battle, 5:64.

6. Order no. 12, Major General Alexander Macomb, Adjutant General's Office.

7. General Order of Battle. Vol. 6, 53, 56, 59.

8. Inspector General Reports, George Croghan's 1831 report from Jefferson Barracks.

9. General Order no. 14, February 12, 1839, U.S. Army Headquarters, Adjutant General's Office.

10. Army Regulations, 1835, 83, 84, National Archives.

11. Order no. 47, Washington, D.C., July 29, 1829, Adjutant General's Office; General Order of Battle. 5: 193.

12. Nassau, N.Y., 1833, Inspector General Reports.

13. The law was ineffective and short lived because the frontier was too extensive to patrol, the army had too few men for the job, and local authorities received little assistance from unsympathetic frontiersmen. William A. Ganoe, *The History of the United States Army* (New York: D. Appleton and Company, 1924), 172.

14. Inspector General Reports, 1833, Record Group no. 624, National Archives.

15. Ibid., Record Group no. 624, Roll no. 3, frame 133.

16. Prucha, *Sword of the Republic*, 329.

17. Croghan, *Army Life on the Western Frontier*, 79.

18. Ibid., 124.

19. Sutlers were first mentioned in 1820, and even then, many inspectors mentioned sutlers only when there was a problem or unusual event. After 1820, many inspectors like George Croghan routinely covered the sutler's services and his demeanor. Inspector General Reports, 3 microfilm rolls, Record Group no. 624, National Archives Roll no. 1, 1812–1822.

20. Mahan, *Old Fort Crawford*, 57–60. During the War of 1812, sutlers accompanied forty-two regulars and sixty-five rangers who ascended the Mississippi to take over Fort Shelby. The fort was subsequently overrun by the British, as was Prairie du Chien.

21. Theodore F. Rodenbough, ed., *From Everglades to Canon with the Second Dragoons, 1836–1875* (New York: A. Van Nostrand, 1875), 35–37, 39; John T. Sprague, *The Florida War* (facsimile of 1848 ed.; Gainesville: University of Florida Press, 1964), 233–34.

22. When Fort Atkinson was closed, the men were relocated to Jefferson Barracks. Prucha, *Sword of the Republic*, 339.

23. Adjutant General's Office, Order no. 12, Major General Alexander Macomb.

24. Nicols, *General Henry Atkinson* 71, 101.

25. Ibid., 165; Prucha, *Broadax and Bayonet*, 27; Prucha, *Sword of the Republic*, 274, 319; Nicols, *General Henry Atkinson*, 165.

26. Prucha, *Broadax and Bayonet*, 22.

27. Prucha, *Sword of the Republic*, 234.

28. Croghan would have been dismayed to learn that forty years later, the Inspector General would argue that the way to keep the soldier from spending everything he had was to pay him less frequently. "The longer you keep soldiers' pay, the longer you prevent them from desertion, and the more seldom they are paid, the fewer drunken irregularities will occur." L. E. Oliva, *Fort Hays, Frontier Outpost, 1865–1889* (Lawrence: Kansas State Historical Society, 1980), 41.

29. Francis Paul Prucha, "Army Sutlers and the American Fur Company," *Minnesota History* 40, no. 1 (Spring 1966): 29.

30. Inspector General Reports.

31. Prucha, *Sword of the Republic*, 324–25.

32. Although this does not sound like much money, it must be remembered that the men who deserted had been on duty for less than two months. The accounts were inspected and verified by Colonel John Ewing and Captain James Bowman. Ellen M. Whitney, ed., *The Blackhawk War, 1831–1832*, 1:254–55n.

33. Records of the Second Auditor's office: Sutlers' claims, Record Group 217. National Archives.

34. Register of Post Traders, 1821–1889. Adjutant General's Office, Record Group 94. National Archives.

35. Lewis E. Atherton, "The Merchant Sutler in the Pre–Civil War Period," *Southwestern Social Science Quarterly* 19, no. 2 (September 1938): 143.

36. Whitney, *Blackhawk War*, 1: 1213, 1214 n. 4, and 284 n.1.

37. From a compilation of biographical material collected on sutlers during research for this book. In the author's possession.

38. Fort Crawford, 1836. Inspector General Reports, 1826–1845 (microfilm), 113, National Archives.

39. Ibid., 106.

40. Atherton, "Merchant Sutler."

41. The record of H. T. Wilson may be found scattered throughout the pages of C. W. Goodlander, *Early Days of Fort Scott* (Fort Scott: Monitor Printing Co., 1900).

42. Historian Francis Paul Prucha called Inspector Croghan's reports

"frank, incisive, critical, and sparked with a military spirit." Croghan, *Army Life on the Western Frontier*, Introduction.

43. Ibid., p. 63; also, see Register of Post Traders, Adjutant General's Office.

44. Ibid., 106.

45. Ibid., 50.

46. Ibid., 54. According to the Register of Post Traders, Jones was sutler from 1828 to 1838.

47. Atherton, "Merchant Sutler," 141.

48. William B. Lees and Kathryn M. Kimery-Lees, "Regional Perspectives on the Fort Towson Sutler's Store and Residence, A Frontier Site in Antebellum Eastern Oklahoma," *Plains Anthropologist* 29 (103) (1984): 13–24.

49. Grant Foreman, *Pioneer Days in the Southwest* (Arthur H. Clark and Co., 1926), 167n.

50. Houston felt pretty confident that he would get the post, so he loaded a keelboat with supplies purchased from New York and Nashville and sent them to the Neosho River. The load included nine barrels of spirits—allegedly for Houston's personal consumption. Amelia W. Williams and Eugene C. Barker, eds., *The Writings of Sam Houston*, 8 vols. (Austin: University of Texas Press, 1938) 1:153–55.

51. Ibid., 99n.

52. John F. McDermott, ed., *The Western Journals of Washington Irving* (Norman: University of Oklahoma, 1944), 150–51.

53. Coffman, *Old Army*, 178.

54. He based his estimate on the 1840 census records.

55. Lewis E. Atherton, "The Services of the Frontier Merchant," *Mississippi Valley Historical Review* (September 1937): 153–70.

56. Lewis E. Atherton, "The Pioneer Merchant in Mid-America," *University of Missouri Studies* 14 (April 1939): 39. No tax burden other than the post-fund assessment could be imposed on the sutler. He was permitted use of an extra building or could build his own, but he had no claim to government quarters, transportation, or allowances. General Regulations, 1841; paragraph no. 189.

57. Atherton, "Merchant Sutler," 150.

58. Whitney, *Blackhawk War*, 2:991.

59. Prucha, "Army Sutlers," 26.

60. Ibid., 31.

61. He resided in the house that formerly belonged to John Kinzie.

62. See Inspector General Reports, Roll no. 3. Subsequent references to Bailey's letter are referred to as Bailey.

63. Register of Indian Trading Licenses, 1847–1873, Record Group 75, National Archives.

64. Prucha, *Broadax and Bayonet*, 8.

65. See Robert A. Trennert, *Indian Traders of the Middle Border: The House of Ewing, 1827–1854* (Lincoln: University of Nebraska Press, 1981).

66. Carter, *Territorial Papers*, 15:190; Barry, *Beginning of the West*, 182, 233, 234.

67. Satterlee Clark, "Early Times at Fort Winnebago," *Wisconsin Historical Collections* 8 (1879): 309–22. Also, M. O. Newberry was the sutler for Jo. Daviess Co. Volunteers during the Blackhawk War. Whitney, *Blackhawk War*, 2:734–35 n. 4.

68. The first postal lines were those leading to the frontier posts, and the first post offices were at the garrisons. The author's sutler statistics show that postmaster and notary public were the most common of all the local offices held by sutlers.

69. Whitney, *Blackhawk War*, 217, 217 n. 3, and 722.

7 Successful Pre–Civil War Sutlers

1. Charles M. Cummings, *Yankee Quaker Confederate General* (Madison: Fairleigh Dickinson University Press, 1971), 109–10.

2. Richard Guentzel, "The Department of the Platte and Western Settlement, 1866–1877," *Nebraska History Magazine* 56 no. 3 (February 1975), 391.

3. John D. Unruh, Jr., *The Plains Across: The Overland Emigrants and the Trans-Mississippi West, 1840–1860* (University of Illinois Press, 1979), 248.

4. Robert W. Frazer, *Mansfield on the Conditions of Forts in the Southwest, 1853–1854* (Norman: University of Oklahoma Press, 1946), 64–65.

5. Ibid., 65.

6. Ibid., 41, 67. Fort Massachusetts' successor was Fort Garland. As for Fort Buchanan, General Garland hoped to obtain some materials from the Tucson area, but was prepared to transport everything from the Rio Grande Valley if necessary. Robert W. Frazer, *Forts and Supplies: The Role of the Army in the Economy of the Southwest, 1846–1861* (Albuquerque: University of New Mexico Press, 1983), 136. High freight costs were not unique to the Southwest. A trooper at Fort Pierre on the Upper Missouri said, "a sutler had set up his store with a miscellaneous stock of goods, also goods for trading with the Indians, but prices were so high that we could not afford to buy much. This was due to the high cost of transportation which amounted to about $50 per ton from St. Louis." Augustus Meyers, *Ten Years in the Ranks of the U.S. Army* (New York: Stirling Press, 1914), 73.

7. Chris Emmet, *Fort Union and the Winning of the Southwest* (Norman: University of Oklahoma Press, 1965), 77.

8. Frazer, *Forts and Supplies*, 96.

9. Ibid., 13–14.

10. Ibid., 88. Not everyone left. Elias Brevoort, who came to New Mexico in 1850, became sutler at Camp Moore, and later at Fort Buchanan. He acquired property and became a great extoller of the virtues of the Southwest, authoring the only known sutler-written book, entitled *New Mexico, Her Natural Resources and Her Attractions* (Santa Fe, 1874). See Frazer, *Forts and Supplies*, 223.

11. Historical Note, "Introduction to Fort Kearny, Nebraska," Archives

Records, Nebraska Historical Society; also, Ray Wilson, *Fort Kearny on the Platte* (Crossroads Communications, 1980), 34–35.

12. George F. Weisel, ed., *Men and Trade on the Northwest Frontier* (Missoula: Montana State University Press, 1955), xxi–xxx, 3.

13. See Rodney C. Loehr, "Franklin Steele, Frontier Businessman," *Minnesota History* 27 (1946): 309–18.

14. Agnes M. Larson, "On the Trail of the Woodsman in Minnesota," *Minnesota History* 13, no. 4 (December 1932), 354.

15. Liza Nagle and Marx Swanholm, "The Buried History of the Sutler's Store," *Chronicles of Fort Snelling,* no. 4 (1976), 2.

16. James G. Soulard (1798–1878) was born in St. Louis. In 1820, he married Elizabeth Hunt, daughter of Colonel Thomas Hunt. During 1821 and 1822, he was the sutler at Snelling. He returned to St. Louis, then settled in Galena, Illinois, as a merchant, lead smelter, postmaster, and a farmer who was known for his nursery. Whitney, *Blackhawk War,* 1:61n.

17. Ibid., 60n.

18. Minnesota Outdoor Recreation Commission, "Fort Snelling" (St. Paul, Minnesota, 1965), 65.

19. Ibid., 66. When the foundations of the sutler's store were unearthed in 1968, archeologists also identified a Spanish coin from 1743, bone toothbrushes, louse combs, cologne and perfume bottles, metal toothpick fragments, brass needles and pins, scissors, hinges, ceramic bowls, various bottles and flasks for alcoholic beverages, gunflints, marbles, dominos made of bone and wood, and a carved chess piece. Nagle and Swanholm, "Buried History," 3.

20. Prucha, "Army Sutler," 27.

21. Clarence W. Rife, "Norman W. Kittson, A Fur Trader at Pembina," *Minnesota History* 6, no. 3 (September 1925), 226.

22. William J. Petersen, "Steamboating in the Upper Mississippi Fur Trade," *Minnesota History* 13, no. 3 (September 1932), 224, 234. About this time period, a Captain Daniel Smith Harris and his brother built steamboats, including one named "The Sutler." See George B. Merrick, *Old Times on the Upper Mississippi River* (Glendale: Arthur H. Clark Company, 1909), 184.

23. Rodney C. Loehr, "Caleb D. Dorr and the Early Minnesota Lumber Industry," *Minnesota History* 24 (1923), 127, 130.

24. Information about Steele's involvement in the sale of Fort Snelling was obtained from the pages of U.S. Congress, House of Representatives, Military Affairs Committee, "The Sale of Fort Snelling." HR no. 351. 35th Cong., 1st sess.

25. Information on the life of John Dougherty was assembled from Hafen, *Mountain Men;* LeRoy Hafen and F. M. Young, *Fort Laramie and the Pageant of the West* (Lincoln: University of Nebraska, 1938); Carter, *Territorial Papers;* Barry, *Beginning of the West.*

26. D. Ray Wilson, *Fort Kearny on the Platte: First Fort Built on the Oregon Trail* (n.p.: Crossroads Communications, 1984), 165.

27. Tutt also had competition from the army commissary, which provided many emigrants with basic foodstuffs for cost and carriage. See Merrill J.

Mattes, "The Sutler's Store at Fort Laramie," *Annals of Wyoming* 4 (1937): 99–133.

28. Tom White et al., "Post Sutlers/Traders at Fort Laramie" (n.p.: Fort Laramie Historical Association, February 28, 1971), 3, 4.

29. Register of Post Traders, 1821–1889, Office of the Adjutant General's Office. National Archives.

30. Eugene Bandel, *Frontier Life in the Army, 1854–1861,* trans. Olga Bandel and Richard Jente, ed. Ralph P. Bieber (Glendale: Arthur H. Clark Co., 1932), 105.

31. Bearss and Gibson, *Fort Smith* 101.

32. Jerry M. Sunder, *The Fur Trade on the Upper Missouri, 1840–1865* (Norman: University of Oklahoma Press, 1965), 183.

33. Robert G. Athearn, *Forts of the Upper Missouri* (Englewood: Prentice Hall, 1967), 57.

8 The Civil War Sutler at Large

1. Charles M. Clark, *The History of the 39th Regiment, Illinois Volunteer Veteran Infantry* (Chicago: n.p., 1889), 122–24. This sutler amassed a fortune and established a bank at Richmond, Virginia, and subsequently had a banking business in Chicago, but he died in 1877 in very reduced circumstances.

2. Whitney, *Blackhawk* War, 1:vii, xi.

3. Nicols, *General Henry Atkinson,* 167.

4. Conclusions drawn from a statistical analysis of data for twenty-four companies from the Third Army of Illinois Volunteers.

5. The allotment included $2.62 base pay, $2.32 travel pay (five days with forage), $4.80 for horse and arms ($0.40 a day), and $2.00 for supplying one's own forage and subsistence for eight days. Whitney, *Blackhawk War,* 1:119n.

6. Whitney, *Blackhawk War,* 1:529n.

7. From sutler indebtedness of 649 soldiers.

8. "Camp Inspection Return Questions," Document no. 19a, *Documents of the United States Sanitary Commission.* 2 vols. (New York: United States Sanitary Commission, 1866), 30.

9. Donald P. Spear, "The Sutler in the Union Army," *Civil War History* (June 16, 1970), 121.

10. Document no. 40, *Documents of the United States Sanitary Commission,* 23. The commission had no legal authority; it did, however, inquire of and report to the Secretary of War on the state of army sanitary conditions, as well as look at inspection principles and practices and conditions surrounding cooks, nurses, hospitals, and related subjects.

11. A ratio of 3,500 men X 3 months to 500,000 men x 4 years=1:16,000.

12. Spear, "Sutler in the Union Army," 121.

13. Ibid., 122–23; Edward G. Longacre, ed., *From Antietam to Fort Fisher* (Madison: Fairleigh Dickinson Press, 1985), 42–43; James C. Nisbet, *Four Years on the Firing Line* (Jackson: McCowat-Mercer Press, 1963), 249.

14. Francis A. Lord, *Civil War Sutlers and Their Wares* (New York:

Yoseloff, 1969), 67; see also Johnson, *Muskets and Medicine, or, Army Life in the Sixties,* 199.

15. Lord, *Civil War Sutlers,* 132ff.

16. Johnson, *Muskets and Medicine,* 178.

17. John D. Billings, *Hardtack and Coffee: The Unwritten Story of Army Life* (Chicago: Lakeside Press, 1960), 243.

18. Ibid., 242.

19. Ibid., 245.

20. Augustus C. Stearns, *Three Years with Company K.,* ed. Arthur A. Kent (Cranbury: Association of University Presses, 1976), 158.

21. Sutlers and private dealers made efforts to sell metal chest plates guaranteed as ironclad life preservers. Such accouterments became popular as frying pans. Robert McAllister, *The Civil War Letters of General Robert McAllister,* ed. James I. Robertson, Jr. (New Brunswick, 1965), 181 and n.

22. Ibid., 148–49.

23. Carlton McCarthy, "Detailed Minutiae of a Soldier's Life," *Southern Historical Society Papers* 6 (July 1878), 5.

24. Bell I. Wiley, *The Life of Johnny Reb* (New York: Bobbs-Merrill, 1943), in *The Common Soldier in the Civil War,* Book no. 2 (New York: Grosset and Dunlap, 1951), 76.

25. Ibid., 355; Longacre, *From Antietam to Fort Fisher,* 42–43.

26. Johnson, *Muskets and Medicine,* 178–79.

27. Lord, *Civil War Sutlers,* 67, 131.

28. Ibid., 294.

29. Frank McNitt, *The Indian Traders* (Norman: University of Oklahoma Press, 1962), 83.

30. David E. Schenkman, *Civil War Sutler Tokens and Cardboard Scrip* (New York: Jade House Publications, 1983), 10, 11, and 15. These firms also made "dog tags," coins that sutlers sold which had soldiers' names and units on them.

31. Leo W. Faller and John I. Faller, *Dear Folks at Home: The Civil War Letters of Leo W. and John I. Faller with an Account of Andersonville,* ed. Milton E. Flower (Harrisburg: Cumberland County Historical Society and Hamilton Library Association, 1963), 70–71; also, see Schenkman, *Civil War Sutler Tokens,* 91.

32. Ibid., 235.

33. Emil Rosenblatt, *Anti-Rebel: The Civil War Letters of Wilbur Fisk* (New York: Croton-on-Hudson, 1983), 10.

34. Spear, "Sutler in the Union Army," 126. For other unusual items, see Charles A. Page, *Letters of a War Correspondent,* ed. James R. Gilmore (Boston: L. C. Page and Company, 1899), 243–44.

35. Frank L. Byrne, ed., *The View from Headquarters: The Civil War Letters of Harvey Reid* (Madison: Wisconsin State Historical Society, 1965), 63. Mr. W. O. Stillman sold his share of his sutlership to his employee, Mr. Shove, and returned to his home in Racine, Wisconsin, because he couldn't sell anything to the boys except beer.

36. Lord, *Civil War Sutlers,* 137.

37. Edwin A. Glover, *Bucktailed Wildcats: A Regiment of Civil War Volunteers* (New York: T. Yoseloff, 1960), 187, 233.

38. Document no. 40, *Documents of the United States Sanitary Commission*, 24.

39. Joseph F. Culver, *Your Affectionate Husband, J. F. Culver*, ed. Wesley W. Dunlap (Iowa City: Friends of the University of Iowa Libraries, 1978), 82.

40. Meyers, *Ten Years in the Ranks*, 187.

41. General LaFayette C. Baker, *History of the United States Secret Service* (Philadelphia: published by the author, 1867), 154–55.

42. United States War Department, *War of the Rebellion: A Compilation of Official Records of the Union and Confederate Armies* (Washington, D.C., 1899), Series 1, 40, 3:55–56.

43. Wilton P. Moore, "The Provost Marshall Goes to War," 67; United States War Department, *War of the Rebellion*, Series 1, 40, no. 3, 55–56.

44. Document no. 40, *Documents of the United States Sanitary Commission*, 24.

45. Ibid.

46. Meyers, *Ten Years in the Ranks*, 187; also, see Van Doren, *Mutiny in January*, 32.

47. Meyers, *Ten Years in the Ranks*, 187.

48. Glover, *Bucktailed Wildcats*, 187.

49. Document no. 40, *Documents of the United States Sanitary Commission*, 24.

50. Billings, *Hardtack and Coffee*, 242.

51. Document no. 40, *Documents of the United States Sanitary Commission*, 23.

52. Ibid., 41.

53. Johnson, *Muskets and Medicine*, 179.

54. Rosenblatt, *Anti-Rebel*, 73.

55. Ibid., 33.

56. Billings, *Hardtack and Coffee*, 242–43; *The United States Army and Navy Journal* 7:278.

57. Rosenblatt, *Anti-Rebel*, 33.

58. Robert E. Park, "The Diary of Captain Robert E. Park, 12th Alabama Regiment," *Southern Historical Society Papers* 3 (1875), 355.

59. Park, "Diary," 2:84, and 26:22.

60. Ibid., 196–97.

61. Longacre, *From Antietam to Fort Fisher*, 42–43, 93; Rosenblatt, *Anti-Rebel*, 33 and 73; Billings, *Hardtack and Coffee*, 243; and Calvin D. Cowles, ed., *Atlas of the war of the Rebellion*. 3 vols. (Washington, D.C.: Atlas Publishing Co., 1892), 254–55.

62. Billings, *Hardtack and Coffee*, 246.

63. Julian W. Hinkley, *A Narrative of Service with the Third Wisconsin Infantry* (originally Vol. 7, *Wisconsin Historical Commission Original Paper* no. 7, 1912) (Madison: Wisconsin Historical Society, 1912), 142.

64. Ibid., 134ff.

65. Records of the Second Auditor's Office, Record Group 217, National Archives.

66. *United States Statutes at Large*, Vol. 33, part 1, 1903–05, 759.

67. Rosenblatt, *Anti-Rebel*, 267.

68. M. H. Dunkelman and M. J. Winey, *The Hardtack Regiment* (Madison: Fairleigh Dickinson Press, 1981), 39.

69. Longacre, *From Antietam to Fort Fisher*, 240.

70. J. W. Mattson, "Orr's South Carolina Rifles," *Southern Historical Society Papers* 27 (January-December 1899), 161.

71. Colonel A. F. Brown, "Van Dorn's Operations in Northern Mississippi: Recollections of a Cavalryman," *Southern Historical Society Papers* 5 (1877), 158.

72. William Hallen, "History of the Campaign of Stonewall Jackson in the Shenandoah Valley of Virginia," *Southern Historical Society Papers* 43 (August 1920), 221–22n, 233n.

73. Longacre, *From Antietam to Fort Fisher*, 34, 42–43, 97.

74. Spear, "Sutler in the Union Army," 136.

75. Rosenblatt, *Anti-Rebel*, 288.

76. Bruce Catton, *Glory Road: The Bloody Route from Fredericksburg to Gettysburg* (Garden City: Doubleday and Co., 1954), 257.

77. John J. Pullen, *The 20th Maine: A Volunteer Regiment in the Civil War* (New York: J. B. Lippincott, 1957), 277–79.

78. Rosenblatt, *Anti-Rebel*, 137–38.

79. Frank L. Byrne, ed., *The View from Headquarters: Civil War Letters of Harvey Reid* (Madison: State Historical Society of Wisconsin, 1965), 114–15.

80. Spear, "Sutler in the Union Army," 122.

81. Frank L. Byrne and Jean P. Soman, eds., *Your Dear Marcus: The Civil War Letters of a Jewish Colonel* (Kent, Ohio: Kent State University Press, 1985), 230, 254, 263, 266.

82. Ibid., 187, 269, and 296–97.

83. "We get our boxes via sutler whose teams goes to the express office in Washington D.C. nearly every day. He charges us 25 cents," said Leo Faller, in Faller and Faller, *Dear Folks at Home*, 36; also, see McAllister, *Civil War Letters*, 295.

84. Spear, "Sutler in the Union Army," 133.

85. Cowles, *Atlas of the War of the Rebellion*, 1:248.

86. United States War Department, *War of the Rebellion*, Series 2, 8:312–13.

87. Park, "Diary," 2 (1874), 84.

88. General Order no. 3, dated February 7, 1865. Jno Winder, HQ, Military Prisons, Columbia, South Carolina. U. S. War Department, War of the Rebellion, Series 2, 8:313.

89. Wiley, *Life of Johnny Reb*, 100; Cowles, *Official Record: Atlas*, 1:255.

90. Dunkelman and Winey, *Hardtack Regiment*, 42.

91. Wiley, *Life of Johnny Reb*, 100; *Harper's Weekly*, 8 (December 10, 1864), 787, col 3.

92. Washington Davis, *Campfire Chats of the Civil War* (Chicago: A. B. Gehman Company, 1886), 151–54.

93. Pullen, *20th Maine*, 278; Billings, *Hardtack and Coffee*, 242.

94. Billings, *Hardtack and Coffee*, 277–79.

95. John C. Gray and John C. Ropes, *War Letters* (Boston; Houghton Mifflin, 1927), 327n; United States War Department, *The War of the Rebellion*, Series 1, 20, 2:104., and also 29, 2:79; Culver, *Your Affectionate Husband*, 54n.

96. Colonel Charles S. Wainwright, *A Diary of Battle: The Personal Journals of Colonel Charles S. Wainwright*, ed. Allan Nevins (N.Y.: Harcourt, Brace and World, 1962), 340, 562.

97. McAllister, *Civil War Letters*, 296.

98. Billings, *Hardtack and Coffee*, 247.

99. E. B. Coddington, *The Gettysburg Campaign: A Study in Command* (New York: Charles Scribner's Sons, 1968), 364n.

100. J. S. Newberry, M.D., ed., "Report on the Condition of the Troops and the Operation of the Sanitary Commission in the Valley of the Mississippi for the three months ending Nov 30 1861," Document no. 36. *Documents of the United States Sanitary Commission*, 5.

101. Rosenblatt, *Anti-Rebel*, 109.

102. McAllister, *Civil War Letters*, 173; Wainwright, *Diary of Battle*, 408, 461.

103. Park, "Diary" 3:250.

104. Coddington, *Gettysburg Campaign*, 364n.

9 Controlling a Necessary Evil

1. An act of Congress, approved on December 24, 1861, in response to Wilson's attack on the sutlers, repealed an act of June 12, 1858, and abrogated all privileges above and beyond the Articles of War, including the sutler's ability to obtain a lien on the soldier's pay. Specifics of the act were identical to controls passed by the Continental Congress in 1776. *War of the Rebellion: A Compilation of Official Documents of the Union and Confederate Armies*, Series 3, 1:764–65.

2. *Congressional Record*, January 11, 1962.

3. Ibid.

4. *Congressional Globe*, January 29, 1862.

5. The discussion on how to control the sutler comes from Senate debates printed in the *Congressional Globe*, 37th Cong., 2d. sess., 17, 68, 182, 199, 271, 377, 538, 1155, 1164, 1180, 1234, and 1297.

6. The Secretary of War told Congress that he wanted total authority and responsibility for hiring and controlling the sutler to belong to each regiment and the Commanding General. "Resolution of the Senate re the appointment of the sutler to General Daniel E. Sickles' brigade," S. Exec. Doc. no. 10, 37th Cong., 2d. sess., 1862.

7. *Congressional Globe*, January 10, 1862; *Statistical Abstracts of the United States* (United States Department of Commerce, 1987); *Historical Abstracts of the United States*, Part 1 (U.S. Department of Commerce).

8. To place the size of the sutler trade in perspective, the purchasing power of one dollar in 1861 was worth $12 to $15 in 1989; thus, the sutler's annual gross sales from the Army of the Potomac alone reached the equivalence of $125 million to $150 million.

9. New York *Tribune*, December 9, 1861.

10. This congressional act was passed December 24, 1861, *United States Statutes*, 12:331.

11. H.R. Misc. Doc. no. 42, 37th Cong., 2d. sess., 1862. At the same time, a congressional committee to investigate the organization and administration of the Medical, Commissary and Quartermaster departments said: "The comfort of the volunteers would be consulted by a definite number of sutlers judiciously selected, properly restricted and a tariff with moderate profits adopted." T. N. Waul's Report, January 29, 1862. *War of the Rebellion*, Series 4. 1:883–91.

12. *Congressional Globe*, January 29, 1862.

13. Document no. 40, *Documents of the United States Sanitary Commission*, 23; *Congressional Globe*, January 27, 1862; A letter of January 12, 1863, from the Adjutant General informed Jesse M. Stone, Fort Abercrombie, Dakota Territory, sutler, that the Wilson bill did not apply to Regular Army sutlers. David McCauly Papers, North Dakota Institute for Regional Studies, North Dakota State University at Fargo.

14. On February 7, 1863, Special Order no. 37 increased the list of items sutlers were allowed to sell to include canned meats, oysters, condiments, pickles, fish, tin plates, cups, cutlery, twine, wrapping paper, uniform clothing for officers, socks, shirts, drawers, and shoes. Francis A. Lord, *They Fought for the Union* (Harrisburg: Stackpole Co., 1960), 130.

15. Act of March 19, 1862: Ch. 47, H.R. Misc. R. no. 43, 37th Cong., 2d. sess. Also, see Cowles, *Official Record, Atlas*, 1:71, 80, 88, 248, 253–55.

16. Article 25, devoted to sutlers, was the same as Union Army Regulations of 1857, sections 196–203, and 202–209, *Regulations for the Army of the Confederate States, 1862* (Richmond: 1862).

17. Lord, *They Fought for the Union*, 112. In the opinion of Colonel Joseph Holt, Judge Advocate General, it seemed that "under the comprehensive and imperative language of the enrolling act, sutlers, together with members of the enrolling board are necessary subject to draft." Circular no. 64, August 6, 1863, from James B. Fry, Provost Marshal General, Washington, D.C., *War of the Rebellion*, Series 3, 2:631. On January 22, 1863, a resolution to enroll and place in the ranks all sutlers between the ages of eighteen and forty-five was introduced at the First Confederate Congress, Third Session, and subsequently adopted by the military committee. *Southern Historical Society Papers* 47 (December 1930), 178.

18. " . . . moreover, citizens who accompany an army for whatever purpose, such as sutlers, editors or reporters of journals . . . if captured may be made prisoners of war and detained as such." April 24, 1863, General Order no.

100, War Department, "Instructions for the Government of Armies," Item 50, Section 3, *War of the Rebellion*, Series 2, 5:671–74. A letter of August 23, 1862, Brigadier-General James S. Wadsworth, HQ, Washington, D.C., to Major-General John A. Dix, Fort Monroe, Va., listed sutlers and sutlers' clerks held prisoner at the Libby Prison at Richmond. Series 2, 4:426–47. See also a letter of December 17, 1862, from Hitchcock, Major General of Volunteers, Commissioner for Exchange of Prisoners, to Secretary of War Stanton, in reference to resolutions of Congress calling for information about the exchange of noncombatants, including sutlers who have been held prisoner at Richmond. He said the cartel of September 25 requires captured sutlers, teamsters, and all civilians in the service of either party to be exchanged for prisoners in similar positions. Ibid., Series 2, 5:91, A letter dated January 28, 1863, from William H. Ludlow, agent for exchange of prisoners, to Colonel William Hoffman, said he expects sutlers and civilian employees to be delivered the following week. Ibid., Series 2, 5:222.

19. *Southern Historical Society Papers* 15 (January-December 1887), 278. The three sutlers were Joseph I. Burgess of the 27th North Carolina Regiment; James H. Corder of the 7th Tennessee Regiment; and H. L. Neal of Barton's Independent Brigade.

20. Allan Nevins, *The War for the Union* (New York: Charles Scribner's Sons, 1971) 2:477.

21. As General Meade wrote to Grant on July 8, 1864: "The objection to permitting [sutlers] to coming to the front is the necessity of either allowing them the use of government wagons . . . or else permitting them to bring their own wagons thus increasing the number of animals to be fed and the number of wagons using the road, some three or four hundred. Another objection is the uncertainty of our own position and the difficulty in getting rid of them in the event of a sudden movement. . . . There are many articles only to be procured from the sutlers, which are necessary to the men's comfort and which they are now in want of and I think it would be well to let the sutlers come up if it is practicable." *War of the Rebellion*, Series 1, 40, Part 3:73.

22. General Order no. 130, September 14, 1862. War of the Rebellion, Series 3, 2:544.

23. *War of the Rebellion*, Series 1, 29, Part 2: 40, 41, August 13, 1863. Letter from Captain W. W. Beckwith, aide-de-camp to Colonel G. H. Sharp, Deputy Provost Marshal General.

24. Baker, *History of the United States Secret Service*, 158–59.

25. Ibid., 160–61.

26. *War of the Rebellion*, Series 1, 29, Part 2:11.

27. General Order no. 79, August 20, 1983, HQ of the Army of Potomac, Assistant Adjutant General Williams. *War of the Rebellion*, Series 1, 9, Part 2:79.

28. General Order no. 23, November 27, 1862, HQ, 14th Army Corps, Dept. of Cumberland, Nashville, Tenn. *War of the Rebellion*, Series 1, 2, Part 2:104–5. Also, see Culver, *Your Affectionate Husband*, 54 n. 9.

29. John Bakeless, *Spies of the Confederacy* (New York: J. P. Lippincott

Co., 1970), 355; Charles James, *An Universal Military Dictionary*. 4th ed. (London: T. Egerton, 1816), 475.

30. On January 9, 10, and 11, 1864, Captain Park wrote, "Our bill of fare consists of bread and tea for breakfast and a small piece of pork and beans and bean soup in a tin cup with one third of a loaf of bread for diner. Sometimes beef and beef soup is furnished in lieu of pork and bean soup for dinner. Some of my roommates have received money from friends and buy cheese, crackers and apples from the sutler." Park, "Diary," 312.

31. Prisoners were creative when it came to fulfilling their needs. "A lot of men wrote articles while in prison and officers would purchase them. They were not allowed to purchase them for money so they would give pass-books to the sutler upon which one was credited to the amount agreed upon. The prisoners could not purchase eatables from the sutler. This mode of trading did not suit the prisoners, so they used 'detailers' from the camp. They created a chain of go-betweens to Baltimore and Washington using runners on the boats." James T. Wells, "Prison Experience," *Southern Historical Society Papers* 7 (January–December 1879), 488.

32. *War of the Rebellion*, Series 2, 6:625.

33. Ibid., 626.

34. Wells, "Prison Experience," 395. At Johnson's Island, another prisoner found the rations abundant, if plain, until the issuance of an order that was said to be in retaliation of treatment of prisoners at Andersonville. He said they were put on half-rations, prohibited the receipt of boxes, and excluded from having a sutler. The result was that they were in a state of sharp hunger all the time. Honorable James F. Crocker, "Prison Reminiscences," *Southern Historical Society*, Paper 34 (January–December 1906): 28–51.

35. Circular no. 2, February 13, 1865, from William Hoffman, Commissary General of Prisoners, *War of the Rebellion*; Series 2, 8:215.

10 Doing Without the Army Sutler

1. "An Act to Increase and Fix the Military Peace Establishment of the United States," *United States Statutes* 14, 39th Cong., 1st sess., July 28, 1866.

2. Letter to the Secretary of War, April 6, 1892. H. R. Exec. Doc. no. 207, 52nd Cong., 2d sess., 1 and 2.

3. *Congressional Globe*, February 5, 1867, 1014; 40th Cong., 2d. sess., H.R. Exec. Doc. no. 1, 581.

4. Edgar N. Carter, "Judge Carter and Old Fort Bridger," *Westerners Brand Book* (Los Angeles: 1950): 180.

5. Raymond L. Welty, "The Policing of the Frontier by the Army, 1860–1870," *Kansas Historical Quarterly* 3 (August 1938), 246.

6. Robert G. Athearn, *William Tecumseh Sherman and the Settlement of the West* (Norman: University of Oklahoma Press, 1967), 15, 36–38.

7. Raymond L. Welty, "Supplying the Frontier Military Posts," *Kansas Historical Quarterly* 7, no. 2 (May 1938), 157.

8. See Robert M. Utley, *Frontier Regulars* (Lincoln: University of Nebraska Press, 1973), chapter 2; and Don Rickey, Jr., *Forty Miles a Days on Beans and*

Hay: The Enlisted Soldier Fighting the Indian Wars (Norman: University of Oklahoma Press, 1963).

9. *Annual Report of the Secretary of War*, 41st Cong., 2d sess., H. R. Exec. Doc. no. 1, 1870, pt. 1; Raymond L. Welty, "The Daily Life of the Frontier Soldier," *Cavalry Journal* 36 (October 1927), 370.

10. *United States Statutes* 14, 39th Cong., 1st sess., July 28, 1866; General Order no. 59, May 30, 1867, *Annual Report of the Secretary of War*, 1867, 40th Cong., 2d. sess., H. R. Exec. Doc. no. 1, 581.

11. The author developed the biographical sketch of William Alexander Carter from the following sources: William A. Carter Manuscript Collection, Wyoming State Archives; Colonel Albert G. Brackett, *Fort Bridger* (n.p., 1870); Carter, "Judge Carter and Old Fort Bridger," 179–82; William A. Carter, Jr., "Fort Bridger in the 70s," *Annals of Wyoming* 11, no. 2 (1939): 111–13; William N. Davis, Jr., "The Sutler at Fort Bridger," *Western Historical Quarterly* 2, no. 1 (January 1971): 37–53; William N. Davis, Jr., "Post Trading in the West," *Explorations in Entrepreneurial History* 6 (October 1953): 30–37; Robert S. Ellison, *Fort Bridger, A Brief History* (Casper: Wyoming Historical Landmark Commission, n.d.); Fred Gowans and E. E. Campbell, *Fort Bridger: Island in the Wilderness* (Provo: Brigham Young University, 1975); Merrill J. Mattes, *Indians, Infants and Infancy* (Denver: Old West Publishing Company, 1960); A. K. McClure, *Three Thousand Miles through the Rocky Mountains* (Philadelphia, 1869); Wallace Shurtleff, "Bridger Country" (Wyoming State Archives, n.p., n.d.).

12. William A. Carter Manuscript Collection.

13. Army HQ, Letters Received, E., 87: 115, 116, March 14, 1867. Appeal by William A. Carter, National Archives.

14. "Inspection of Military Posts, 1867," 39th Cong. 2d sess. H. R. Exec. Doc. no. 20, 7.

15. Senate Joint Resolution no. 25. *Congressional Globe*, 40th Cong., 1st sess. March 30, 1867, 459n. Read at length, and passed as 15 *United States Statutes at Large*, 29.

16. Public Resolution no. 33. General Order no. 58, U.S. Army HQ, Washington, D.C., May 24, 1867.

17. General Order no. 68, U.S. Army HQ, Adjutant General's Office, August 22, 1867.

18. Register of Post Traders, 1821–1889; Clayton W. Williams, *Texas' Last Frontier: Fort Stockton and the Trans-Pecos, 1861–1895* (Texas A&M University Press, 1982), 105.

19. Letter entry, Post Records, Fort Hays, Kansas, November 4, 1868.

20. Open letter from Brevet Major Buchannan, Fifth Military District, *United States Army and Navy Journal* 6 (August 22, 1868), 2.

21. Ibid., 150.

22. Ibid., Letter of October 3, 1868.

23. "Quartermaster General Report," *Annual Report of the Secretary of War*, 40th Cong., 2d sess., 1869, pt. 1, 31.

24. Data compiled from H.R. Document no. 2568.

25. Davis, "Sutler at Fort Bridger," 34.

26. Public Resolution no. 332, *United States Statutes*, 15: 29.

27. "Index of Reports to House Committees," H.R. Document no. 2568, 44th Cong., 1st sess., 1876, 2. The law rescinded Public Resolution no. 332, 15, *United States Statutes*, March 30, 1867, 29.

28. H.R. Exec. Doc. no. 249, 41st Cong., 2d sess., 1870.

29. Even after the Civil War, the sutler's store was often located outside the fortified compound. In bivouacs and temporary camps, the sutler kept a tent. In her book, *Tenting on the Plains*, Elizabeth Custer, the wife of Lieutenant Colonel George Armstrong Custer, wrote that at Fort Hays, the sutler's tent was the last in the row but within easy reach of soldiers. See Raymond L. Welty, "The Army Fort on the Frontier, 1860–70," *North Dakota History* 2, no. 3 (April 1928), 165. James K. Moore located his Fort Washakie trading post and home a quarter-mile from the drill field, out of the way but within reach of the garrison. James K. Moore Collection, Wyoming State Archives.

30. Adjutant General of the Army E. D. Townsend's testimony for the House of Representatives committee investigating the sale of post traderships, "Index of Reports to House Committees," June 7, 1871, 150. The trader was appointed under the authority given by the act of July 15, 1870, and was furnished a letter of appointment from the Secretary of War, which designated the post where he was appointed.

31. Parts 1–6, March 25, 1872, Circular, Adjutant General's Office.

11 Patronage and the Military Post Trader

1. New York *Times*, March 8, 1876, p. 1:2.

2. Letter from the Adjutant General to the Secretary of War, H. Exec. Doc. no. 207, 52d Cong., 2d sess. 1, 1892

3. Gen. John McDonald, *The Secrets of the Great Whiskey Ring* (Chicago: Belford, Clarke and Co., 1880), iv, 17–18, and 339.

4. See E. I. Stewart, *Custer's Luck* (Norman: University of Oklahoma Press, 1955), and J. S. Gray, *Centennial Campaign: The Sioux Indian War of 1876* (Colorado: Old Army Press), chapter 6.

5. Gray, *Centennial Campaign*, 235.

6. Letter from Fort Hays, Kansas, February 4, 1782. Marvin E. Kroeker, *Great Plains Command: William B. Hazen in the Frontier West* (Norman: University of Oklahoma Press, 1976), 106. Also, see Stewart, *Custer's Luck*, 116.

7. Kroeker, *Great Plains Command*, 109–10.

8. Brevet Major General William B. Hazen, *The School and the Army in Germany and France* (New York: Harper and Bros., 1872), 235.

9. Kroeker, *Great Plains Command*, 108.

10. New York *Tribune*, March 27, 1872; Dept. of War Circular, March 25, 1872.

11. New York *Tribune*, April 6, 1876; Stewart, *Custer's Luck*, 143–48.

12. Testimony by General George Armstrong Custer, April 4, 1876, Committee on Military Affairs, "Management of the War Department," H.R. no. 799. 44th Cong., 1st sess., August 5, 1876, 163.

13. New York *Times*, March 2, 1876.

14. New York *Times*, March 3, 1876.

15. Stewart, *Custer's Luck*, 143.

16. New York *Times*, March 4, 1876, 1:1 and 1:5

17. New York *Times*, March 6, 1876, 1:1

18. Ibid. At Fort Bowie, General McClennan backed post trader Sidney De-long by saying that he "need not be removed," but a significant turnover in post traders may have occurred at this time. Randy Kane, "An Honorable and Upright Man," *Journal of Arizona History* 19, no. 3 (1978), 307.

19. New York *Times*, March 7, 1876, 1:6

20. New York *Times*: May 10, 1876, 1:5

21. Ibid., 15, 52.

22. "Management of the War Department," 52d Cong., 2d sess., 3.

23. Ibid., 3ff. Hedrick secured appointments for James Trainor at Fort Conchos for $2,500; for A. E. Reynolds at Camp Supply for $4,500; for R. C. Seip at Fort Abraham Lincoln for $3,700, and for A. C. Leighton at Fort Buford and Fetterman for $10,000. He also held a one-third interest in sutler profits at Forts Buford, Lincoln, Griffin, and Fetterman. Rice introduced J. S. Evans to the Secretary of War for $1,000; secured appointments for Joseph Loeb at Fort Conchos for $2,000; for Henry Reed at Fort Wingate for $1,500, and for Major Hicks at Fort Griffin for $5,000. For his share in the Fort Richardson tradership, he received $2,000 from L. M. Gregory, $2,000 for sale of his interest in the tradership at Fort Abraham Lincoln, and $3,750 from R. C. Seip.

24. Alvin C. Leighton was extensively involved in post-tradership dealings from Wyoming to Texas.

25. Committee on Military Affairs, "Management of the War Department," 4.

26. Ibid., 8, 18–21.

27. Ibid. Without investing a cent in trading posts, Orvil Grant obtained a one-third interest in Standing Rock, was an equal partner with A. C. Leighton at Fort Peck, sold his interest at Berthold for one thousand dollars to Raymond, and at Fort Belknap insisted a man named Conrad receive the license. Orvil Grant's testimony in front of the congressional investigating committee, March 9, 1876; also see chapter 6 in Gray, *Centennial Campaign*.

28. Indian Trade: Act of July 26, 1866, *United States Statutes*, sec. 2128, 374, says that any loyal person of good moral character can trade with the Indians with a bond of from five to ten thousand dollars and at least two good sureties approved by the Indian Supervisor, U.S. District Judge, or District Attorney; U.S. Congress, Committee on Military Affairs, "Management of the War Department," 4.

29. U.S. Congress, Committee on Military Affairs, "Management of the War Department," 127.

30. Ibid., 145. See David M. Delo, "Post Trader, Indian Trader," Part 2, *Wind River Mountaineer* 2, no. 4 (October–December 1986): 9–11.

31. See John Collins, *My Experiences in the West*. ed. Colton Storm (Chicago: Lakeside Press, 1970).

32. Committee on Military Affairs, "Management of the War Department," 173–74.

33. Ibid., 67.

34. Davis, "Sutler at Fort Bridger," 33.

12 The Military Post Trader as Entrepreneur

1. National Park Service historian Merrill Mattes suggests that the sutler's heyday was from 1849 to 1876. See Merrill Mattes, "Sutler's Store," 94.

2. Athearn, *William Tecumseh Sherman*, 5.

3. See Alexander Toponce, *The Reminiscences of Alexander Toponce* (Ogden: Mrs. Kate Toponce, 1923).

4. Jack D. Foner, "The Socializing Role of the Military," *The American Military on the Frontier*, U.S.Air Force Academy Symposium, 1976. (Washington, D.C. U.S.Air Force Academy, 1978), 85.

5. Oliva, *Fort Hays,* 40; David P. Robrock, "A History of Fort Fetterman, Wyoming, 1867–1882," *Annals of Wyoming* 48 no. 1 (Spring 1976): 5–76;.also, see Kane, "Honorable and Upright Man," 297–307.

6. Merrill Mattes, "Sutler's Store," 94.

7. Margaret Carrington, *Absaroka, Home of the Crows* (Chicago: Lakeside Press, 1950), 85.

8. Merrill J. Mattes, "Guardian of the Oregon Trail," *Annals of Wyoming* 17, no. 1 (January 1945), 15.

9. Fort Laramie National Historical Site, 5 556, 3;.Collins, *My Experiences in the West*, 105.

10. Letter from G. O. Reid to Merrill J. Mattes, December 20, 1945. Mattes, "Sutler's Store," 128–29.

11. Ibid., 115.

12. Jerry M. Sullivan, *Fort McKavett: A Texas Frontier Post.* (n.p.: West Texas Museum, 1981), 53.

13. W. F. Pride, *The History of Fort Riley* (n.p., 1926), 180.

14. Wooster, *Soldiers, Sutlers and Settlers* (College Station: Texas A & M University Press, 1987), 77.

15. Collins, *My Experiences in the West*, XVI.

16. Alson B. Ostrander, *An Army Boy of the Sixties* (New York: World Book Co., 1924), 207–8.

17. Dee Brown, *Fort Phil Kearny: An American Saga* (New York: G. P. Putnam, 1962), 42.

18. Carrington, *Absaroka*, 86.

19. "There is a scarcity of funds at western forts. Creditors are suffering, including the government. Discounting of 'certified vouchers,' forces the doubling of prices; public credit becomes depreciated, and private people suffer." Letter from Rufus Ingalls, 1866. H. Exec. Doc. no. 1111, 15–16.

20. Captain W. S. Nye, *Carbine and Lance: The Story of Old Fort Sill* (Norman: University of Oklahoma Press, 1938), 374–76.

21. Ibid., 376.

22. Colonel William Bullock, "Old Letter Book," ed. Agnes Wright Spring, *Annals of Wyoming* 13, no. 4 (October 1941), 318.

23. James W. Jones, "Seth E. Ward," *Annals of Wyoming* 5 (1927), 10.

24. Bullock, "Old Letter Book," 257.

25. For more detail on the life of Seth Ward, see Hafen, *Mountain Men*, and Mattes, "Sutler's Store."

26. Charles Larpenteur, *Forty Years a Fur Trader* (Chicago: Lakeside Press, 1933), 325.

27. Athearn, *Forts of the Upper Missouri*, 157, 165, 170.

28. Larpenteur, *Forty Years a Fur Trader*, 323–25.

29. Wooster, *Soldiers, Sutlers, and Settlers*, 4.

30. Raymond L. Welty, "The Frontier Army on the Missouri River, 1860–70," *North Dakota History* 2, no. 2 (January 1928), 86.

31. Raymond L. Welty, "Army Fort of the Frontier," 156.

32. Ibid., 154.

33. Ibid., 156.

34. Register of Post Traders, 1821–1889, Adjutant General's Office, National Archives..

35. Jane R. Kendall, "The History of Fort Francis E. Warren," *Annals of Wyoming* 18, no. 1 (January 1946), 12.

36. Robrock, "History of Fort Fetterman," 33; L. G. (Pat) Flannery, ed., *John Hunton's* Diary, 4 vols. (Lingle, Wyoming: Guide-Review, 1960), 4:116.

37. Ray H. Mattison, "Old Fort Stevenson," *North Dakota History* 18, no. 2, 75.

38. Wooster, *Soldiers, Sutlers and Settlers*, 120.

39. Ibid., 121.

40. Larpenteur, *Forty Years a Fur Trader*, 323–25.

41. Based on statistics included in the 1876 congressional investigating committee's report published as "Management of the War Department," August 5, 1876, Committee on Expenditures in the War Dept, 44th Cong., 1st sess., H.R. no. 799.

42. James K. Moore Manuscript Collection, Denver Public Library.

43. Index of Reports to House Committees. House Document 2568, 44th Cong., 1st sess., 1876, 60.

44. James K. Moore, Jr., "Indian Trader Tokens," James K. Moore Collection, Denver Public Library.

45. Hafen and Young, *Fort Laramie*, 349–50.

46. Annual Report of the Secretary of War, 41st Cong., 2d.sess., 1870, pt. 1, 41.

47. Welty, "Supplying the Frontier Military Posts," 167.

48. Letter of agreement, July 21, 1859, Bullock, "Old Letter Book," 237–330.

49. John Hunton, "Letter," *Annals of Wyoming* 4, no. 2 (October 1926), 315. Also, see Flannery, *John Hunton's Diary*, 2:183–84; and Article of Agreement, June 1874; and letter, Quartermaster, HQ, Dept. of Dakota, St. Paul, Minn., April 1880, to J. H. McKnight, post trader, Fort Shaw, in J. H. McK-

night and Co. Records, 1865–1914, Manuscript Collection no. 56, Montana Historical Society Archives. For a 100-year comparison, baled hay in Wyoming in 1981 cost $65 per ton of delivered hay.

50. Kane, "Honorable and Upright Man," 304.

51. U. L. Burdick, *Tales From Buffalo Land: The Story of Fort Buford* (Baltimore: Wirth Brothers, 1940), 133.

52. Ibid., 136.

53. Bullock, "Old Letter Book," 237–330.

54. Ibid., 330.

55. Griffen, *My Life,* 149–50.

56. Nye, *Carbine and Lance,* 374–76.

57. Bullock, "Old Letter Book," 330.

58. That ranch was later owned by Buffalo Bill Cody.

59. Burdick, *Tales From Buffalo Land,* 139.

60. The William Carter Collection, Wyoming State Archives.

61. Ibid.

62. Nye, *Carbine and Lance,* 376.

63. Martin F. Schmitt, *General George Crook, His Autobiography* (Norman: University of Oklahoma Press, 1946), 238.

64. Nye, *Carbine and Lance,* 373.

65. Charles Schuchert and Clara Mae LaVene, *O. C. Marsh, Pioneer in Paleontology* (New Haven: Yale University Press, 1940), 109, 177.

66. Rickey, *Forty Miles a Day,* 202.

67. William N. Davis, Jr., "Post trading in the West," *Explorations in Entrepreneurial History* 6 (October 1963),32.

68. Index of Reports to House Committees. Document no. 2568. 44th Cong., 1st sess., 1876, 15, 52.

69. Letter from John London, February 3, 1881, to his wife, London Family Papers, University of North Carolina at Chapel Hill, North Carolina.

70. Ibid., 149, 167.

71. Davis, "Sutler at Fort Bridger," 32.

13 The Beginning of Hard Times

1. *Army-Navy Journal* 4 (1866–1867), 233.

2. Ibid.

3. Letter from Fort Monroe. *Army–Navy Journal* 4 (November 1866).

4. Jay Monaghan, *The Life of General George Armstrong Custer* (New York: Little, Brown and Co., 1959), 341–42.

5. Ibid., 252.

6. Pride, *History of Fort Riley,* 110.

7. Ibid., 198.

8. Mari Sandoz, *The Buffalo Hunters* (New York: Hastings House, 1954), 101–2.

9. Professor Francis Paul Prucha wrote that a decrease in whiskey resulted in an increase in discipline and health. See Prucha, *Sword of the Republic,* 329.

10. Abstracts from *Personal Recollections of General Miles*, quoted in U.S. Congress, S.R. Doc. 51, 57th Cong., 2d sess., 1900.

11. Ibid.

12. November 16, 1847, letter from Albuquerque to the *Daily Herald*, Newberrypost, Mass. (January 31, 1848).

13. Letters from personnel at Fort Hays State Park, Fort Hays, Kansas.

14. Athearn, *Forts of the Upper Missouri*, 286–87.

15. Quoted from John C. Fremont, *An Exploring Expedition, 1842,* in Hafen and Young, *Fort Laramie*, 40.

16. See Robert A. Trennert, Jr., *Alternative to Extinction: Federal Indian Policy and the Beginning of the Reservation System, 1846–1851* (Philadelphia: Temple University Press, 1975), 22. See also Francis Paul Prucha, *American Indian Policy in the Formative Years: The Indian Trade and Intercourse Acts, 1790–1834* (Harvard University Press, 1962), Chapter 6, "The Crusade against Whiskey"; M. M. Quaife, ed., *Army Life in Dakota, The Diary of Phillipe R. D. de Tobriand* (Chicago: Lakeside Press, 1941), 93 and 116.

17. U.S. District Court, Evanston, Wyoming, Cases no. 142–145. Records of Uinta County Clerk District Court.

18. Adjutant General's Office, February 1, 1876, to James K..Moore, Post Trader, Camp Brown. The order was endorsed by Lieutenant General Philip H. Sheridan and the post's commanding officer. James K. Moore Collection, Denver Public Library.

19. See David M. Delo, "Camp Stambaugh: The Miner's Delight," *Wind River Mountaineer* (June-August 1987), 10.

20. James K. Moore Collection, Cheyenne, Wyoming.

21. Kane, "Honorable and Upright Man," 311. The Post Adjutant's Order of October 24, 1879, defined the blacklist. Rickey, *Forty Miles A Day*, 202.

22. Meyers, *Ten Years in the Ranks*, 128.

23. Robert T. Granger, "Fort Robinson, Outpost on the Plains," *Chronicles of Oklahoma* 36, no. 1 (1958), 21.

24. Ralph P. Bieber, *Marching with the Army of the West* (Glendale: Arthur H. Clark Co., 1936), 77.

25. Grant Foreman, *Pioneer Days in the Southwest* (Glendale: Arthur H. Clark Co., 1926), 174.

26. Letter from John London, Post Trader, Fort Laramie, Wyoming, to his wife in North Carolina, March 2, 1881, John London Papers, University of North Carolina at Chapel Hill.

27. Letter, December 27, 1878, Governor Hoyt to James Patten, Indian agent, Camp Brown, Letters Received, Shoshone Agency, 1871–1880.

28. See David Delo, "The Fiery Demise of the Frontier Index," *Old West Magazine* (Spring 1988): 18–24.

29. For more details of Moore's life, see Delo, "Post Trader, Indian Trader," *Wind River Mountaineer* 2, no. 3 (July-September 1986): 4–7, and 3, no. 1 (January-March 1987): 4–12; James K. Moore Collection, Denver Public Library and Wyoming State Archives; and William A. Carter Collection, Wyoming State Archives.

30. Letter to Carl Schurz, January 7, 1879. Copy Book of John Hoyt, Governor, Territory of Wyoming.

31. Letter from Joseph M. Carey, Cheyenne, Wyoming, December 20, 1878, to Secretary of Interior Carl Schurz.

32. Letter from James Patten, Shoshone Indian Agent, to Commissioner of Indian Affairs, February 5, 1879.

33. James K. Moore Collection, Denver Public Library.

34. Senate Select Committee on Indian Traders (1886). S.R. no. 2707, 50th Cong., 2d sess., 1889.

35. Prucha, "Army Sutlers," 25–26.

36. Davis, "Post Trading in the West," 36.

37. Atherton, Lewis E., "The Pioneer Merchant in Mid-America," *University of Missouri Studies* 14 (April 1939), 126.

38. Department of the Army, Adjutant General's Office, April 6, 1892.

14 The End of an Era

1. "Camp Baker," *Montana Magazine of History* 27, no. 2, (April 1977), 40.

2. Athearn, *Forts of the Upper Missouri*, 286–87.

3. Letter of February 8, 1876. An Address to the American public on the subject of the Canteen together with newspaper extracts, reports, speeches related to the Post Exchange and Army Canteen, S.R. no. 51, 57th Cong., 2d sess., 1900, printed December 20, 1902.

4. T. G. Steward, "The Canteen in the Army," *Harper's Weekly* 36 (April 9, 1892).

5. The British Canteen, a refreshment house in barracks for soldiers, permitted the sale of malt liquor at low prices. Between 1836 and 1845, income from the canteen was valued at seventy thousand pounds sterling, but the experiment resulted in great intoxication. Liquor was finally prohibited in 1847. *Farrow's Military Encyclopedia*, 1:281–82.

6. Register of Post Traders 2, Circular no. 3, HQ, Department of Dakota, January 17, 1882.

7. Fort Sullivan. *Reports of the Inspector General*, 1828, Roll no. 1, 172.

8. General Order no. 24, February 22, 1881, Adjutant General's Office; Kane, "Upright and Honorable Man," 303.

9. *The Army-Navy Journal*, February 9, 1881. The Senate Military Committee reported against a bill to repeal section 3, paragraph 225, *United States Statutes at Large* (July 24, 1876), which provided for one post trader to be appointed by the Secretary of War.

10. Steward, "Canteen in the Army."

11. Richard Upton, *Fort Custer on the Big Horn, 1877–1898* (Glendale: Arthur H. Clark Co., 1973), 285–86.

12. Article 39, paragraph no. 328ff., U.S. Army Regulations (Washington, D.C., 1889).

13. Ibid., Article 40, paragraphs 350, 352, 355, 357.

14. Register of Post Trader, 2, AGO, October 18, 1889; "Memorandum: Post Trader and the Canteen," Letters Received, February 10–May 10, 1889, Secretary of War.

15. Register of Post Trader, 2, AGO, October 18, 1889: "Memorandum: Post Trader and the Canteen," Letters Received, February 10–May 10, 1889, Secretary of War.

16. Only two letters were actually sent—to Meyer, Va., and Washington Barracks on December 2, 1889—and only the latter post-trader's position was closed. Adjutant General's Office, April 6, 1892; Adjutant General report of February 1, 1889, authorized the canteen.

17. Register of Post Traders, 2, December 20, 1889.

18. Ibid., 405.

19. Ibid., 271.

20. Upton, *Fort Custer*, 796.

21. Ibid., 285–86.

22. Z, "The Canteen Criticized," *Army and Navy Journal* 27 (1889–1890), 617.

23. Ibid., 617.

24. Register of Post Traders, 2, MS, NA 46.

25. Pride, *History of Fort Riley*, 207.

26. Ibid.

27. Ibid., 68.

28. General Order no. 10, October 7, 1890. Report of Adjutant General, H.R. Exec. Doc. no. 1, 1, Part 2, 64–65, 51st Cong., 2d sess., 1890; Committee on Military Affairs. Purchasing of Post Traders' Buildings, April 22, 1892, 52d Cong., 1st sess., H.R. Exec. Doc. no. 207; also, H.R. no. 2203, January 6, 1893, 52d Cong., 2d sess. to accompany S.B. no. 3117, Abolishment of Post Traderships.

29. *Army-Navy Journal*, November 9, 1889, 211–13.

30. H. Exec. Doc no. 1, 1, Part 2:16, *Annual Report of the Secretary of War*, 51st Cong., 2d sess., November 15, 1890; H. Exec. Doc no. 1, *Annual Report of the Secretary of War*, 56th Cong., 2d sess. 1891.

31. Letter from the Secretary of War, May 14, 1892.

32. Letter from the Secretary of War accompanying Senate Committee on Military Affairs. S.R. no. 713, May 23, 1892, to accompany S.B. no. 3117, May 14, 1892, with extract from 1891 Annual Report of the Secretary of War.

33. Purchasing of Post Traders' Buildings, H.R. Exec Doc. no. 207. 52d Cong., 1st sess, April 22, 1892; Committee on Military Affairs Senate Bill no. 3117 to abolish post traderships, H.R. no. 2203, 52d Cong., 2d sess., January 6, 1893.

34. Closure was based on the Bureau of Census ruling that it could no longer delineate the line of furthest advance of western settlement.

35. Hafen and Young, Fort Laramie, 396.

15 A Niche in American History

1. Matthew Prior, "The Viceroy: A Ballad," *The Literary Works of*

Matthew Prior, ed. H. Bunker Wright and Monroe K. Spears (Oxford: Clarendon Press, 1959), 1:424–25.

2. Correlli Barnett, *Britain and Her Army, 1509 to 1970* (London: Allen Lane, Penguin Press, 1970), 144–45; Scouller, *Armies of Queen Anne*, 22, 217.

3. Ibid., 686.

4. O. W., "Sutlers in the Camp," *Fraser's Magazine for Towne and Country* (London) LII (December 1855), 687–88.

5. Ibid., 694.

6. Ibid., 695.

7. Atherton, "Pioneer Merchant," 10, 21.

8. Ibid., 15.

9. Ibid., 16.

10. Ibid., 17.

11. Frazer, *Forts and Supplies*, 233.

12. Elvid Hunt, *History of Fort Leavenworth, 1827–1927* (Fort Leavenworth: Service Schools Press, 1926), 263.

13. Thomas G. Maghee, "J. K. Moore Dies in California," *Lander State Journal*, Fremont County, Wyoming, February 6, 1920. James K. Moore Collection, Wyoming State Historical Society, Cheyenne, Wyoming.

Epilogue

1. *Annual Report of the Secretary of War.* House Doc. no. 2, 38–39. 56th Cong., 1st sess.,1899.

2. Ibid.

3. "Annual Report of the Lt. General Commanding of the Army to the Secretary of War," 1901, 8.

4. Committee of Military Affairs. "Prohibiting the sale of Alcoholic Beverages at the canteen." 56th Cong., 1st sess., H.R. no. 1701, May 24, 1900.

5. Littlefield Amendment, December 14, 1900, "Annual Report of the Lt. General Commanding of the Army to the Secretary of War," 1901.

6. Committee of Military Affairs, "Prohibiting the Sale of Alcoholic Beverages at the Canteen"; "An Address to the American Public on the Subject of the Canteen Together with Newspaper Extracts, Reports, Speeches Related to the Post Exchange and Army Canteen," Senate Document no. 51, 57th Cong., 2d sess., 1900, printed December 20, 1902.

7. "The Sale of Beer and Light Wines in the Post Exchange," 5th Cong., 2d sess., H.R. no. 252, January 9, 1903.

8. "An Address to the American Public on the Subject of the Canteen."

BIBLIOGRAPHY

Books

Adams, George W. *Doctors in Blue: The Medical History of the Union Army in the Civil War*. New York: Henry Schuman, 1952.

Athearn, Robert G. *William Tecumseh Sherman and the Settlement of the West*. Norman: University of Oklahoma Press, 1956.

Forts of the Upper Missouri. Englewood, N. J.: Prentice-Hall, 1967.

Bakeless, John. *Spies of the Confederacy*. New York: J. B. Lippincott Co., 1970.

Baker, General LaFayette C. *History of the United States Secret Service*. Philadelphia: published by the author, 1867.

Bandel, Eugene. *Frontier Life in the Army, 1854–1861*. Translated by Olga Bandel and Richard Jente, and edited by Ralph P. Bibier. Glendale, Calif.: Arthur H. Clark Company, 1932.

Barnett, Correlli. *Britain and Her Army, 1509 to 1970*. London: Allen Lane, Penguin Press, 1970.

Barry, Louise. *The Beginning of the West: Annals of the Kansas Gateway to the American West, 1540–1854*. Lawrence: Kansas Historical Society, 1972.

Bearss, Edwin C., and Arrell M. Gibson. *Fort Smith: Little Gibraltar on the Arkansas*. Norman: University of Oklahoma Press, 1969.

Bedford, New Hampshire. *The History of Bedford, New Hampshire*. The Runford Printing Company, 1903.

Beers, Henry P. *The Western Military Frontier: 1815–1846*. Philadelphia (University of Pennsylvania thesis): published by the author, 1935.

Bieber, Ralph P. *A Documentary Account of the Utah Expedition, 1857–1858*,

247

The Far West and the Rockies Series, 1820–1875. Glendale, Calif.: Arthur H. Clark Company, 1958.

Bieber, Ralph P. *Marching with the Army of the West.* Southwest Historical Series, 8 vols. Glendale, Calif.: Arthur H. Clark Company, 1936.

Billings, John D. *Hardtack and Coffee: The Unwritten Story of Army Life.* Chicago: Lakeside Press, 1960.

Billon, Frederick L. *Annals of St. Louis, 1804–1821.* St. Louis: G. I. Jones and Company, 1886.

Birge, J. C. *The Awakening of the Deseret.* Boston: R. G. Badger, 1912.

Blumenthal, Walter H. *Women Camp Followers of the American Revolution.* Philadelphia: G. S. MacManus Company, 1952.

Botkin, B. A., ed. *A Civil War Treasury of Tales, Legends, and Folklore.* New York: Random House, 1960.

Bowler, Arthur. *Logistics and the Failure of the British Army in America, 1775–1783.* Princeton, N. J.: Princeton University Press, 1975.

Brevoort, Elias. *New Mexico, Her Natural Resources and Her Attractions.* Santa Fe: n.p., 1874.

Brown, Dee. *Fort Phil Kearny: An American Saga.* New York: G. P. Putnam, 1962.

Buffum, Francis H. *A Memorial of the Great Rebellion: Being a History of the Fourteenth Regiment, New Hampshire Volunteers, Covering Its Three Years of Service, With Original Sketches of Army Life, 1862–1865.* Boston: Rand, Avery and Company, 1882.

Burdick, U. L. *Tales from Buffalo Land: The Story of Fort Buford.* Baltimore: Wirth Brothers, 1940.

Byrne Frank L., ed. *The View from Headquarters: Civil War Letters of Harvey Reid.* Madison: State Historical Society of Wisconsin, 1965.

Byrne, Frank L., and Jean P. Soman, eds. *Your Dear Marcus: The Civil War Letters of a Jewish Colonel.* Kent, Ohio: Kent State University Press, 1985.

Callan, John F., ed. *Military Laws of the United States Relating to the Army and Volunteers Militia and to Bounty, Lands and Pensions.* Philadelphia: G. W. Childs, 1864.

Calvert, Henry M. *Reminiscences of a Boy in Blue, 1862–1865.* New York: G. P. Putnam Sons, 1920.

Canfield, Silas S. *History of the 21st Regiment Ohio Volunteer Infantry in the War of the Rebellion.* Toledo, Ohio:Vrooman, Anderson and Batesman, 1893.

Carriker, Robert C. *Fort Supply Indian Territory: Frontier Outpost on the Plains.* Norman: University of Oklahoma Press, 1970.

Carrington, Margaret. *Absaroka, Home of the Crows.* Chicago: Lakeside Press, 1950.

Carter, Clarence Edwin, ed. *Territorial Papers of the United States.* 28 vols. Washington, D.C.: U.S. Government Printing Office, 1934–

Castle, Henry A. *The Army Mule and Other War Sketches.* Indianapolis: Bowen-Merrill Company, 1897.

Catton, Bruce. *The Army of the Potomac; Glory Road: The Bloody Trail from Fredericksburg to Gettysburg.* Garden City, N.Y.: Doubleday and Company, 1954.

———. *Mr. Lincoln's Army*. Garden City, N.Y.: Doubleday and Company, 1955.

Clark, Charles M., M.D. *The History of the 39th Regiment, Illinois Volunteer Veteran Infantry*. Chicago: n.p., 1889.

Coddington, E. B. *The Gettysburg Campaign: A Study in Command*. New York: Charles Scribner's Sons, 1968.

Coffman, Edward M. *The Old Army*. New York: Oxford University Press, 1986.

Collins, John. *My Experiences in the West*, ed. Colton Storm, Chicago: Lakeside Press, 1970.

Copp, Elbridge J. *Reminiscences of the War of the Rebellion, 1861–1865*. Nashua: Telegraph Publishing Company, 1911.

Cowles, Calvin D'. Comp. *Atlas of the War of the Rebellion*. New York: Atlas Publishing Co., 1892.

Crackel, Theodore J. *Mr. Jefferson's Army*. New York: New York University Press, 1987.

Croghan, George. *Army Life on the Western Frontier: Selections from the Official Reports Made Between 1826 and 1845*. Edited by Francis Paul Prucha. Norman: University of Oklahoma Press, 1958.

Culver, Joseph F. *Your Affectionate Husband, J. F. Culver*. Edited by Wesley W. Dunlap. Iowa City: Friends of the University of Iowa Libraries, 1978.

Cummings, Charles M. *Yankee Quaker Confederate General*. Madison: Fairleigh Dickinson Press, 1971.

Currey, J. Seymour. *The Story of Old Fort Dearborn*. Chicago: A. C. McClurg and Company, 1912.

———*Chicago: Its History and Its Builders*. 6 vols. Chicago: S. J. Clarke Publishing Company, 1912.

Davis, Washington. *Campfire Chats of the Civil War*. Chicago: A. B. Gehman and Company, 1886.

Delbruck, Hans. *History of the Art of War*. 3 vols. Translated by Walter J. Renfroe, Jr. Westport, Conn.: Greenwood Press, 1982.

Donald, David H., ed. *Gone for a Soldier: The Civil War Memories of Private Alfred Bellard*. Boston: Little, Brown and Company, 1975.

Ducrey, Pierre. *Warfare in Ancient Greece*. New York: Schocken Books, 1986.

Duffy, Christopher. *The Army of Frederick the Great*. London: David and Charles Newton Abbott, 1974.

Dunkelman, M. H., and M. J. Winey. *The Hardtack Regiment*. Madison: Fairleigh Dickinson Press, 1981.

Eastman, Mary (Henderson), *Dahcotah: Or, Life and Legends of the Sioux around Fort Snelling*. New York: J. Wiley, 1849.

Edwards, Richard, and M. Hopewell, M.D. *Edward's Great West and Her Commercial Metropolis*. St. Louis: Edward's Monthly, 1860.

Ellison, Robert S. *Fort Bridger, A Brief History*. Casper: Wyoming Historical Landmark Commission, n.d.

Emmet, Chris. *Fort Union and the Winning of the Southwest*. Norman: University of Oklahoma Press, 1965.

Esmond, Henry. *The History of Henry Esmond, Esq.* 2 vols. Edited by William M. Thackeray. New York: Charles Scribner's Sons, 1904.

Faller, Leo W., and John I. Faller. *Dear Folks at Home: The Civil War Letters of Leo W. and John I. Faller with an Account of Andersonville.* Edited by Milton E. Flower. Harrisburg: Cumberland County Historical Society and Hamilton Library Association, 1963.

Farrow, Ed. S., ed. *Farrow's Military Encyclopedia: A Dictionary of Military Knowledge.* 3 vols. New York: Military-Naval Publishing, 1885.

Flannery, L. G. (Pat), ed. *John Hunton's Diary.* 6 vols. Lingle, Wyoming: 1958–1963.

Folwell, William W. *A History of Minnesota.* 4 vols. St. Paul: Minnesota Historical Society, 1922–1930.

Foreman, Grant. *Pioneer Days in the Southwest.* Glendale, Calif.: Arthur H. Clark Company, 1926.

Forsyth, George A. *Story of a Soldier.* New York: D. Appleton and Company, 1900.

Frazer, Robert W. *Forts and Supplies, The Role of the Army in the Economy of the Southwest, 1846–1861.* Albuquerque: University of New Mexico Press, 1983.

———, ed. *Mansfield on the Conditions of the Western Forts, 1853–1854.* Norman: University of Oklahoma Press, 1946.

Frey, Silvia R. *The British Soldier in America: A Social History of Military Life in the Revolutionary Period.* Austin: University of Texas Press, 1981.

Ganoe, William A. *The History of the United States Army.* New York: D. Appleton and Company, 1924.

Gardner, Charles K. *A Dictionary of All Officers of the United States, 1789–1853.* New York: Putnam, 1853.

General Orders of the War Department, 1861–1863. New York: n.p., 1864.

Glazier, Williard. *Three Years in the Federal Cavalry.* N.Y.: R. H. Ferguson and Company, 1870.

Glover, Edwin A. *Bucktailed Wildcats: A Regiment of Civil War Volunteers.* New York: T. Yoseloff, 1960.

Gooch, John. *Armies in Europe.* London: Routeledge and Kegan Paul, 1980.

Goodlander, W. C. *Early Days of Fort Scott.* Fort Scott: Monitor Printing Company, 1900.

Gowans, Fred R., and Eugene E. Campbell. *Fort Bridger: Island in the Wilderness.* Provo, Utah: Brigham Young University, 1975.

Gray, John Chipman, and John C. Ropes. *War Letters.* Boston: Houghton Mifflin Company, 1927.

Gray, John S. *Centennial Campaign: The Sioux Indian War of 1876.* Norman: University of Oklahoma Press, 1986.

Griffen, Robert A., ed. *My Life in the Mountains and on the Plains.* Norman: University of Oklahoma Press, 1965.

Grismer, Karl H. *The Story of Fort Myers.* St. Petersburg, Fla.: St. Petersburg Printing Company, 1949.

Griswold, Bert J., ed. *Fort Wayne, Gateway of the West, 1802–1813.* Indianapolis: Indiana Library and Historical Department, 1927.

————. *The Pictorial History of Fort Wayne, Indiana.* Chicago: Robert O. Law Company, 1917.

Hafen, Leroy, ed. *Mountain Men and the Fur Trade.* 10 vols. Glendale, Calif.: Arthur H. Clark Company, 1972.

Hafen, Leroy, and F. M. Young. *Fort Laramie and the Pageant of the West.* Lincoln: University of Nebraska Press, 1938.

Hart, Herbert M. *Old Forts of the Southwest.* Seattle: Superior, 1954.

Hazen, Colonel William B. *The School and the Army in Germany and France.* New York: Harper Bros., 1872.

Hebard, Grace. *The Bozeman Trail.* Glendale: Arthur H. Clark Company, 1922.

Hemphill, W. Edwin, ed. *The Papers of John C. Calhoun.* 10 vols. Columbia: University of South Carolina Press, 1959–1989.

Hesseltime, William. *Ulysses S. Grant, Politican.* New York: Dodd, Mead and Company, 1935.

Hill, William H. *Old Fort Edward Before 1800.* Fort Edward: privately printed, 1929.

Hinkley, Julian W. *A Narrative of Service with the Third Wisconsin Infantry.* Madison: Wisconsin Historical Society, 1912.

Hollister, Ovando J. *Boldly They Rode: A History of the First Colorado Regimental Volunteers.* Lakewood: Golden Press, 1949.

Houck, Louis. *A History of Missouri.* 3 vols. Chicago: R. R. Donnelly and Sons Co., 1908.

Hunt, Elvid. *History of Fort Leavenworth, 1827–1927.* Fort Leavenworth: Service Schools Press, 1926.

Hunton, Marcus. *Old Fort Snelling, 1819–1858.* Iowa City: State Historical Society of Iowa, 1918.

Irving, Pierre M. *Life and Letters of Washington Irving.* 3 vols. Princeton, N.J.: Princeton University Press, 1947.

Jacobs, James R. *The Beginning of the U.S. Army, 1780–1812.* Princeton: Princeton University Press, 1947.

James, Charles. *An Universal Military Dictionary.* 4th ed. London: T. Egerton, 1816.

Johns, Henry T. *Life with the Forty-Ninth Massachusetts Volunteers.* Washington, D.C.: n.p., 1890.

Johnson, Charles B., M.D. *Muskets and Medicine; or, Army Life in the Sixties.* Philadelphia: F. A. Davis Co., 1917.

Johnson, Sir John. *The Orderly Book of Sir John Johnson during the Oriskany Campaign, 1776–77.* Edited by William L. Stone. Albany, N.Y.: J. Munsell's Sons, 1882.

Jones, Evan. *Citadel in the Wilderness.* New York: Coward-McCann, 1966.

Jones, John B. *The Western Merchant.* Philadelphia: Gregg Elliot and Co., 1849.

————. *The Life and Adventures of a Country Merchant.* Philadelphia: J. B. Lippincott and Co., 1882.

Kagan, Donald. *The Peace of Nicias and the Sicilian Expedition.* Ithaca, N.Y.: University of Cornell University Press, 1981.

Keim, Debenneville R. *Sheridan's Troopers on the Border*. Philadelphia: D. McKay, 1891.

Kemp, Allen. *The British Army in the American Revolution*. London: Almark Publishing Co., 1973.

Kennerly, William C. *Persimmon Hill*. Edited by Elizabeth Russell. Norman: University of Oklahoma Press, 1948.

Kieffer, Harry M. *The Recollections of a Drummer Boy*. 6th ed. Boston: Ticknor and Company, 1889.

Kinzie, Mrs. John. *Wau-Bun: The "Early Day" in the Northwest*. Chicago: Lakeside Press, 1932.

Kirkland, Joseph. *The Chicago Massacre of 1812*. Chicago: Dibble Press, 1893.

Knight, Oliver. *Following the Indian Wars*. Norman: University of Oklahoma Press, 1960.

Knopf, Richard C., ed. *Anthony Wayne*. Pittsburgh: University of Pittsburgh Press, 1960.

Kroeker, Marvin E. *Great Plains Command: William B. Hazen in the Frontier West*. Norman: University of Oklahoma Press, 1976.

Lamar, Howard R. *The Trader on the American Frontier—Myth's Victim*. College Station: Texas A & M University Press, 1977.

Larpenteur, Charles. *Forty Years a Fur Trader*. Chicago: Lakeside Press, 1933.

Lass, William E. *A History of Steamboating on the Upper Missouri*. Lincoln: University of Nebraska Press, 1962.

Locke, E. W. *Three Years in Camp and Hospital*. Boston: G. D. Russell Company, 1870.

Longacre, Edward G., ed. *From Antietam to Fort Fisher*. Madison, Wisc.: Fairleigh Dickinson Press, 1985.

Lord, Francis A. *Civil War Sutlers and Their Wares*. New York: T. Yoseloff, 1969.

———. *They Fought for the Union*. Harrisburg: Stackpole Company, 1960.

Lounsberry, Clement A. *The Early History of North Dakota*. Washington, D.C.: Liberty Press, 1919.

Magnusson, Daniel O. *Peter Thompson's Narrative of the Little Bighorn Campaign, 1876*. Glendale, Calif.: Arthur H. Clark Company, 1974.

Mahan, Bruce E. *Old Fort Crawford and the Frontier*. Iowa City: State Historical Society of Iowa, 1926.

Mason, Philip. *A Matter of Honor*. London: Jonathan Cape, 1974.

Matloff, Maurice, ed. *American Military History*. Washington, D.C.: Office of the Chief of Military History, U.S. Army, 1969.

Mattes, Merrill J. *Indians, Infants and Infancy*. Denver: Old West Publishing Co., 1960.

McAfee, Robert B. *History of the Late War in the Western Country*. Bowling Green: University of Ohio Press, 1919.

McAllister, Robert. *The Civil War Letters of General Robert McAllister*. Edited by James I. Robertson, Jr. New Brunswick, N.J.: Rutgers University Press, 1965.

McClure, A. K. *Three Thousand Miles Through the Rocky Mountains*. Philadelphia: J. B. Lippincott & Company, 1869.

McDermott, John F., ed. *The Western Journals of Washington Irving*. Norman: University of Oklahoma Press, 1944.

McDonald, General John. *The Secrets of the Great Whiskey Ring*. Chicago: Belford, Clark and Company, 1880.

McIntyre, Benjamin F. *Federals on the Frontier: The Diary of Benjamin F. McIntyre*. Edited by Nannie M. Tilley. Austin: University of Texas Press, 1963.

McNitt, Frank. *The Indian Traders*. Norman: University of Oklahoma Press, 1962.

Merrick, George B. *Old Times on the Upper Mississippi*. Glendale, Calif.: Arthur H. Clark Company, 1909.

Meyers, Augustus. *Ten Years in the Ranks of the U.S. Army*. New York: Stirling Press, 1914.

Minnesota Outdoor Recreational Resources and Minnesota Historical Society. *Fort Snelling*. St. Paul: Minnesota Historical Society, 1965.

Mohr, Richard E., ed. *The Cormany Diaries: A Northern Family in the Civil War*. Pittsburgh: University of Pittsburgh Press, 1982.

Monaghan, Jay. *The Life and Times of General George Armstrong Custer*. Boston: Little, Brown and Company, 1959.

Moore, Frank, ed. *The Rebellion Record: A Diary of American Events, with Documents, Narratives, Illustrative Incidents, Poetry, etc.* 10 vols. New York: Van Nostrand, 1864–68.

Morford, H. *Red Tape and Pigeon-Hole Generals: As seen from the Ranks during a Campaign in the Army of the Potomac*. New York: Carlton, 1864.

Murray, Robert A. *Brief Guide to Research on Army Posts*. Phoenix: Council on Abandoned Posts, 1969.

———. *Military Posts in the Powder River Country of Wyoming, 1865–1894*. Lincoln: University of Nebraska Press, 1968.

Nadeau, Remi. *Fort Laramie and the Sioux*. Lincoln: University of Nebraska Press, 1967.

Nason, Reverend Elisas, and the Honorable Thomas Russell. *The Life and Public Services of Henry Wilson*. New York: Negro Universities Press, 1969.

Nevins, Allan. *The War for the Union*. 6 vols. New York: Charles Scribner's Sons, 1971.

Nichols, James M. *Perry's Saints, or the Fighting Parson's Regiment in the War of the Rebellion*. Boston: n.p., 1886.

Nicols, Roger B. *General Henry Atkinson: A Western Military Career*. Norman: University of Oklahoma Press, 1965.

Nisbet, Jame C. *Four Years on the Firing Line*. Jackson: McCowat-Mercer Press, 1963.

Nye, Captain W. S., *Carbine and Lance: The Story of Old Fort Sill*. Norman: University of Oklahoma Press, 1938.

Oliva, L. E. *Fort Hays, Frontier Army Outpost, 1865–1889*. Lawrence: Kansas State Historical Society, 1980.

———. *Fort Larned on the Santa Fe Trail*. Lawrence: Kansas State Historical Society, 1982.

Ostrander, Alson B. *An Army Boy of the Sixties*. New York: World Book Company, 1924.

Ostrowe, R., and S. R. Smith. *The Dictionary of Retailing*. New York: Fairchild Publishing Company, 1985.

Oxford English Dictionary. London: Oxford at the Clarendon Press, 1970.

Page, Charles A. *Letters of a War Correspondent*. Edited by James R. Gilmore. Boston: L. C. Page and Company, 1899.

Page, Charles D. *History of the Fourteenth Regiment, Connecticut Volunteer Infantry*. Meriden: Horton Printing Company, 1906.

Parker, Geoffrey, and Angela Parker. *European Soldiers, 1550–1650*. Cambridge: Cambridge University Press, 1977.

Parker, James. *The Old Army: Memories, 1872–1918*. Philadelphia: Dorrance and Company, 1929.

Pathways to the Old Northwest: Conference Proceedings. Franklin College of Indiana, July 10–11, 1987. Indianapolis: Indiana Historical Society, 1988.

Patrick, David, and William Geddie. *Chamber's Encyclopedia: Dictionary of Universal Knowledge*. Philadelphia: J. B. Lippincott, 1923.

Pirtle, Caleb, and M. Cusak. *Fort Clark on Texas' Western Frontier: The Lonely Sentinel*. Austin: Eakin Press, 1985.

Price, Isaiah. *History of the Ninety-Seventh Pennsylvania Infantry Volunteers during the War of the Rebellion, 1861–1865*. Philadelphia: n.p., 1875.

Price, George F. *Across the Continent with the Fifth Cavalry*. New York Antiquarian Press, 1959.

Pride, Captain William F., *The History of Fort Riley*. N.p., 1926.

Prucha, Francis P. *American Indian Policy in the Formative Years: The Indian Trade and Intercourse Acts, 1790–1834*. Cambridge, Mass.: Harvard University Press, 1962.

———. *Broadax and Bayonet: The Role of the United States Army in the Development of the Northwest, 1815–1860*. Madison: Wisconsin Historical Society, 1953.

———. *A Guide to the Military Posts of the United States*. Madison: Historical Society of Wisconsin, 1964.

———. *The Sword of the Republic: The United States Army on the Frontier, 1783–1846*. Bloomington: Indiana University Press, 1969.

Pullen, John J. *The 20th Maine: A Volunteer Regiment in the Civil War*. New York: J. B. Lippincott, 1957.

Quaife, M. M., ed. *Army Life in Dakota, The Diary of Phillipe R. D. de Keredern de Tobriand*. Chicago: Lakeside Press, 1941.

———. *Checagou: From Indian Wigwam to Modern City, 1673–1835*. Chicago: University of Chicago Press, 1933.

———. *Checaugo and the Old Northwest*. Chicago: n.p., 1913.

Regulations for the Army of the Confederate States, 1862. Richmond: 1862.

Regulations for the Army of the United States. New York: n.p., 1857.

Rickey, Don, Jr. *Forty Miles a Day on Beans and Hay: The Enlisted Soldier Fighting the Indian Wars*. Norman: University of Oklahoma Press, 1963

Risch, Erna. *Quartermaster Support of the Army: A History of the Corps.* Washington, D.C.: War Department, 1962.

Roberts, Robert B. *Encyclopedia of Historical Forts: The Military, Pioneer and Trading Posts of the United States.* New York: Macmillan, 1987.

Rodenbough, Theodore F., ed. *From Everglades to Canon with the Second Dragoons, 1836–1875.* New York: A. Van Nostrand, 1875.

Rosenblatt, Emil. *Anti-Rebel: The Civil War Letters of Wilbur Fisk.* New York: Croton-on-Hudson, 1983.

Royster, Charles. *A Revolutionary People at War: The Continental Army and American Character, 1775–1783.* Chapel Hill: University of North Carolina Press, 1979.

Saunier, Joseph A., ed. *A History of the 47th Regiment Ohio Veteran Volunteer Infantry, Second Brigade, Fifteenth Army Corps, Army of the Tennessee.* Hillsboro, Ohio: Lyle Printing Co., 1903.

Scharf, J. T., ed. *History of St. Louis City and County.* 3 vols. Philadelphia: Louis H. Everts and Co., 1883.

Schenkman, David E. *Civil War Sutler Tokens and Cardboard Scrip.* New York: Jade House Publications, 1983.

Schmitt, Martin F. *General George Crook, His Autobiography.* Norman: University of Oklahoma Press, 1946.

Schuchert, Charles and Clara Mae LaVene. *O. C. Marsh, Pioneer in Paleontology.* New Haven: Yale University Press, 1940.

Scobee, Barry. *Old Fort Davis.* San Antonio: Naylor Company, 1947.

Scouller, Major R. E. *The Armies of Queen Anne.* London: Oxford University Press, 1966.

Sewell, Robert. *Practice in the Executive Departments of the Government under the Pension, Bounty and Prize Laws of the United States, with Forms and Instructions for Collecting Arrear of Pay, Bounty and Prize Money, and for Obtaining Pensions.* New York: D. Appleton and Company, 1864.

Shannon, Fred A., ed. *Organization and Administration of the Union Army.* 3 vols. Glendale, Calif.: Arthur H. Clarke Company, 1928.

Simon, John Y., ed. *The Papers of Ulysses S. Grant.* 15 vols. Carbondale: Southern Illinois University Press, 1969–.

Sparks, Jared. *Correspondence of the American Revolution.* Boston: Little, Brown and Company, 1953.

Sprague, John T. *The Florida War.* Gainesville: University of Florida Press, 1964 (facsimile copy of 1848 edition).

Spring, Agnes W. *The Cheyenne and Black Hills Stage and Express Routes.* Clendale, Calif.: Arthur H. Clark Company, 1949.

Stearns, Augustus C. *Three Years with Company K.* Edited by Arthur A. Kent. Cranbury, N.J.: Association of University Presses, 1976.

Steffen, Jerome O. *William Clark, Jeffersonian Man on the Frontier.* Norman: University of Oklahoma Press, 1977.

Stewart, E. I. *Custer's Luck.* Norman: University of Oklahoma Press, 1955.

Stiles, Henry R., ed. *Affairs at Fort Chartres, 1768–1781.* Albany, N.Y.: n.p., 1864.

Stillwell, Leander. *The Story of a Common Soldier of the Army Life in the Civil War: 1861–1865.* Erie: Franklin Hudson Publishing Company, 1920.

Sullivan, Jerry M. *Fort McKavett: A Texas Frontier Post.* West Texas Museum, 1981.

Sunder, John E. *The Fur Trade on the Upper Missouri, 1840–1865.* Norman: University of Oklahoma Press, 1965.

Swanson, Evadene B. *Fort Collins Yesterday.* Published by the author, 1975.

Sword, Wiley. *President Washington's Indian War.* Norman: University of Oklahoma, 1985.

Thiebault, Paul. *An Explanation on the Duties of the Several Etat-majors in the French Army . . .* London: T. Egerton, 1801.

Thwaites, Reuben G., ed. *Early Western Travels, 1748–1846.* 32 vols. Cleveland: A. H. Clark Company, 1904-1907.

Tilley, Nannie M. *Federals on the Frontier: The Diary of Benjamin F. McIntyre.* Austin: University of Texas Press, 1963.

Toponce, Alexander. *Reminiscences of Alexander Toponce, 1839–1923.* Ogden, Utah: Mrs. Kate Toponce, 1923.

Trennert, Robert A., Jr. *Alternative to Extinction: Federal Indian Policy and the Beginning of the Reservation System, 1846–1851.* Philadelphia: Temple University Press, 1975.

———. *Indian Traders on the Middle Border: The House of Ewing, 1827–1854.* Lincoln: University of Nebraska Press, 1981.

Trustram, Myna. *Women of the Regiment: Marriage and the Victorian Army.* London: Cambridge Press, 1984.

United States, Continental Congress. *Journals of the Continental Congress, 1774–1789.* Washington, D.C.: U.S. Government Printing Office, 1904–1937.

United States Sanitary Commission. *Documents of the U.S. Sanitary Commission.* 2 vols. New York: n.p., 1866.

Unruh, John D., Jr. *The Plains Across.* Urbana: The University of Illinois Press, 1979.

Upton, Richard. *Fort Custer on the Big Horn, 1877–1898.* Glendale, Calif.: Arthur H. Clark Co., 1973.

Van Cleve, Charlotte O. *Three Score Years and Ten: Lifelong Memories of Fort Snelling, Minnesota.* 3d ed. N.p., 1895.

Van Doren, Carl. *Mutiny in January.* New York: Viking Press, 1943.

Wainwright, Colonel Charles S. *A Diary of Battle: The Personal Journals of Colonel Charles S. Wainwright.* Edited by Allan Nevins. New York: Harcourt, Brace and World, 1962.

Ware, Eugene. *The Indian War of 1864.* New York: St. Martin's Press, 1960.

Weisel, George F. *Men and Trade of the Northwest Frontier.* Missoula: Montana State University Press, 1955.

Wesley, Edgar W. *Guarding the Frontier, A Study of Frontier Defense from 1815 to 1825.* Westport, Conn.: Greenwood Press, 1970.

Western, J. R. *The English Militia in the Eighteenth Century: The Story of a Political Issue, 1660–1802.* Toronto, Ontario: University of Toronto Press, 1965.

Whitney, Ellen M., ed. *The Blackhawk War, 1831–32.* 3 vols. Collections of the Illinois State Historical Society, vol. 35. Springfield: Illinois State Historical Library, 1970.

Wildes, Harry E. *Valley Forge.* New York: Macmillan Company, 1938.

Wiley, Bell I. *The Life of Johnny Reb.* New York: Bobbs-Merrill, 1943. In *The Common Soldier in the Civil War,* Book no. 2. New York: Grosset and Dunlap, 1951.

Wilkeson, Frank. *Recollections of a Private Solder in the Army of the Potomac.* New York and London: G. P. Putnam's Sons, 1898.

Williams, Amelia W., and Eugene C. Barker, eds. *The Writings of Sam Houston.* 8 vols. Austin: University of Texas Press, 1938.

Williams, Clayton W. *Texas' Last Frontier: Fort Stockton and the Trans-Pecos, 1861–1895.* College Station: Texas A & M University Press, 1982.

Wilson, D. Ray. *Fort Kearny on the Platte: First Fort Built on the Oregon Trail.* N.p.: Crossroads Communications, 1984.

Wooster, Robert. *Soldiers, Sutlers and Settlers: Garrison Life on the Texas Frontier.* College Station: Texas A & M University Press, 1987.

Wormser, Yellow Legs. *The Story of the U.S. Cavalry.* Garden City, N.Y.: Doubleday and Company, 1966.

Wright, H. Bunker, and Monroe K. Spears, eds. *The Literary Works of Matthew Prior.* 2 vols. Oxford: Clarendon Press, 1959.

Yates, Elizabeth. *With Sherman to the Sea: A Drummer's Story of the Civil War.* New York: John Day Company, 1960.

Young, Otis E. *The West of Philip St. George Cooke.* Glendale, Calif.: Arthur H. Clark Company, 1955.

———. *The First Military Escort on the Santa Fe Trail, 1829.* Glendale, Calif.: Arthur H. Clark Company, 1952.

Articles and Newspapers

Atherton, Lewis E. "The Merchant Sutler in the Pre–Civil War Period." *Southwestern Social Science Quarterly* 19, no. 2 (September 1938): 140–51.

———. "The Pioneer Merchant in Mid-America." *University of Missouri Studies* 14 (April 1939): 1–135.

———. "The Services of the Frontier Merchant." *Mississippi Valley Historical Review* 24 (September 1937): 153–70.

Barry, Louise, ed. "William Clark's Diary." *Kansas Historical Quarterly* 16 (1948). 4 Parts: (February 1948):1–39; (May 1948): 136–74; (August 1948): 274–305; (November 1948): 384–410.

Beard, Daniel W. "With Forrest in West Tennessee." *Southern Historical Society Papers* 37 (January-December 1909): 304–8.

Brown, Colonel A. F. "Van Dorn's Operations in Northern Mississipi: Recollections of a Cavalryman." *Southern Historical Society Papers* 5: 151–61.

Bullock, Colonel William. "Old Letter Book." Edited by Agnes Wright Spring. *Annals of Wyoming* 13, no. 4 (October 1941): 237–330.

Caldwell, Norman W. "Civilian Personnel at the Frontier Military Post (1790–1814)." *Mid-America* 38, no. 2 (October 1955): 111–18.

Campbell, John. "The Diary of John Campbell." *Annals of Wyoming* 10 (January 1938): 5–12; (July 1938): 59–78.

Capron, Cynthia J. "The Indian Border War of 1876." *Journal of the Illinois State Historical Society* 13: 477–79.

Carter, Edgar N. "Judge Carter and Old Fort Bridger." *Westerners Brand Book Los Angeles* (1950): 179–82.

Carter, William A., Jr. "Diary of Judge William Carter." *Annals of Wyoming* 11, no. 2 (1939) :75–110.

———. "Fort Bridger in the 70s." *Annals of Wyoming* 11, no. 2 (1939): 111–13.

Cheyenne *Daily Leader*, 1880.

Clark, Satterlee. "Early Times at Fort Winnebago." *Collections of the State Historical Society of Wisconsin* 8 (1879): 309–21.

Clark, William. "Journal of General Wayne's Campaign of 1793–94." *Mississippi Valley Historical Review* 1 (December 1914): 418–44.

Collier, Charles F. "The Story of the Evacuation of Petersburg, by an Eye Witness." *Southern Historical Society Papers* 22 (January-December 1894): 69–73.

Confederate Congress. House of Representatives. First Confederate Congress— Third Session, January 22, 1863. *Southern Historical Society Papers* 47 (December 1930): 178.

Conniss, I. R., ed. "Recollections of Taylor Pennock." *Annals of Wyoming* 6, nos. 1 and 2:199–212.

Crocker, Honorable James F. "Prison Reminiscences." *Southern Historical Society Papers* 34 (January-December 1906): 28-51.

Davis, William N., Jr. "Post Trading in the West." *Explorations in Entrepreneurial History* 6 (October 1953): 30–37.

———. "The Sutler at Fort Bridger." *Western Historical Quarterly* 2, no. 1 (January 1971): 37–53.

Delo, David M. "Camp Stambaugh: The Miner's Delight." *Wind River Mountaineer* 3, no. 4 (October-December 1987): 4–14.

———. "Post Trader, Indian Trader." *Wind River Mountaineer* 2, no. 3 (July-September 1986): 4–7, 3, no. 1 (January-March 1987): 4–12.

———. "Regimental Rip-Off Artist Supreme." *Army Magazine* (January 1989): 40–48

———. "The Road to Yellowstone." *Wind River Mountaineer* 2, no. 2 (April-June 1986): 4–11.

Dodge City *Times*, 1880, 1881, 1882.

Dorsey, Dorothy B. "The Panic of 1819 in Missouri." *Missouri Historical Review* 30: 77–91.

Ellers, H. W. "Old Fort Atkinson." *Nebraska State Historical Society Transactions and Reports* 4 (1892): 18–29.

Folwell, William W. "Minnesota in 1849: An Imaginary Letter." *Minnesota History* 6, no. 1 (March 1925): 34–40.

———. "The Sale of Fort Snelling." *Minnesota Historical Society Collections* 15: 393–409.

Foner, Jack D. "The Socializing Role of the Military." *The American Military on the Frontier.* U.S. Air Force Academy Symposium, 1976. Washington, D.C.: U.S. Air Force, 1978.

Foreman, Carolyn T. "General John Nicks and His Wife Sarah Perkins." *Chronicles of Oklahoma* 8: 389–406.

Forsyth, T. "Journal of a Voyage from St. Louis to the Falls of St. Anthony." *Wisconsin Historical Collections* 6 (1872): 188–219.

"Fort Winnebago Orderly Book 1834–36." *Annals of Life in Wisconsin Territory* (1898): 103–17.

Frank Leslie's *Illustrated Newspaper*, 1862, 1863.

"Frontier Officer's Military Order Book." *Mississippi Valley Historical Review* 6: 260–67.

Gettys, M. "Historical Background on the Fort Towson Sutler's Store." An address given before the Society for Historical Archeology, Denver, Colorado, 1983.

Granger, Roger T. "Fort Robinson, Outpost on the Plains." *Nebraska History* 39, no. 3 (1958): 191–240.

Griswold, Gillet. "Old Fort Sill: The First Seven Years." *The Chronicles of Oklahoma* 36, no. 1(1958): 2-15.

Guentzel, Richard. "Department of the Platte and Western Settlement, 1866–1877." *Nebraska History Magazine* 56, no. 3 (February 1975): 389–418.

Hacker, Barton C. "Women and Military Institutions in Early Modern Europe: A Reconnaissance." *Signs* 6, no. 4 (1980): 643–71.

Hallen, William. "History of the Campaign of Stonewall Jackson in the Shenandoah Valley of Va." *Southern Historical Society Papers* 43 (August 1920): 111–294.

Hammond, Major Paul F. "Kirby Smith's Ky Campaign." *Southern Historical Society Papers* 9 (July-August 1881): 290.

Harper's Weekly, 1861-1865.

Henshaw,Lieutenant William. "The Orderly Book of Lt. William Henshaw, May 9, 1759–Nov 28, 1759." *Transactions and Collections of the American Antiquarian Society* 11 (1909): 185–254.

Hoekman, S. "The History of Fort Sully." *South Dakota Historical Collections* 26: 222–77.

Hunton, John. "History of the Old Sutler Store Coins." *Fort Laramie Scout*, December 12, 1928.

———. "Letter." *Annals of Wyoming* 4, no. 2 (October 1926): 314–17.

Huston, James A. "Logistical Support of Federal Armies in the Field." *Civil War History* 7 (March 1961): 36–47.

Innis, Ben. "The Fort Buford Diary of Pvt. Sanford." *North Dakota History* 33, no. 4 (Fall 1966): 335–78.

Jackson, D. "Old Fort Madison—1808-1813" *Palimpsest* 39 (January 1958): 1–64.

Jerabek, E., comp. "A Bibliography of Minnesota Territorial Documents." St. Paul: Minnesota Historical Society, 1936. Vol. 3, Minnesota Historical Society Publications. Vols. 1–4, 1935–36.

Johnson, General B. T., "The Memoirs of the First Maryland Regiment." Paper no. 4: The Battle of Winchester. *Southern Historical Society Papers* 10, no. 3 (March 1882): 97–107.

Johnson, General Richard W., "Fort Snelling." *Collections of the Minnesota Historical Society* 8: 427–48.

Johnson, Sally A. "Cantonment Missouri—1819–1820." *Nebraska History* 37 (June 1956): 121–33.

———. "The Sixth's Elysian Fields—Fort Atkinson on the Council Bluff." *Nebraska History* 40 (March 1959): 1–38.

Jones, Hoyle, "Seth E. Ward." *Annals of Wyoming* 5 (1927): 5–18.

Jones, James W. "The Kirkpatrick–Dahlgren Raid against Richmond." *Southern Historical Society Papers* 13 (1883): 515–60.

Kane, Randy. "An Honorable and Upright Man." *Journal of Arizona History* 19, no. 3 (1978): 297–314.

Kendall, Jane R. "The History of Fort Francis E. Warren." *Annals of Wyoming* 18, no. 1 (January 1946): 3–66.

Kennerly, William C. "Early Days in St. Louis." *Missouri Historical Society Collections* 3: 407–22.

Lander Clipper.

Lander State Journal

Lane, Brigadier General J. H., "Glimpses of Army Life in 1864." *Southern Historical Society Papers* 18 (1890): 406–22.

Larson, Agnes M. "On the Trail of the Woodsman in Minnesota." *Minnesota History* 13, no. 4 (December 1932): 349–66.

Lees, William B., and Kathryn M. Kimery-Lees. "Regional Perspectives on the Fort Towson Sutler's Store and Residence, A Frontier Site in Antebellum Eastern Oklahoma." *Plains Anthropologist* 29 (103) (1984): 13–24.

Lewis, K. E., ed. "Fort Washita from Past to Present: An Archeological Report." *Oklahoma Historical Society Series in Anthropology* 1. Oklahoma City: Oklahoma Historical Society. 1975.

Loehr, Rodney C. "Caleb D. Dorr and the Early Minnesota Lumber Industry." *Minnesota History* 24 (1943): 125–41.

Lorstad, Erling. "Personal Politics in the Origin of Minnesota's Democratic Party." *Minnesota History* 36: 256–70.

Mattes, Merrill. "Fort Laramie, Guardian of the Oregon Trail." *Annals of Wyoming* 17, no. 1 (January 1945): 3–23.

———. "The Sutler's Store at Fort Laramie." *Annals of Wyoming* 18, no. 2 (July 1946): 92–133.

Mattison, Ray H. "Fort Rice—North Dakota's First Missouri River Military Post." *North Dakota History* 20, no. 2 (April 1953): 87–108.

———. "The Letters of Henry A. Boller: Upper Missouri Fur Trader." *North Dakota History* 33, no. 2 (Spring 1966): 106–219.

———. "Old Fort Stevenson." *North Dakota History* 18, nos. 2, 3 (April-July 1951): 53–92.

Mattson, J. W. "Orr's South Carolina Rifles." *Southern Historical Society Papers* 27 (January-December 1899): 157–65.

McCarthy, Carlton. "Detailed Minutiae of a Soldier's Life." *Southern Historical Society Papers* 6 (July 1878): 1–10, 93–214.

Mentzer, Raymond R., Jr. "Camp Baker/Fort Logan: Microcosm of the Frontier Military Experience." *Montana Magazine of History* 27, no. 2 (April 1977): 34–43.

Merrell, Honorable Henry. "Pioneer Life in Wisconsin." *Report and Collections of the State Historical Society of Wisconsin* 7 (1873–1876): 366–402.

Moore, Wilton P. "The Provost Marshall Goes to War." *Civil War History* 5 (March 1959): 62–71.

Murray, Robert A. "The Hazen Inspection of 1866." *Montana Magazine of Western History* 18, no. 1: 25–33.

Newberry, J. S., M.D. "Report on the Condition of the Troops and the Operation of the Sanitary Commission in the Alley of the Mississippi for the Three Months Ending November 30, 1861." *Documents of the United States Sanitary Commission* 1, Report no. 36.

New York *Herald*, 1872, 1876.

New York *Times*, 1872, 1876.

New York *Tribune*, 1872, 1875, 1876.

"Old Fort Madison: Some Source Materials." *Iowa Journal of History and Politics* 11 (1913): 517–45.

Park, Robert E. "The Diary of Captain Robert E. Park, 12th Alabama Regiment." *Southern Historical Society Papers* 1: 370–86, 430–37; 2: 25–31, 78–85, 172–80, 232–39, 306–15; 3: 43–46, 55–61, 123–27, 183–89, 244–54; 26: 1–31.

"Paroles of the Army of Northern Virginia at the Time of Surrender." *Southern Historical Society Papers* 15 (January-December 1890): 1–508.

Pattee, John. "The Reminiscences of John Pattee." *South Dakota Historical Collections* 5 (1910): 275–350.

Petersen, William J. "Steamboating in the Upper Mississippi Fur Trade." *Minnesota History* 13, no. 3 (September 1932) :221–44.

Phillips, George H. "The Indian Ring in Dakota Territory, 1870–1890." *South Dakota History* 2, no. 4 (Fall 1972): 345–76.

Prucha, Francis Paul. "Army Sutlers and the American Fur Company." *Minnesota History* 40, no. 1 (Spring 1966): 22–31.

Rife, Clarence W. "Norman W. Kittson, A Fur Trader at Pembina." *Minnesota History* 6, no. 3 (September 1925): 225–52.

Robrock, David P. "A History of Fort Fetterman, Wyoming, 1867–1882." *Annals of Wyoming* 48, no. 1 (Spring 1976): 5–76.

Russell, Mrs. Daniel R., ed. "Early Days in St. Louis, from the Memories of an Old Citizen." *Missouri Historical Society Collections* 3 (1908–1911): 407–22.

Sangamo Journal (Springfield, Ill.), 1832, 1833.

Sioux City, Iowa, *Eagle*: 1857, 1858.

Spear, Donald P. "The Sutler in the Union Army." *Civil War History* (June 16, 1970): 121–38.

Steward, Chaplain T. G. "The Canteen in the Army." Harper's Weekly 36, no. 1842 (April 9, 1892): 350–51.

Trenholm, V. "The Bordeau Story." *Annals of Wyoming* 26, no. 2 (July 1954): 119.

W.O. "Sutlers in the Camp." *Fraser's Magazine for Towne and Country,* 52, (December 1855): 685–95.

Way, Royal B. "The United States Factory System for Trading with the Indians, 1796–1822." *Mississippi Valley Historical Review* 6: 220–35.

Wayne, Anthony. "General Wayne's Orderly Book." *Michigan Pioneer and Historical Society Collections* 34 (1900): 341–733.

Wells, James T. "Prison Experience." *Southern Historical Society Papers* 7 (January-December 1879): 393–98.

Welty, Raymond L. "The Army Fort of the Frontier, 1860–70." *North Dakota History* 2, no. 3 (April 1928): 155–67.

———. "The Daily Life of the Frontier Soldier." *Cavalry Journal* 36 (October 1927): 367–81.

———. "The Frontier Army on the Missouri River, 1860-70." *North Dakota History* 2, no. 2 (January 1928): 85–94.

——— . "The Policing of the Frontier by the Army, 1860–1870." *Kansas Historical Quarterly* 3 (August 1938): 246–57.

———. "Supplying the Frontier Miliary Posts." *Kansas Historical Quarterly* 7, no. 2 (May 1938): 154–69.

Wesley, Edgar, ed. "The Diary of James Kennerly." *Missouri Historical Society Collections* 6 (1928–1931): 41–97.

———. "Life at Fort Atkinson." *Nebraska History* 30 (December 1949): 348–58.

Williams, M. "John Kinzie's Narrative of the Fort Dearborn Massacre." *Journal of the Illinois State Historical Society* 46 (Winter 1953): 342–62.

Young, Will H. "Journals of Travel of Will H. Young, 1865." *Annals of Wyoming* 7 (1930): 378–82.

Government Documents

Congressional Globe. 46 vols. Washington, D.C., 1843–73.

Congressional Record. Washington, D.C., 1873–.

Fort McKavett Post Records. Record Group no. 393, National Archives.

Fort Hays Post Records. Fort Hays Historic Site, Fort Hays, Kansas.

Hazen, William B., "Report of Inspection of Fort Phil Kearny, August 28th and 29th, 1866," to Adjutant General Major H. G. Litchfield, August 29, 1866. LR, HQ, Dept. of the Platte, Record Group 98, National Archives.

———. "Report of Inspection of Fort Reno (August 22) Kearny (August 29) and C.F. Smith (September 2) 1866."

Inspector General's Reports, 1812–1846. 3 Rolls, Record Group no. 624, National Archives.

Pattee, John. Report of Major John Pattee upon a Letter of Charges of J. B. S. Todd, Delegate in Congress from Dakota Territory, to the Adjutant General, U.S.A., March 18, 1883. Des Moines, Iowa, 1883.

Second Auditor's Office, Army Records, Letter Book, National Archives.

U.S. Congress, *American State Papers*, 38 vols. (1789–1838).

———. *Annual Reports of the Secretary of War.*

U.S. Congress. House of Representatives. Order no. 9, August 2, 1846. House Exec. Doc. no. 60.

———. Military Affairs Committee. "The Sale of Fort Snelling." 35th Cong., 1st sess., H.R. no. 351.

———. 37th Cong., 2d sess., H.R. Misc. Doc. no. 42, 1862.

———. Act of March 19, 1862. 37th Cong., 2d sess., H. Misc. Doc. no. 43.

———. Resolution to Look into Release of Non-combattants Held at Richmond, Va. December 12, 1862. 37th Cong., 3d sess., H.R. Exec. Doc. no. 17.

———. "Annual Report of the General-in-Chief." November 15, 1863. *Annual Report of the Secretary of War.* 38th Cong., 1st sess., House Exec. Doc. no. 1.

———. Report of Rufus Ingalls, November 7, 1866. 39th Cong., 2d sess., House Exec. Doc. no. 111.

———. Inspection Report of Delos B. Sackett, 1866. 39th Cong., 2d sess., House Exec. Doc. no. 23.

———. "The Sale of Fort Snelling Reservation." 40th Cong., 3d sess., House Exec. Doc. 9.

———. Report of Commissary General of Subsistence. In *Annual Report of the Secretary of War.* 41st Cong., 2d sess., House Exec. Doc. no. 1, 1869.

———. Letter from the Secretary of War to the Committee on Military Affairs re. sales to enlisted men by Post Traders. 41st Cong., 2d sess., House Exec. Doc. no. 249, April 1870.

———. Committee on Expenditures in the War Department. "Management of the War Department," August 5, 1876. H.R. no. 799. 44th Cong., 1st sess., 1876.

———. Reorganization of the U.S. Army. 44th Cong., 1st sess., H.R. no. 354.

———. *Annual Report, Commissioner of Indian Affairs.* 1878.

———. "Reorganization of the Army, March 21, 1878." 45th Cong., 2d sess. H. Misc. Doc. no. 56.

———. Committee on Indian Affairs. The Management of the Indian Dept. H. Misc. Doc. no. 167, 1886.

———. Report of the Adjutant General. In *Annual Report of the Secretary of War.* 51st Cong., 2d sess., House Exec. Doc. no. 1, pt. 2, October 7, 1890.

———. "Purchasing of Post Traders' Buildings." 52d Cong., 1st sess., H.R. Exec. Doc. no. 207, April 22, 1892.

———. "Report of the Adjutant General Office," Annual Report of the Secretary of War, 1892, 52d Cong., 1st sess., House Exec. Doc. no. 1.

———. "Abolishment of Post Traderships." Committee on Military Affairs, 52d Cong., 2d sess. January 6, 1893. H.R. no. 2203.

———. Military Affairs Committee, Committee Hearing—January 9, 1913. Y4.M59/1:C16.

U.S. Congress. Senate. Doniphan Expedition—1st Regiment, Missouri Cavalry. 36th Cong., 2d sess., Sen. Doc. no. 608.

———. Senate. "Resolution of the Senate re. the Appointment of the Sutler to

General Daniel E. Sickles' Brigade." 37th Cong., 2d sess., S. Exec. Doc. no. 10, January 1862.

———. S.R. no. 829, "Regulations on Post Traders," 1880.

———. Select Committee on Indian Traders. 50th Cong., 2d sess., S.R. no. 2707, 1886. Printed 1889.

———. Committee on Military Affairs. S.R. no. 713, May 23, 1892, to accompany S.B. no. 3117, with letter from Secretary of War and extract from 1891 *Annual Report of the Secretary of War.*

———. Committee on Military Affairs. Bill to abolish Post Traderships, January 6, 1893, 52d Cong. 2d sess., S.B. no. 3117.

———. Address on subject of Army Canteen and sale of liquor, with newspaper extracts. 57th Cong., 2d sess., S.B. no. 51. 1900.

U.S. Department of Commerce. *Statistical Abstracts of the United States.* 1987.

———. *Historical Abstracts of the United States.*

U.S. District Court, Evanston, Wyoming.

U.S. Secretary of War. Register of Post Traders, 3 vols.

———. *The War of the Rebellion: A Compilation of the Official Records of the Union and Confederate Armies.* Series 1, 2, and 3. War Department. U.S. Government Printing Office, 1880.

U.S. Surgeon General's Office. *Medical and Surgical History of the War of the Rebellion.*

———. "Hygiene of the U.S. Army and Description of Military Posts." Circular no. 8. Sol-Lewis: New York, N.Y., 1974.

U.S. War Department. Adjutant General's Office. Regulations Regarding Post Traders and Registers of Post Traders, 1821–1889. Record Group 94, National Archives.

———. Applications for Appointments for Sutlers, 1829.

———. Applications for Appointments in the Army, 1836–46.

———. General Order Book, January 16, 1857–March 20, 1861.

———. *General Orders Affecting the Volunteer Force.* Washington, D.C.: Government Printing Office.

———. General Orders and Circulars. 1881, 1887, 1888, 1889, 1891.

———. Register of Appointments of Sutlers made by the Secretary of War, 1828.

———. Register of Sutler Appointments, 1831–Late 1860s.

———. Register of Post Traders—Centered on 1876 for the Belknap Period.

———. Regulations. 1889. Washington, D.C.: Government Printing Office, 1889.

———. Regulations Regarding Post traders, Register of Post Traders, 1821–1889. Microfilm 1952, Record Group 94.

———. Revised United States Army Regulations of 1861, with an Appendix containing the Changes and Laws Affecting Army Regulations and Articles of War to June 25, 1863. Washington, D.C.; 1863.

Manuscripts

Boller, Henry A. State Historical Society of North Dakota.

Brackett, Colonel Albert G. Fort Bridger. N.p., n.d., 1870. Typed manuscript. Wyoming State Archives.

Carter, William A. University of Oregon; Wyoming Archives and Historical Department; and Bancroft Library, University of California, Berkeley.

Dougherty, John. Missouri Historical Society Collections, St. Louis.

Durfee and Peck. James Boyd Hubbell Papers, 1865–1906. Minnesota Historical Society.

Evans, Neal. Hensley Collection, University of Tulsa.

Fort Union Records. Arrott Collection, Donnelly Library, New Mexico Highlands University.

Frisco, John M. State Historical Society of Colorado Collections, Denver.

Gaddis, William. Montana State Historical Society Collections, Helena.

Hooker, W. F. "John Hunton, Bull Team Freighter, Ranch Owner, Army Post Trader, and Contractor." Wyoming Historical Society.

Hoyt, John, Governor, Territory of Wyoming. Copy Book, 1879, 1880. Wyoming State Archives.

Hugus Family. Charles B. Carroll Collection, Wyoming State Archives.

Hunton, John (1839–1928). American Heritage Center, University of Wyoming; and Wyoming State Archives.

Kennerly, James and George. Missouri State Historical Society, St. Louis.

Kinzie, John. Chicago Historical Society.

Larpenteur, Charles. Minnesota Historical Society Manuscript Collections, St. Paul.

London, John. London Family Papers. Southern Historical Collections. University of North Carolina, Chapel Hill.

McCauley, David. North Dakota Institute for Regional Studies. North Dakota State University, Fargo.

McNair, Alexander. Missouri State Historical Society, St. Louis.

Meyer, Ferdinand. State Historical Society of Colorado Collections, Denver.

Moore, James Kerr. Denver Public Library; and Wyoming State Archives.

Moore, James K., Jr. "Indian trader Tokens." James K. Moore Collection, Wyoming State Archives.

Moran, Thomas F. Montana Historical Society Collections, Helena.

O'Fallon, John and Benjamin. Manuscript Collection, Missouri Historical Society, Columbia.

Parker, Daniel. Historical Society of Pennsylvania Collections. 1300 Locust St., Philadelphia, Pa. 19107.

Parkin, Henry Sid. Historical Society of North Dakota, Bismarck.

Randolph, Edward B. (1792–1848). Randolph–Sherman papers, Mitchell Memorial Library, Mississippi State College, State, Mississippi.

Shurtleff, Wallace. "Bridger Country." N.p., n.d. Wyoming State Archives.

Sibley, Alexander Hamilton. Detroit Public Library, Burton Historical Collection.

Sibley, Henry H. Draper Collection, Newberry Libary, Chicago; and Minnesota Historical Society Manuscript Collections, St. Paul.

Speigelberg Brothers (Emmanual, Lehman, and Willi). Michael Stephan Martinez Memorial Collection, Rio Grande Historical Collections, New Mexico State University Library, Las Cruces; and American Jewish Archives, Cincinnati.

Speigel, Marcus M. American Jewish Archives, Cincinnati.

Spiegelberg family. American Jewish Archives, Cincinnati.

Steele, Franklin. Minnesota Historical Society Manuscript Collections, St. Paul.

Symmes, John C. Draper Collection, Wisconsin Historical Society; and Newberry Library, Chicago.

Ward, Giles Frederick. Papers. Duke University Library, Durham, N.C.

White, Tom, et al. "Post Sutlers/Traders at Fort Laramie." N.p.: Fort Laramie Historical Association, February 28, 1971.

INDEX